I0569720

THE FORGOTTEN CAREGIVER OF MENTAL CRISIS

NAVIGATING **SUICIDALITY AFTER TRAUMA** WITH INCREASED HOPE, RESILIENCE, & PRACTICAL STRATEGIES

INCLUDES FOCUSED SECTIONS ON MILITARY AND VETERAN PTSD AND SUICIDE

AMBER J. PARKER, PA-C, MPAS

©2025 by Amber J. Parker, PA-C

Published by hope*books
2217 Matthews Township Pkwy
Suite D302
Matthews, NC 28105
www.hopebooks.com

hope*books is a division of hope*media

Printed in the United States of America

First paperback edition.
Paperback ISBN: 979-8-89185-311-9
Hardcover ISBN: 979-8-89185-312-6
Ebook ISBN: 979-8-89185-313-3
Library of Congress Number: 2025945034

hope*books

ADVANCE PRAISE
For *The Forgotten Caregiver Of Mental Crisis*

"This is far more than a "how to" book. It is multi-layered—academic and professional guidance as well as in-depth understanding of the issues—wrapped with personal experience in an empathetic tone. It is a one-of-a-kind book! Every Caregiver regardless of the particular issue will benefit and will care for their own mental and physical health by reading this book."

—Dr. Jo Anne Lyon, MA-LPC, D.Min. (Honorary)
General Superintendent Emerita and Ambassador
of the Wesleyan Church
Founder of World Hope International
Author of *The Ultimate Blessing: My Journey to
Discover God's Presence*

"This incredible resource by Amber Parker fills a huge void in resources for people facing the incredible challenges of loving a person who struggles with thoughts of suicide. I have walked with many spouses, parents, adult children, siblings, friends and pastors who carry a huge burden as they walk alongside those who struggle with suicidal ideation and the painful mental health issues that often lead to thoughts of suicide. I have not had a book I felt comfortable sharing with these people, especially Christians....until now. Amber Parker's courageous and vulnerable book speaks directly to all the fear, pain, frustration and determination felt by those who face the possibility of losing a loved one to suicide. Using both her personal experience and exceptional research in the field, Amber's presence in the book comes alongside the reader like an experienced and trusted friend sharing her own journey down the same dark and winding path they currently walk. She offers insight, wisdom, understanding and practical tools without being heavy handed. This book is a God send for anyone who has a family member or loved one battling the significant mental health issues that can lead to suicide."

—Jennifer Ellers, MA
Christian Counselor, Professional Life Coach, and Crisis
Responder/Trainer focusing on grief, crisis, trauma,
and suicide
Instructor and Faculty with the International
Critical Incident Stress Foundation
Co-Author of *CISM Courses: "Understanding Suicide: Effective
Tools for Prevention, Intervention and Survivor Support"* and
"The First 48 Hours: Spiritual Caregivers as First Responders"

"A book that has been a long time in the waiting. The author has exposed her and her husbands' lives in this much needed book dealing with PTSD. It is well researched and very personal in walking the reader through the battles of Post Traumatic Stress Disorder caused by the trauma of war. This book is very well blended with both medical treatments, as well as religious prayer and God's help in dealing with not only her husband's needs, but also her own. It is beautifully written and easy to read and understand. You can tell it is written with love. This is a book that will help many people suffering with PTSD."

—Ronald E. Bowers Jr., DHSc, PA-E (Emeritus)
US Army, Captain (Retired)
Physician Assistant (PA-C), Retired
Retired Faculty Kettering College Physician
Assistant Masters degree Program
Medical Officer, Veterans' Social Command

"In *The Forgotten Caregiver of Mental Crisis: Navigating Suicidality After Trauma with Increased Hope, Resilience, & Practical Strategies,* Amber J. Parker shares the challenges she faced as a caregiver for her husband who struggled with PTSD, mental health issues, and suicidality after trauma. With eloquence and sensitivity, Amber shares her fight to save her husband's life as she searched and advocated for the treatments and resources he needed. Within the book's pages, she thoughtfully acknowledges her own personal struggles and need for support in her role as his caregiver. Bravely addressing issues such as civilian and combat trauma, veteran and military mental health barriers, and alcohol and substance addiction, Amber speaks into the lives of caregivers who are desperate to help their loved ones, while experiencing exhaustion and burnout themselves. Not only does she address these complex issues, she shares the various treatments available to both the loved one and their caregiver as well. Finally, Amber shares her deep faith in God and how He strengthened her and brought her family through the darkest of circumstances to a place where she can share hope and healing with others. I highly recommend this book to anyone who is a caregiver to a loved one affected by severe mental health issues, trauma, and suicidality."

—Dawn R. Ward, CCLC, CMHC
Author of *From Guilt to Grace: Hope and Healing for Christian Moms of Addicted Children*
Founder of The Faith to Flourish Ministry
Certified Christian Life Coach and Christian Mental Health Coach

"The Forgotten Caregiver of Mental Crisis addresses the extreme difficulties of caring for your spouse, or a loved one, in the face of suicide, from the perspective of someone who has lived this experience, and how it changed her own life. Guided by her faith in God, a community of support, and mental health resources, the author walks the caregiver through the important steps of how to care for their loved one and equally as important, how to care for themselves. This book offers the reader a friend, and endless supportive grace, in navigating suicidality, suicide attempts, and the road to healing. A much-needed comprehensive manual for the caregiver of mental health crisis."

—Janelle Martin, DFM, LPC-A, LCDC, ICP
Author of *Losing Her, Finding Us: A Mother's Fight, A Daughter's Journey and the Road to Recovery*
Owner and Founder of: The Mind Connection: Brain Health Center
IASIS Microcurrent Neurofeedback Certified Provider

"With tender honesty and hard-earned wisdom, Amber J. Parker blends medical research and personal experience to offer caregivers a lifeline through the overwhelming journey of a loved one's mental health crisis. Her compassionate guidance reminds us that healing begins not just with helping others, but also by caring for our own hearts along the way."

—Alicia Michelle, ACC, CPLC
multi-award-winning podcast host of
The Christian Mindset Coach
Author of *Emotional Confidence: 3 Simple Steps to Manage Emotions with Science and Scripture*

"Caregivers supporting a loved one with mental illness often face a wide range of difficult and overwhelming emotions. *The Forgotten Caregiver of Mental Crisis* by Amber Parker captures this reality with honesty and insight, drawing from her own experience caring for her husband. I appreciate her candid portrayal of the caregiver's role—the emotional complexity, the practical strategies she offers, and most importantly, the message we need most: hope."

—Jesslyn McCutcheon, BCMHC
Author of *Fighting Goliath: Slaying the Giant of Bipolar Disorder*
Founder of Fighting Goliath for Mental Illness, Inc.
Certified Mental Health Coach (AACC)

DISCLAIMER

A Note for the Reader: This book is not intended to take the place of professional medical or psychological advice or be the replacement for pursuing appropriate and necessary psychotherapy and/or medical interventions for mental health (i.e., behavioral health) treatment and diagnosis. This book is a guide and support. Reach out and access the mental health care you or your loved one needs. Don't wait to pursue healing. If you or a loved one are having a mental health or suicide emergency or increased mental health symptoms, call 988 or go to your nearest emergency room immediately for care and support. Don't wait to get necessary care.

DEDICATION

To my husband. Thank you for entrusting me with your story too. Thank you for allowing me the honor of being vulnerable on the page with both of our pain and stories. God's grace has kept you and me, though the enemy has tried to break us. May you continue walking with God and me—sober, faith-filled, stronger, pointing others to the only One who can truly save us. I love you. I choose you.

To my four children. I am blessed beyond measure. May you know how loved and championed each of you are. May the healing work I have done and your dad has done be a bridge for you to pursue healing and wholeness in your own life as you grow and face further challenges and struggles. I know the Lord has mighty things for each of you as you have already faced so much. Children—This is my prayer for you: *"May the God of hope fill you with all joy and peace as you trust in Him, so that you may overflow with hope by the power of the Holy Spirit"* (Romans 15:13).

To my parents. Thank you for your unwavering support, love, and personal sacrifice. Your example of perseverance, resilience, faith, and advocacy paved the way for my own caregiving story.

This book is also dedicated to you—the caregiver of crisis. You are seen. You are valued. May you be supported and have authentic, safe community around you as you persevere in this fight for life for your loved one and care for yourself as well.

TABLE OF CONTENTS

INTRODUCTION

The Silent Battle

There is a silent battle raging in the minds and hearts of a vast number of people, and they haven't told a single soul. Or maybe they sent out a couple SOSs via a joke or a self-deprecating comment—a statement thrown out—to test the waters and see what the response was to 'that' kind of issue, the issue of harming themselves or ending it all.

They may laugh heartily and act as if things are fine to cover over it, to mask it, but inside, they are screaming for someone to hear them. To see them. Screaming for the emotional pain they feel to abate. Not knowing what to do or how to fix it. Feeling so utterly alone.

[If you, yourself, feel this way, 988 is the Suicide and Crisis Lifeline in the U.S. Reach out and get help for yourself. Don't suffer in silence.]

And so, they may turn to something, anything, to numb the pain, to distract from it, or even to feel alive again after feeling so dead inside. They are screaming inside for the pain to stop, whatever the pain is, wherever the pain came from. They want it to go away. They can't handle how raw and intense it feels. They are scared to feel it, even worried it will overwhelm them.

And so, they try to dull the pain.[1] They try to numb themselves from the emotions and feelings.[1] They look for outs to make it better. They self-medicate with whatever may temporarily cover over the noise of the pain in their life and in their head. They distract or numb by alcohol, drugs, sex, food, movies or tv shows, work, exercise, control, or anything to make the pain go away.[1] To lessen. But the emotional pain returns as the numbing subsides. Eventually, they may begin to turn to thoughts of suicide...and so...

When no one hears and understands their SOS as a cry for help and validation of their pain, the hurting person may go forward and end their pain.[2] Die by suicide.[2] It is absolutely heartbreaking and not a rare occurrence.

We have a mental health epidemic on our hands in this country.

Those who die by suicide leave a wake of pain behind them—all those who love them and fought for them. These left behind loved ones, or survivors of suicide, must now carry the grief and hollow whittled out inside of them—aching with the pain and shock of loss and the sting of not being able to go back in time and save that person, to grab them back from the abyss of death.

The thing is...there is a way to change the tide. To slowly push back against the devastating deaths by suicide.

We Can Make a Change

I believe—the toll of death by suicide can be decreased if suicide awareness and mental health education increases within society. If regular, ordinary people learn suicide risk symptoms and how to support someone in mental crisis and get them emergency care. If 988 was talked about as widely as 911.

[988 is the suicide and crisis lifeline in the U.S. you can call or text for help.]

What if we learned how to spot the signs of suicide risk and self-harm and respond appropriately? What if we got over our uncomfortable feelings and the awkwardness of asking how someone is doing and truly took the time to care, to listen?

If we began to change how we approached mental health conditions, lives could be saved. Even one additional life saved makes all the difference. Placing a person on the path toward healing with the appropriate mental health care in their life makes an incredible difference.

One life changed can create a cascade of healing in other lives as well.

Increasing awareness has the ability to save many more lives than one though, if people band together in solidarity to speak out and speak up on suicide risk and warning symptoms of suicide risk and self-harm. When we overcome our own reservations and distractions to choose to see the people around us—their pain, their struggle—we have the power to help. We have the power to help someone get mental health care before they enter into suicidality and the potential for suicide. Or before they die by suicide.

When we give voice to those who are hurting emotionally and choose to be a voice for the silent, we empower those fighting the silent battle against suicide. We help them feel seen, cared about, and important to somebody.

Important enough to hopefully receive the mental health care they need to heal and get better. As a result, they may also see themselves as important in their own eyes.

Those hurting from significant emotional pain need support from others as they pursue healing.

We must break down the barriers to seeking mental health care. Break down the stigma surrounding someone having a mental health condition. It's not hush-hush. Or it shouldn't be.

We must throw away judgment, condemnation, and self-righteousness.

People are hurting, fighting inner battles they don't know what to do with.

We must step into the fight with them and be a support for them, a voice, a friend.

The Loved One, the Caregiver, of Suicidality

In the battle against suicide, there are close loved ones and support people of the person struggling with mental illness. These people are the caregivers. There is the primary support person, the primary caregiver, who offers the most tangible and emotional support to the one struggling. Next, there are additional support people surrounding the one who is ill and their primary caregiver. These additional people are the secondary and tertiary caregivers who help come alongside both the one struggling and primary caregiver.

The primary caregiver of mental crisis desperately needs support and championing too. They need to be seen and given the proper tools, resources, and knowledge to fight for their loved one's life—creating a caregiver who is empowered, valued, and educated on mental health symptoms. When the primary caregiver is empowered in their role, they can advocate, caregive, and fight for their loved one's life more effectively. They won't know everything right away; therefore, they must seek to educate themselves on mental health symptoms and care through professional support and organizations to aid in that growth.

The primary caregiver is the one standing in the gap at home and away from the hospital and medical spaces. They are standing in the gap, supporting their loved one, looking for signs of suicide, and trying to hold life together for everyone. The burden on their shoulders is great. They need support too.

I wrote this book for them. I wrote this book for the primary caregiver of mental crisis.

If you are the primary support person, the caregiver, of mental health crisis—know this:

You matter.

You are mighty.

And you are doing important work, friend.

You are a caregiver warrior.

I see you. I was in the trenches myself with suicidal caregiving for my husband.

You are not alone in your battle. Read on. My words are for you.

Would you give me permission to come alongside you as the friend and support you need as you navigate the chaos and turmoil of life right now?

I pray this book is a lifeline for you, to lift you up and propel you forward in your battle.

I pray through these words you have increased strength, hope, and resilience to keep going and fighting for life, goodness, and healing. I am cheering you on.

And now, let's get comfy and grab some coffee.

We're going to be hanging out for a while together.

Meeting for Coffee

Friend, I'm so glad you picked up my book and are choosing to consider my words and story to help you in your own story. If you can picture us meeting for coffee or you inviting me over to your home, make sure to go and brew a coffee or tea for yourself before we dive in. Take my book with you as you grab your drink and maybe grab a snack to munch on also. Get comfortable. Make sure you have a pen to underline with and/ or a highlighter to emphasize areas of particular importance for you. This book is your guide to help you in your own journey.

I'm sure I have a different background than you and different lived experience. Some of the perspectives I have or recommendations I offer may not be applicable or helpful for you in your specific situation. If so, take the recommendations you need and leave the opinions you don't need. My book is not intended to take the place of professional advice. I will ask you, though, to strongly consider the professional recommendations I share from research, experts, or professional associations—whether medical or psychology-based. I am passionate about this subject, and if we met, I would adapt some of my words to be more fully applicable to your situation. That would be my preference.

Instead, we meet through the pages of this book. Stark white pages. Black letters. Hope-filled words praying they land well and help you in the midst of the chaos, pain, and turmoil you are walking through right now. That's how it was for me at least. Chaotic. Overwhelming. Uncertain. Intense. Scared I would miss something or not do what I needed to and the consequences would be dire. Death. Suicide. The weight of responsibility was heavy, but I slowly made it bit by bit.

A Lifeline and Vital Resource

I searched for wisdom and insight on PTSD and found some through at least one book (I share its name in Chapter 1) that was crucial during that time for me—one that gave me wisdom, insight, background, and a better grasp of what I was dealing with. By understanding the background of the issues more fully, I was better equipped to care for my husband through his combat trauma, PTSD and trauma responses, suicidal ideation, suicide attempts, and hospitalizations.

I pray this book will be that for you. I pray this book will be a lifeline and vital resource for you in the mental health battle you are in right now, helping you be better equipped to fight for your loved one's life.

Whether your loved one (or the person you care about) is a spouse, fiancée, partner, boyfriend/girlfriend, friend, acquaintance, brother, sister, cousin, mom, dad, grandparent, child, other family member, co-worker, or a relationship I didn't mention in your life, know this person you care deeply about desperately needs your support and care. You are coming alongside them in their mental health battle, and it won't always be pretty through the caregiving. In fact, it will likely be far from it often.

Know this—*You are doing the brave thing.*

You are standing beside them and trying to help them seek healing, treatment, and the care they need to get better. You are learning to be an advocate if you weren't one before. You are likely learning about topics and diagnoses you never knew about but now care deeply about because they affect someone you care for deeply. I know because it happened for me.

My person was in trouble, and I fought with all my resources, and God's alongside, to support him and fight for his life, even when my loved one was self-sabotaging efforts through negative choices—choices focused on numbing or stopping the pain, memories, and intrusive nightmares he was plagued with.[1]

We Are All on a Healing Journey

We are all on a healing journey, one of personal growth, if we choose to pursue it.

Take your time with this content, allowing room for growth and application in your life.

I pray none of my words land offensively or cause hurt. If they do, please forgive me. Each of us are made uniquely with different personalities, backgrounds, and lived experience. I speak from my own background and perspective but also strive to be considerate and show empathy towards others' perspectives.

We are interacting on very difficult and painful subject matters. I know this full well. There are still painful places within me that I know future EMDR (Eye Movement Desensitization and Reprocessing) work will uncover and help to integrate and heal.[3] [4] That is not for me to be ashamed of but realistic about—I have done a lot of healing work myself and am proud of my growth. I am still on a healing and growth journey.

I hope you can be honest about your own self too. There is more to uncover, in layers, as you continue forward in your healing journey. Make a continued promise to yourself to keep pursuing health, for yourself and your loved ones.

The Raw, Sacred Story

You are a trusted guest entering into our sacred story.

As you enter into the painful parts of our specific story, please know you are doing so as a guest, as a trusted friend, and one who, I know, will respect and honor us and our story with their words and conversation…

You are being welcomed into our painfully raw "sanctuary" of a military family navigating combat PTSD, self-medicating, depression, suicidality, mental crisis, and the caregiving of it all. It's messy. Not all is shared.

Some parts are held back for privacy or because they aren't necessary in order to help you move forward in your own story. Other difficult parts are too sacred or not fully healed yet and therefore also held in privacy.

May we mutually choose to honor each other, trust each other—I with my words and personal and professional insights and you with the story you hold, with all its details and nuanced struggle and pain. May we find hope and healing together, friend.

It is my honor to come alongside and support you in the specific challenges and struggles you are facing. I know full well the struggle of not having all the support I needed in the caregiving journey. I had a few wonderful and trusted people in the thick of it, but I needed a more robust support system in the midst of the caregiving.

I am honored you would welcome me into the painful parts of your story and am grieved you are in the midst of such deep and difficult waters. It is hard. It is not easy.

Keep going. Keep persevering.

I pray my words, vulnerability, and resources help you as you go forward in this battle. I pray you find strength to continue, hope to carry you, and the right combination of medical and mental health care treatments for your loved one's care, in order for them to improve and get better.

You, friend, are strong. You are a caregiver warrior.

I can't promise you the ending of your story, but I can promise you won't be walking it alone anymore.

With care,

Amber

REFERENCES

[1] van der Kolk, B. A. (2014). *The Body Keeps the Score: Brain, Mind, and Body In the Healing of Trauma.* Penguin Books, 268.

[2] van der Kolk, 244.

[3] van der Kolk, 222, 230.

[4] Brayer, R. (2023). *The Art and Science of EMDR: Helping Clinicians Bridge the Path from Protocol to Practice.* PESI Publishing, Inc., 2-13.

HOW TO USE THIS BOOK

First off, this book is a guide based on one person's lived experience, opinions, insight, and recommendations. You should read it knowing that it is not intended to be professional advice or take the place of professional therapeutic mental health or medical care.

Verify all information with trusted medical and mental health recommendations and best evidence-based practices. Always seek the appropriate medical and psychological or mental health care and do not use this book in lieu of or in place of seeking the appropriate professional services you or your loved one needs for treatment and healing.

You will notice me speaking authoritatively as I communicate on the different subject matter with conviction and strength. I still expect you to verify and research my words against evidence-based medical and mental health best practices and research in order for you to access the best care for you and your loved one. You should also become your own researcher to educate yourself from professionally reputable sources.

That said—this book is supposed to be the friend by your side sharing experiences, science, and hard-fought insight to help you pursue the best care, treatment, and support for you and your loved one. You are not alone in your mental health battle, friend. As you implement recommendations from these pages, I hope you will find hope and strength for the journey.

Hopefully, my words and recommendations will be the springboard to new ideas for you as you continue pursuing the care your loved one needs. My words can be a catalyst in your search for the exact resources and treatment needed in your unique situation. This book will aid you in that process.

You may disagree with me on different points. I hope we can respect each other if there are differences of opinion. I am cheering you on to find the best healing modalities for your loved one or you. Be brave in the pursuit.

The Book's Organizational Structure

While this book builds on itself, each chapter focuses on specific topics. If you need help right away on a topic covered later in the book, it's okay to flip to that chapter and begin reading that topic. You have my permission. Just realize you may need to reference an earlier chapter to understand more fully what is communicated later. Many of the concepts build on previous information shared.

If you flip ahead, please promise me you will head back to where you were originally and read the skipped material to not miss necessary context and background information. If we were talking in a conversation, we would jump around to topics that were most applicable to your situation at that moment anyway. Feel free to do the same, but come back to the spot you were at before you jumped ahead.

Revisiting any missed chapters will provide a more comprehensive view of suicidal and trauma caregiving, understanding of professional recommendations, and assist you in implementing the necessary strategies needed for your own caregiving role.

While different topics may make more sense to you in a different order, I will be unveiling the mental health topics as they occurred in our life. You will learn our story piece by piece as a portion is pertinent to the topic we are discussing. You are headed on a journey with me and my husband in the way life unfolded for us with mental crisis. I hope that's okay and my explanation helps you understand my format and why specific chapters are where they are in the book. Our story is used to introduce many of the chapters' subject matter or as examples within.

- Part 1, Chapters 1—5, lays the groundwork and foundation of mental crisis caregiving in covering a myriad of topics including: what a caregiver is and their role, how a mental health condition can begin, caregiver burden and burnout, trauma and neuroscience, and specific struggles in the military and veteran community.
- Part 2, Chapters 6—12, focuses on caring for your loved one struggling with suicidality, trauma, and comorbidities such as alcoholism and addiction. Chapter 11 discusses EMDR and other psychotherapies, and Chapter 12 demystifies aspects of a psychiatric hospitalization.
- Part 3, Chapters 13—16, focuses on caring for yourself, the caregiver. It covers my faith background, safe, trusted community, boundaries in crisis, and the impact caregiving had on me. Chapter 16 covers my own trauma and mental health struggles, including a negative belief which came out of survival.

The Conclusion of the book, Chapter 17, is a balanced long-term view of doing life after crisis. You won't want to miss it as it's for the caregiver and the one struggling. It focuses on relapses, resilience, and redemption. Learning how to do life after crisis can be challenging as you are both changed from what you have walked through. There is newness to learn together including how to apply new skills and tools gained from therapy or interactions with mental health professionals. In this section, I share from our own story and address relapses of symptoms, supporting self-advocacy of your loved one, and the long-term focus of living a more balanced, healthier life together as you continue forward. I also share Josh's Saul to Paul moment—a moment of redemption.

- The chapters specifically on caring for your loved one's mental health are: Chapter 2 & Chapters 4—12.
- The chapters specifically on caring for yourself, the caregiver, are: Chapter 1, Chapter 3, & Chapters 13—16.
- Chapter 17 is for both of you as you learn to support each other and grow together.

I know you also want your loved one to stay alive and are in a fight against time like we were. Your story will unfold differently than mine, but there will be overlaps and commonalities between the struggles we face. I pray my vulnerability and sharing offer some of the support you need or will help you identify an additional resource, treatment, or way forward that springs forth for you as you caregive.

Chapter Topics, Bold, and Italics

The chapter names line up closely with the topics they cover. Reference the Table of Contents.

Bold and/or *Italics* - You will find **bold** and/or *italicized* sentences or phrases in certain sections. These are phrases or sentences I find especially powerful and want to draw your attention to as you are reading. Feel free to quote those which resonate the most with you online, on social media, etc. Tag me.

Connect with Me

I would love to hear from you and what words and sections were especially meaningful to you.

You can sign up for my email newsletter, receive free resources, and contact me through my author website.

Website: **amberjparker.com**

You can also follow and send me a message on social media or send an email:

Instagram: **@amberjparker_**
@choosejoyinthemidst

Facebook: **@amberjparker**
@choosejoyinthemidst

Youtube: **@amberjparker**

Email: **theforgottencaregiver@gmail.com**

Your Free Gifts- Spotify Playlist and E-book Guide

Here are your Free Gifts to accompany this book and your and your loved one's journey toward health and wellness. They are my thank you to you for purchasing this book.

- "You Are Not Alone In Your Battle" Spotify playlist
- "How To Find A Mental Health Therapist"—your free E-book guide

Scan this QR code to access your gifts:

You can also type in this website for access:
amberjparker.com/theforgottencaregiver/gifts

The QR code and link to access both are also in the Appendix at the back of the book. This E-book guide has my tried-and-true steps in finding the right mental health therapist. They are the steps I took to find a therapist for my husband when he was in the midst of crisis. In the guide, you will find the two websites I use to research and find the right mental health professionals. Go grab your copy right now!

There is a song title at the beginning of each chapter. These songs are meaningful songs to me which I have compiled into a Spotify playlist for you to download.

The reason I share it with you is because powerful truth-filled words were incredibly necessary for me during caregiving. They brought strength and perseverance.

The Spotify playlist has the songs at the beginning of each chapter and additional powerful bonus songs to bolster you up in your own battle.

Many of the songs' words sustained me. Download the playlist right now so you can play it whenever you need strength or when life is hard. You can listen while reading the book too, if you'd like.

Approach to Healing: Integration of Faith and Science

I believe in the powerful integration of faith and psychology for trauma and emotional healing. I weave both scientific and faith aspects throughout this book, as I believe it is the strongest approach for healing from difficult memories, emotions, and struggles. I have personally experienced the power of healing from traumatic memories and PTSD through faith-supported psychotherapy. When we tap into both modalities, faith and psychology, we have a stronger stance in the fight against mental health struggles, including suicidality and mental crisis.

Faith in God was my lifeline, and it's a vital part of our story as I fought for my husband's life and health. Chapter 13 focuses in depth on my faith background, spiritual battles, and prayer.

Science (including medicine, psychology, neuroscience, mental health therapy, and research) has a significant purpose in this fight for life as well. Chapter 4 is technical in nature and crucial to read as it lays the groundwork for understanding integral information on trauma including: trauma definitions, the neuroscience of trauma, where trauma is processed and stored in the brain, and how that knowledge can assist in choosing the best therapy for treatment. It also covers how this knowledge can help a person begin to gain control back when trauma or PTSD responses try to take control in a moment.

EMDR therapy (Eye Movement Desensitization & Reprocessing) is discussed in Chapters 4 and 11. I am a strong advocate for EMDR therapy as I have witnessed its effectiveness, both in my husband and myself, as well as studied evidence-based research supporting its use in trauma treatment and other conditions. It's powerful and incredibly helpful for trauma and emotional healing.

Chapter 11 is technical with focus on EMDR and other psychotherapies using our story as groundwork. Chapter 12 shares the purpose of behavioral health medications (psychiatric medications) and helps demystify some aspects of a psychiatric admission and hospitalization to better equip the caregiver in supporting their loved one through a hospitalization if needed.

Promise me you'll read Chapter 4 and later Chapter 11 and continue to reference them as you work through the book.

There is a reason why I incorporate technical chapters into this book. When we educate ourselves, we have knowledge to help us understand what is occurring to us and help guide us in making informed decisions for our health and healing. When I don't know something, I research it using professional, reputable sources. I offer the same approach to you. You will find in the appendix additional resources such as websites, authors, books, and organizations to assist you in your continued pursuit of healing and health for yourself and your loved one.

My hope for you is to not be alone anymore in your battle for life for your loved one and in your pursuit of healing. May you be supported through my words and find a way forward. You are not alone in your battle, friend.

PART 1: LAYING THE FOUNDATION OF MENTAL CRISIS CAREGIVING

Ch. 1—5

Chapter 1

WHAT IS A CAREGIVER? YOU ARE NOT FORGOTTEN OR ALONE ANYMORE

Song: "Good Plans" by: Red Rocks Worship, Cody Carnes

I can't promise you the ending of your story, but I can promise you won't be walking it alone anymore.

Mental health caregiving is bone-wearingly brutal, especially when fighting against the leviathan of suicide. Suicide—that taunting, scary threat of death. Shifting shadows, elusive enemy—and you fighting for life, praying for healing, advocating for treatment, caregiving in the dark bits and pieces of life where no one sees you, being on suicide watch. The unseen sacrifices, the worries, the silent fight you are in, trying your best to keep your loved one alive so they have a fighting chance at getting better. Clinging to hope in the midst of it.

Our battle began years before the start of this book—in the middle of war.

Combat trauma for him from an IED explosion killing his buddy. Memories and moments compartmentalized and pushed down for years until they wouldn't be quieted anymore. Nightmares ensuing. Worsening mental health. PTSD. Self-medicating. Depression. Suicidality*.[1] Medications. Therapy.

Fighting for life and caregiving in the urgent darkness for me.

Let's peel back the layers of our story—each new chapter another necessary stepping-stone in the fight for life and healing.

*Suicidality is a term encompassing all words and topics surrounding suicide including suicidal ideation, intention, plan, attempt, and hospitalization.[1]

Why We Share Vulnerably

I desire healing and health for your loved one and you.

My husband, also, wholeheartedly supports this message and gave me permission to share his story because your loved one's healing and life are that important.

Important enough to be vulnerable and open.

My prayer is by my/our choosing to be vulnerable that it will welcome you into being seen in your pain and less alone. I hope my sharing vulnerably about our story gives you the courage to speak out and find the support and help you and your loved one need—the mental health therapy needed, medical care or medication needed, community support, and hopefully faith support as well in order to pursue healing and (I pray) begin to redeem part of your own story.

Not every person approaches mental health crisis the same way.

Some of my words may not land quite right for you. If that's the case, please set those specific words aside and keep going forward, finding the nuggets of truth you were supposed to glean along the way.

Be open to what I share, not close-minded, and mull over the parts I share you aren't sure of yet. Sit with them. Consider them.

I believe we can support one another even if we have very different backgrounds, beliefs, or perspectives. After all, the common thread is we are fighting a similar foe: suicidality and mental crisis. We are in a similar battle. We can respect and show kindness to one another along the way.

You Need a Friend in Your Current Battle

If you are reading this book, chances are you are in an intensely lonely and heavy battle for yourself or someone you care deeply about.

You are in a fight for life and need a beacon of hope, a proverbial life raft.

Maybe some tools to help along the way.

You need a friend with experiential knowledge because they have traversed the deep darkness of mental crisis and suicidality caregiving. Somehow, they are still standing—having gained costly insight to help you in your battle.

I am that friend.

I wish I'd had that friend myself when I was in the thick of intense mental crisis caregiving. It would have made such a difference.

My preference is for us to meet in person, over coffee. For you to share your story with me—the parts you feel comfortable telling.

I want for us to enter into conversation with mutual respect, discernment, and care—listening with intention, understanding, and deep compassion. Never pity.

I choose to share vulnerably from my own story to offer insight and support to you. It isn't easy to share vulnerably, but it's necessary.

Validation and active listening are a part of our conversation.

Minimizing or judging has no place. Sometimes, few words are needed, but another's presence and understanding speak volumes.

If you are anything like I was, you are grasping for a semblance of normalcy and a feeling of security while your life crumbles around you.

Your reality is chaotic, unpredictable. You can't count on your day and night being calm or certain. Your loved one's symptoms are what set the pace and atmosphere for life. Charged tension is under wraps to not trigger emotional distress or crisis. Fear and uncertainty ebb and flow while overwhelmingness presses in.

You don't choose to walk into this type of battle but find yourself squarely in the middle of it. Choosing to rise up, you accept the battle before you. You must fight for your loved one's life and healing.

You pray for guidance in finding the best therapists, doctors, and treatment to aid your loved one in healing. You feel unprepared for this mighty undertaking of mental health crisis but hope you can learn quickly how to caregive* well. The stakes are too high. Their life is too precious.

This is why we enter into sharing our story, supporting one another, while caregiving for our loved ones. Having a friend who "gets" it is such a gift in the midst of swirling turmoil. You need resources and tools to help you through. You shouldn't try to do it alone.

Entering into someone's story of pain is a sacred endeavor. An honor. It is not something taken lightly.

[*I have coined the term, *caregive*, which means: the act of giving care to another, specifically as a caregiver of a significant health condition.]

An Ill-Defined Role Creates Confusion in Care.

There is not a specific term universally used at present to refer to the loved one or primary support person of mental crisis. Different people throw around different terms.

Family member, caretaker, carer, family caregiver, loved one, and caregiver are all ones I have seen or heard.[2][3] It is confusing when there is not a specific, universally used term to describe this significant role.

I was at a mental health conference where the term 'caregiver' was used to describe the therapists, psychologists, and other behavioral health staff who cared for the patients while they were inpatient at the hospital. The term 'family member' was used to describe the person or people who gave care to their loved one regularly, day in and day out, when the patient was not hospitalized.

I have read research articles focused on the family member or support person which use the terms 'caregiver' and 'carer'.[2] [3] Within the elderly population, when a spouse or adult relative begins to care for their spouse or elderly family member declining in health or with increasing physical ailments, they are commonly referred to as the 'caregiver' or 'caretaker'.

It is confusing to throw around so many different terms continuously when referring to the same role and function.

I believe the correct term to use for this support person of the ill loved one is: *caregiver.* The term caregiver defines the role well.

By definition, you give care continuously to your loved one who is ill or has limitations requiring assistance.

Hence, you are a giver of care.

Caregiver.

I am drawing this point out because this is a significant and empowering moment for you to accept and identify yourself and your role as a caregiver.

What you do is valuable, and it matters.

Acknowledging the Caregiver in Their Own Right

Let us call this person from now on—the caregiver. Let us not muddy up the waters and confuse who is being referenced in conversations.

Let us acknowledge the caregiver in their own right.

Let us allow mental health professionals to be defined by their role and job title. Let us allow the loved one and support person of mental crisis to be defined by their role, to call themselves a caregiver of mental crisis.

A well-defined title affords a sense of identity and ownership and allows this person, the caregiver, to be seen in their own right. They aren't lumped together with everyone who supports the loved one. They are seen. Their role is known, by others and by themselves.

The Primary Caregiver

The primary caregiver is the one who gives the most care and support to their ill loved one—the most invested emotional, mental, and physical care. They are the primary support person, the primary caregiver.

There may a secondary person who is very invested also, especially when two parents care for their ill child, but even in this setting, there will be a primary person giving the most care and support, often, but not always, the mother, in that scenario.

Identifying the person who gives the most care and support as the primary caregiver is incredibly important as it also allows conversations with mental health professionals to focus on asking the patient or client who their primary support person/caregiver is to interact with and be given permission to contact about their care.

It becomes a clearly defined question on an intake form:

"Who is your primary caregiver at home?

Who is the one who offers the most support and care to you, emotionally and tangibly, for your mental health struggles?"

The caregiver becomes seen, and when they are seen, their own needs can begin to be addressed also. They are not swallowed up and forgotten, grouped into "the family members". The other additional family members and friends who give care are secondary and tertiary caregivers and support people. They are also important people who are affected by the mental health condition and care deeply, however, their role's function is as support people for both the person who is ill and the primary caregiver of the ill person.

In understanding these delineations, confusion is decreased when decisions must be made and care discussed. It is incredibly important for the primary caregiver to realize what their role is and see themselves in that light. It is important for each person to take on and understand their role in the battle for life and improved health. This can decrease confusion and conflict. The caregiver's role matters. This knowledge is impactful. It affects how decisions are made. The patient or ill loved one still has a voice or say in their care, but their primary caregiver is communicated with and can be brought into conversations with professionals (with patient approval), which helps to streamline care.

Have You Accepted the Title of *Caregiver* Yet?

Friend, you may not have viewed yourself as a caregiver before, because in the thick of it, I didn't label myself one either, but you ***are*** a mental health caregiver.

You are a caregiver.

Mental health caregiving is such a unique and difficult role. It is vital and necessary. Emotional, mental, tangible, and logistical support, as well as spiritual support are needed.

You are often unseen by others but are one of the most important, or likely, the most important person in your loved one's life right now. If suicidality is part of the struggle, you are a mental crisis caregiver and fighting for your loved one to stay alive. You can't do it alone. Chapter 3 and Chapters 13—16 are on caring for yourself.

Your loved one needs support—both professional and personal support. You also need your own support including people in your corner who understand the fight and are willing to enter into it with a growth and learning mindset. They are often secondary and tertiary caregivers, precious people who willingly and humbly come alongside to support you, the primary caregiver, and to also support your loved one struggling with mental illness. They choose to learn about the diagnosis and help carry the burden alongside you. They don't make it more difficult on you or your loved one. They respect both of you and support emotionally, tangibly, and spiritually. They advocate on both of your behalf, if needed, and willingly come alongside. They enter into the fight with you without preconceived notions or their own personal agenda in the situation.

You need people who will validate and champion you and your loved one at the same time. These people are rare gold, and they don't come along often.

Recognize them and thank them for being who they are.

Hopefully, by now you are accepting the truth that: You are a caregiver.

Identifying yourself as such does something within you. It changes your perspective and allows you to acknowledge the importance of what you do for your loved one.

Caregiver is a proud and mighty title that is also very weighty.

You are needed and important, and I'm so grateful your loved one has you in their life.

Please don't dismiss my words about your role with a pleasantry. "Oh, anyone would." Or the like.

Accept my truth-filled words. Allow them to settle on you—to permeate your being with their validity and realness.

You are a mental crisis caregiver.

A caregiver.

Your role is crucial.

The role you play is essential to your loved one's wellbeing and continued health and healing. And you shouldn't do it alone. You need trusted, safe, and supportive secondary and tertiary caregivers in your and your loved one's life as well as professional medical and mental health providers and therapists to aid you and your loved one in appropriate care and healing.

The Forgotten Caregiver in Mental Crisis

When mental health crisis hits, the primary caregiver is often forgotten in the midst of and in the aftermath of crisis.

The focus is usually placed solely on the person who is in crisis and struggling with suicide intention or attempts. The caregiver's needs are often placed on the backburner of priorities because the crisis is about the loved one receiving help, medication, and therapy as well as navigating their hospitalization and outpatient care once they are discharged.

The caregiver often diminishes and ignores their own care and needs in crisis too.

The primary caregiver (you) rarely has another person present to recognize and support the caregiver's mental or emotional needs, to make sure the caregiver receives the help or care they need also.

Tangible, physical care is often the need most easily seen and offered—meals or child care offered by those who know about the incident or mental crisis. Usually, though, very few, if anyone, know about it because suicide attempts and crises aren't widely communicated, and therefore the support for the primary caregiver is significantly diminished.

If a person had a physical emergency and hospitalization, meal trains and public prayers over a loved one in the hospital are widely offered, but in mental health crisis and hospitalization, there are quiet and whispered hushed tones with the few trusted people in one's life. It is difficult to navigate.

The caregiver needs a larger level of support, but the sensitive subject matter at hand [suicide] automatically decreases access to support due to its private nature and limited public knowledge. Some of this privacy is to protect the loved one's life and future mental health and is necessary when they are very ill. It does not make it easy though.

Awareness of this disparity of support during a physical versus mental health hospitalization need not discourage us, but instead help us plan for our needs as a result. You, the caregiver, must be your own support person and advocate to seek the mental and emotional care you need for yourself. Pro-actively taking notice of how you are feeling, and what you need at different points, can help you address your needs before you enter burnout with nothing left to offer and no additional energy to give. No one will likely recognize or realize how important your need is for self-care and mental health support. It's not fair, but I know you can fight for your own needs too, friend.

To act as if you are strong and have it all together is not being strong, but holding up a façade, hiding or ignoring the real needs that you have. A façade can only be held up for so long before it begins to crack under the weight of continued upheaval and battering.

Before we splinter and break fully ourselves, let us be brave and honest about how the battle is affecting our own self too. You are not weak to need support, to need community, to cry, or to say how hard this situation truly is.

You are human.

Let us find solidarity together and true strength through *validation and authenticity.*

I delve into this further in Chapter 3 on caregiver burden and burnout and in Chapter 14 on safe, trusted community.

Valid Feelings

Caregiving for mental crisis brings with it a lot of feelings and emotions. You are not alone in those feelings. You may feel utterly alone at times in this battle—desperate, weary, uncertain. I felt those ways. Those are valid feelings.

You may not be sure of the right way forward, and I'm so thankful you are here reading my words. Because as you are beginning to realize, I've been through the hell of suicide caregiving and lengthy mental health crisis. I have my scars and own traumas to prove it. I don't say that lightly, just truthfully. I go into more detail on how it affected me and the scars I carry and mental health struggles I had from it in Chapter 16.

I am so grateful that, because of all that I've been through, I can now "sit down with you" and be able to speak into your own life. This is experiential knowledge, the knowledge that comes only when we have walked through a difficult experience ourselves and truly "know" the depth of feeling and struggle in it. We then can say to someone presently walking through it, "I've been where you're at."

The details may be different, but there is a shared struggle and understanding, gleaned from a hard-fought battle.

It is an honor to speak into your present struggle and not a responsibility I take lightly. We can "sit together" in solidarity and acknowledgment of how hard and difficult it is. You are seen, friend, and you are not alone. Neither am I. I can share from my own story—from our own painful, uncertain story—to help you in yours.

The Gift of Validation and True Connection

As we enter into connection and shared stories, we must do so with a mutual understanding in place. When we mutually choose to respect one another and offer validation, understanding, and compassionate listening to one another, we enter into being seen and known, a vital need as humans. We have not walked the exact story of another, but we may have some commonalities or can listen and learn from someone's story, by giving the gift of presence and community.

We can do this in our relationship, between myself, and you, the reader, and you can also practice this gift of true connection with others in your in-person interactions as well.

The gift of validation and authenticity must be done in *safe, trusted spaces* where you can open up and be honest, knowing you will *receive validation, love, and support* from the ones you choose to share your sacred pain with.

I pray you can find those who are safe in your own circles or begin to search for a group that will be safe. Those who can be trusted with your story and who don't try to force you to "look on the bright side" or make the darkness appear better to help themselves feel more comfortable. Those who sit in the hard with you are rare and a gift.

What a gift it is for another to acknowledge the hard, the pain, the brokenness, without trying to gloss over, ignore, or "fix" it for you. Without pitying you either. To not be alone in the difficult anymore and still be accepted and in community is a gift.

Sometimes, we also need to allow ourselves permission to be in a safe space and feel and acknowledge the negative emotions we hide in front of our ill loved one. Those emotions can be difficult for our loved one to hear about while ill. I pray it won't always be that way and there will be mutual openness in the future at some point, when our loved one is healthier. As we work toward that, though, there still must be time and space for us too, friend, for self-care; for space to be honest, for us to stay healthy in order to caregive and have strength to give out of. It's not selfish. In fact, self-care is lifegiving and incredibly important.

You don't have to do it alone. By my own experience, I know I couldn't do it alone. And you can't either. I can't wait to tell you in Chapters 13 and 14 about faith and community support and how they can support you in your battles as they did for me.

The power of another person sharing about their own similar struggle and pain is a beautiful concert of souls.

Truly. I've been a part of a group where someone else shared a feeling, emotion, or personal insight I'd never voiced out-loud yet, and all of a sudden, I was ushered into feeling seen, "normal", and connected. Validated. Whole.

"You too? I thought I was the only one."[4]

There is power in shared connection.

As we grow in trusted, safe friendship and community, we also need resources and increased knowledge about the diagnoses we are caring for.

The Right Resources & Tools Help Us Not be Alone

When we have the right resources and tools in this new battle, we don't feel so alone in our caregiving. I needed faith in God and psychology, simultaneously. An integrated, holistic approach to mental health treatment accelerates the healing of trauma and emotional pain. My integrated perspective combines reliance on faith in God and medical/ mental health treatment for healing. Both allow us to not be alone as we caregive.

This book is specifically written for the primary person caregiving for someone with mental health crisis. That is the focus. This book is absolutely for you if you don't have faith in God. It is also absolutely for you if you do have faith in God.

We who find ourselves on this battle against trauma and suicide didn't choose it, but we need a way forward and need hope and strength. My ultimate hope is God.

My belief in and perspective on God was the anchor for my soul, as the desperate winds of death clamored at our door.

My faith anchored me.

Redemption Moment & Access to Another's Pain

I asked God in the middle of crisis to redeem our story.

I saw the miracles He was doing, and I knew our story was not just for us. I didn't know when or if I'd ever be able to share publicly about the battle we walked through and declare what God did in it.

But guess what—here I am.

I'm stepping out of the silence and shadows finally to have the honor to share publicly now—for your healing and your story.

A full redemption moment, sharing from our story, not because it is now perfect and we are fully healed from all we walked through. No. It is a redemption full-circle moment because we are further down the road now and have done a lot of trauma work and healing—both my husband and myself. I now have the opportunity and privilege to help you in the midst of the crisis you are walking through right now.

A friend once said, *"I only have access to his pain because of my own pain."* (speaking of my husband). It's true.

Likewise, because of my pain, I have access to yours and can speak experientially into your pain.

There will be differences between our pain and stories, but I'm thankful my pain finds purpose in connecting with and helping you in yours. I'm grateful I can come alongside you in the midst of your battle to *help hold your arms up* * when you can't any longer.

[*Reference is to Exodus 17:11-13 during a battle for the Israelites where God said they would win if Moses held his arms up. His arms began to tire and fall down. The Israelites began to lose their advantage. Aaron and Hur came on either side of Moses and lifted up his arms as the battle raged on, for the Israelites to win the battle against the Amalekites. What a picture of obedience to God and also of others' literally supporting and lifting up Moses' arms when he grew weary and couldn't anymore.

I've been there myself so many times, but how grateful am I for God's strength and help. I'm thankful for how He brings others into my path to encourage and uplift me and vice-versa. We can comfort others with the comfort we have received from God.]

Now, you may be asking: How did you make it through still standing Amber—with all you were up against—crisis & suicidality for your husband, while caring for young children too?

My answer—*Barely.*

But God.

God's strength, my reliance on Him, asking God for discernment and truth, listening to worship music when my mind couldn't focus on the words in scripture or I had no time to sit. And prayer. Praying mighty prayers of deliverance and protection over my husband against the enemy's plan for him.

The enemy was after his life. I have no idea how I would have made it through without my reliance on and faith in God. I share more in depth on my faith in Chapter 13.

My Anchor & Sustenance in Doing the Next Right Thing

Truly—my faith and trust in God were what got me through still standing. This is not a trite statement but the crux of my existence through deep turmoil and uncertainty. God was the One who carried me and was my anchor when the mental illness and subsequent comorbidities swirling around me were beyond my own abilities to handle.

Psalm 69 from the Bible eloquently captures this sentiment:

"Save me, O God, for the waters have come up to my neck. I sink in the miry depths, where there is no foothold. I have come into the deep waters; the floods engulf me. I am worn out calling for help; my throat is parched. My eyes fail, looking for my God" (Psalm 69:1-3).

What I was facing felt overwhelming too.

Later in the chapter, the psalmist calls out:

"Answer me, Lord, out of the goodness of your love; in your great mercy turn to me…answer me quickly, for I am in trouble. Come near and rescue me" (Psalm 69:16-18a).

Truly—my strength and sustenance to keep going day after day came from God's goodness and *His renewal of my capacity to do the next right thing.*

To do the next right thing—To have the capacity to advocate and research the diagnoses and treatment. To care for our young children. To protect my husband from himself and the dangers of his illness.

There were so many days it was hard to function with the overwhelming, consuming nature of the battle I was in, fighting for my husband's life, day in and day out, and the nights too.

Asking God for discernment, for leading, that I wouldn't miss something, and the result be that my husband takes his life. It was stressful, naturally. It was a constant battle, one that did not give rest. And God didn't leave me in it. He walked with me through it.

You don't have to do everything this moment.

You only need to—

Do the next right thing.

A Vital Mental Health Resource

As I grew in my knowledge about trauma and PTSD and cared for my husband's symptoms, one book that was a vital resource for me was "Once A Warrior Always A Warrior" by Charles W. Hoge, a doctor in the U.S. Army.[5] His book was integral to my understanding of the difference between civilian trauma and combat trauma, as well as how PTSD (Post Traumatic Stress Disorder) symptoms presented for different people. We will talk more on those trauma types and specific considerations in the military and veteran population in Chapters 4 and 5, respectively.

Informed Caregiving

I learned all that I could to understand what we were facing in order to approach the issues before us with active, informed caregiving.[6]

> [Informed caregiving is my own coined term with the definition being: caregiving of a diagnosis using evidence-based medicine, research articles, reputable sites, and scholarly articles to inform and guide one's advocacy decisions for a person with an ongoing diagnosis. There is an active role and advocacy present along with education and research on the subject matters in order to be an active, informed participant for the purpose of pursuing the best possible care for the person you are supporting, while respecting their wishes and desires as well.][6]

Some people may approach their caregiving very differently to this though. Their caregiving could be carried out passively and in rote fashion or reactively supporting and caring for their loved one. There can still be great love and a desire to get better but an uncertainty with knowing how to ask questions, research, or find answers. They may take all information and recommendations given at face value, not asking questions of professionals or engaging in active thinking or deductive reasoning and problem-solving. For those who tend more toward this approach, they can still learn and grow in how to research and educate themselves and ask questions to receive answers they need from professionals.

Informed caregiving, on the other hand, denotes being an active participant and actively engaging with the diagnosis, seeking out the best up to date care and researching new and promising evidence-based treatments and adjunctive therapies. It is an interactive, problem-solving pursuit with a desire to understand the why and how behind the symptoms and diagnoses in order to find the best treatments. I believe knowledge is the first step to having an informed caregiver approach. With increased understanding of the neuroscience and physiology of a mental health diagnosis (read more on this in Chapter 4), we can begin to pursue the best evidence-based treatment that matches the issue at hand. We can fight more effectively for our loved one's care and treatment.

Support in Research & Treatment—EMDR Therapy

Researching your loved one's symptoms and educating yourself on their diagnoses from trusted, reputable resources brings necessary support. There is a wealth of knowledge at our fingertips through the internet to support us in growing as informed caregivers, empowered and able to speak on behalf of our loved one's best interests. Using evidence-based scholarly articles, national organizations' mental health education and resources, and medical sites, you can identify information to aid you and your loved one in making informed decisions and pursuing best treatments.

For me, God guided my research and steps as I slowly learned more through reading and researching. As I researched treatment modalities, I came across **https://emdr.com/** and read about this promising therapy that could help my husband significantly.[7] EMDR stands for Eye Movement Desensitization and Reprocessing.[7]

The hope of a promising treatment can help us not feel alone but supported, with a way forward. After I read about and researched EMDR therapy, it was clear it would help my husband. I read on **emdr.com** about different research articles indicating such promise for EMDR treating combat trauma and combat PTSD in veterans.[8] It was extremely hopeful. Chapters 4 and 11 delve further into this powerful therapy, EMDR.

During our lengthy crisis, I searched extensively to find a mental health professional near us with EMDR training and combat trauma/ PTSD experience. It became a disheartening endeavor as likely therapists told me they did EMDR therapy but were not experienced with treating combat trauma and war PTSD. The few clinicians that held such promise in my search ended up not being the right professionals. Neither did they have any recommendations for therapists to pursue.

I knew what my husband needed for treatment but couldn't access the treatment. I did all that was in my own power but still couldn't find someone. It took over 6 months to finally find a psychologist with the right skill set—experienced with combat trauma and trained with EMDR therapy. When my husband was finally able to begin EMDR therapy, we saw significant reduction in my husband's PTSD symptoms after only a few EMDR sessions. Read more in Chapter 11 on psychotherapy (mental health therapy).

Feeling Desperate, but Not Forgotten

I knew what it was like to feel desperate, to know the treatment my loved one needed but not be able to get it for him. I also knew God had not forgotten me, had not forgotten us, through all the difficult ups and downs, waiting, painful moments, and excruciating places of uncertainty.

God has not forgotten you either, friend, in the midst of your uncertainty, your questioning, your whys, your doubts, and your weariness. He is right there with you, and He hears you when you call out to Him. I am certain of that, because He heard my cry also.

"He will respond to the prayer of the destitute; He will not despise their plea" (Psalm 102:17).

Different Days' Focus and Living in the Trenches

As you navigate the correct treatment for your loved one and continue to support them as they go through therapy, it can be wearying day in and day out. It is natural to feel worn down at times from the constant care. Different days call for different focus though when caregiving. Many days for me were not days of researching or calling medical or therapy leads or advocating in appointments, but they were instead days doing life in the trenches, alone, with a heavy weight.

I was in the trenches of living with a young family, being mother, wife, and also caregiver with the stress and constant, pressing question of *"Is he okay right now?"* on repeat in my head, especially when he was elsewhere.

This question was reinforced by his ability to look perfectly okay on the outside, give no external or body indicators, facial expression, etc., while considering on the inside a suicide plan to end his life. I couldn't rely on my ability to "read others" or my intuition always.

I couldn't rely on his words reassuring me he was okay either (because as time went on, he would say one thing yet inside be having increased suicidal ideation or a plan).

His words and inner world might not match, which was incredibly difficult as a caregiver. I would have to gently ask the hard question of him and pray he'd be truthful with me

*"**How are you doing on the inside?**"* became our important question since nothing on the outside belayed what was on the inside.

"Are you thinking of hurting yourself?"

"Do you have thoughts or have you had thoughts of hurting yourself?"

The follow-up question: *"Do you have a plan? Are you telling me the truth right now?"*

"Are you sure?"

These questions were asked very gently and respectfully with care and kindness, never in an accusatory tone. They were asked with seriousness also. I discuss this further in Chapter 10.

Professional Support in Caregiving Helps You Not be Alone

If you are walking through these difficult conversations right now, or may soon, Chapter 6 and Chapter 10 will aid you in approaching your loved one's suicidal thoughts and potential increased risk for suicide intent with a plan or attempt.

It is crucial to be aware of the warning signs of increased suicide risk. It is not all that different from becoming aware of symptoms of a heart attack, a stroke, an anaphylactic reaction, or any other emergency requiring immediate care.

When we begin to view mental health symptoms and conditions *within the construct of other medical conditions,* especially emergent ones, it becomes more able to be *recognized and addressed*, rather than symptoms *explained away or overlooked*.

To be ***empowered*** to know what to do when your loved one is exhibiting signs and symptoms of increased suicide risk is incredibly important.

I can't stress enough the importance of reaching out beyond the two of you for professional support when you are uncertain or thinking there may be increased mental health or suicide symptoms. Consider what you would do if they were cardiac related symptoms. You would call and ask or help your loved one go in to get checked out.

You can call or text 988 in the United States to reach the Suicide and Crisis Lifeline for support. You as the caregiver also need support in navigating an emotionally charged moment or knowing if symptoms qualify as increased suicide risk. Reach out and get the support you need to support your loved one well.

You are not alone in supporting your loved one. Reaching out and contacting a mental health therapy office or hospital and asking for guidance from a therapist or professional helps support you as you give support to your loved one.

Referring to trusted national mental health organization's websites to understand warning signs of suicide risk and finding contact information for support for your loved one and yourself is crucial. You shouldn't walk this journey by yourself. You need support.

Your loved one may try to tell you not to talk to anyone or reach out to anyone for assistance. If so, you are in a difficult position. You do need to be discerning in how to navigate that circumstance to try to respect and keep trust present with your loved one but also get the care and information needed to support them.

- *Be honest* with your loved one and share that what they are dealing with is bigger than them or than you.
- *Share* that you need support to know how to care for them and understand the symptoms they are having.
- *Reassure them* you care for them and know they are struggling.
- *Validate* that what they are dealing with is not easy.
- *Contact* to get support and try to get connected with assistance for yourself and them.

If it is in fact an emergency with increased suicide risk, your loved one will need immediate emergency care. A mental health professional can help you and your loved one navigate that. In Chapter 12, I share some aspects of psychiatric hospitalizations to help demystify some of that experience.

Your Silent Inner Battle

You may feel all alone and wish others knew your silent inner battle. I get it. For me, I wanted others to know. I wanted to be connected and have the tangible and relational support and most definitely the prayer support of others praying over us. Instead, I was/we were cut off from that support in the beginning months of caregiving for him with PTSD and self-medication because my husband asked me not to share. He couldn't have anyone know about his trauma or PTSD.

He would have felt too exposed if anyone knew. What do you do with that? For me, I accepted and honored his request and caregave alone until he finally months later confessed that yes, he struggled with suicidal ideation. Then, I was able to reach out to one support person for prayer. Our support circle slowly grew.

If I had realized there were professional organizations or mental health professionals I could reach out to for support for myself in those lonely first few months, it would have made a huge difference for me. I wouldn't have been caregiving alone, with the burden of caregiving only on my shoulders. He likely would have been open to me talking to a mental health professional even when he wasn't comfortable with people we knew knowing about his struggle.

The Weight of Caregiving

I will say, the weight of caregiving can have large ramifications upon you as the caregiver, upon yourself. I myself have my own trauma from specific events I'll share about later, which occurred during the intense almost 2-year period of fighting for my husband's life. There were also many mini-traumas and the chronic stress of continued, ever-present caregiving.

The walking on eggshells around him (to not potentially be the interaction pushing him over the brink and into a suicide thought pathway, plan, and attempt) was constant. Walking on eggshells was ever-present, my wall up of careful interactions, trying at perfection and hiding my own self, in order to keep him alive. It was hard, friend.

It left me with my own scars, my own triggers and PTSD, and my own journey of healing and growth as well. Ultimately, it led me to writing this book for you and wanting more for you in your journey.

We will focus on those incredibly important topics for the caregiver themselves in Chapter 3 on caregiver burden and burnout and in Part 3: Chapters 13—16.

You yourself must be strong in order to continue long-term caregiving.

Please choose to be honest with yourself and recognize there is nothing flawed about you if you yourself have been affected by the incredibly difficult and life-threatening struggles you have faced.

In fact, *that makes you human.*

Survival Skills

It is a normal and protective response in the face of great danger and stress to develop new ways of coping and survival skills which may or may not be healthy, and thereby could incur new struggles and even trauma to work through as a result.

During crisis caregiving, I developed a survival belief I had to dismantle later through therapy—I talk on this in Chapter 16: My Indelible Scars and Mental Health Struggles.

Friend—You are not super-human.

You and I were never meant to carry such significant weight upon us— the emotional heaviness, physical and mental taxation, and spiritual weariness of fighting for our loved one's life.

Also, **our loved one didn't choose to have mental illness.** They just do.

It is an honor to fight for their life, to come alongside, and to love them through it.

Mental crisis caregiving can be far from pretty. It is hard, but the battle is worthwhile. Because they matter. You matter, too.

It's okay to acknowledge the scars you have as a result of caregiving.

Those scars occurred through battle.

Your battle for the life and healing of your loved one.

I'll leave you with this:

The enemy wanted death for Josh, but God wanted life.

God used me to come alongside my husband to fight for life when he couldn't. I am humbled and grateful. I am praying you will also lean into God in this time—no matter your belief about God—God is there. He hasn't forgotten about you or your loved one—truly.

I can't promise the future for us or for you. We've dealt with suicidal ideation and plan years after the initial lengthy crisis. I talk on relapse in Chapter 17. It is hard.

Know that *you aren't alone* in your battle, friend, and I hope, neither am I.

REFERENCES

[1] "Suicidality." APA Dictionary of Psychology, American Psychological Association. https://dictionary.apa.org/suicidality. Accessed 17 February 2025.

[2] Phillips, R., Durkin, M., Engward, H., Cable, G., and Iancu, M. (2023) The impact of caring for family members with mental illnesses on the caregiver: a scoping review. *Health Promotion International,* **38** (3), June 2023, 1-23. https://doi.org/10.1093/heapro/daac049.

[3] Wayland, S., Coker, S., and Maple, M. (2021). The human approach to supportive interventions: The lived experience of people who care for others who suicide attempt. *International Journal of Mental Health Nursing,* **30** (3), June 2021, 667-682. https://doi.org/10.1111/inm.12829.

[4] Lewis, C. S. (1960). *The Four Loves.* Harcourt Brace, 83.

[5] Hoge, C. W. (2010). *Once A Warrior Always A Warrior: Navigating the Transition from Combat to Home—Including Combat Stress, PTSD, and mTBI*. Lyon Press.

[6] My own coined term and definition for 'informed caregiving', encompassing the important aspects necessary to caregive from a pro-active and educated, informed approach

[7] EMDR Institute, Inc. http://www.emdr.com/. Accessed 17 February 2025.

[8] "Research Overview: Treatment of Military Personnel." EMDR Institute, Inc. https://www.emdr.com/research-overview/. Accessed 17 February 2025.

Chapter 2

BECOMING A MENTAL CRISIS CAREGIVER & FACING NEGATIVE COPING STRATEGIES

Song: "Don't Fight Alone" by: Jon Reddick

We were married with two young kids, doing life until that God-ordained night when the Lord allowed me to discover the nightmares and the Ambien.

My husband wouldn't have told me. He was trying to take care of it on his own, by himself, since the previous year. But, God was bringing me to a specific moment that was led by Him, to reveal the inner battle my husband was fighting on his own.

It was a gut punch to know as a medical provider that my husband had PTSD as he told me the symptoms he was struggling with. It was another gut punch to learn he was taking Ambien to try and cope with it. As a provider, I had strongly cautioned my husband years prior about taking it innocuously for deployment time zone adjustments if possible due to its addiction potential. Ambien was routinely prescribed for military members for upcoming deployments to help them quickly adjust to time zone changes. His unit was no different with Ambien being prescribed for time zone adjustments. Ambien is a sleep medication used for short-term insomnia in patients. It is a controlled substance and has an addiction potential. I was careful and sparing with prescribing it to my own patients for sleep hygiene issues because of its addiction potential. Josh knew my stance on it, and yet, he was taking it, desperate to block out his nightmares. This increased my alarm and alerted me to the severity of my husband's distress.

Finding out in the same moment about my husband's nightmares, recognizing all the symptoms of PTSD for him, and finding out he was taking a medication I had strong reservations against was a lot to take in.

It was a pivotal moment. I had to set my emotions and convictions concerning the Ambien aside in that moment to process through later. The uneasiness, the frustration, the feelings of betrayal couldn't cloud my present judgment. I knew coming off that medication was a fight for another day. I needed to be discerning and careful in my word choices. My husband was hurting in front of me, in emotional pain, with such fear of the nightmares coming to engulf him upon sleeping that he was desperate for anything to increase his courage to face sleep.

In that moment of discovery, he needed his pain to be validated rather than his behavior choices pinpointed.

I wasn't enabling behavior but instead *making a critical judgment call at a difficult moment.* I had to take it one step at a time.

My husband needed me. He needed my support. He needed my empathy, my compassion. I thanked him for telling me. I knew he wouldn't have told me had the Ambien and alcohol not already been beginning to work, decreasing his inhibition in sharing that information with me. Yes, he was also using alcohol to cope. Liquid courage as it's been referred to by some.

'Ambien courage' plus liquid courage was a tough combination.

In assessing the symptoms and the behavior choices, one last question had to be asked. It was one of the most important questions of the night. An emergent question.

"Do you have any thoughts of harming yourself or any thoughts or a plan of suicide?"

The second question also of urgent importance: *"Have you ever had thoughts of harming yourself or had thoughts of or a plan of suicide?"*

When I asked him that night, he denied having present suicidal thoughts or plans or ever having thoughts in the past either. He assured me he didn't struggle with that and hadn't ever dealt with thoughts of suicide or of taking his life.

I accepted his answer. *"Okay."* I was relieved.

I knew we had a lot on our plate, but one issue wasn't present. The life-threatening one. Suicide. Or so I thought.

I helped my husband to bed as the combination of alcohol and his sleep medication kicked in further.

I sat with the newfound knowledge of what we were facing.

It was a mundane and regular night that turned momentous.

An Aside for You

Don't be afraid to ask your loved one the same questions about thoughts of harming themselves or thoughts or plans of suicide right now or ever in the past.

Both are incredibly important to know about as they are warning signs of potential suicide risk in the future. It is incredibly important. Your loved one may not reveal the truth right away if they are, in fact, struggling with suicidal ideation or if they have ever had thoughts of harming themselves or thoughts about suicide or of being dead.

Your asking and being aware of the potential of suicidal thoughts, intention, or plans is incredibly necessary as you support your loved one. Asking once is not enough.

It is important to have an open discussion on it. Tell your loved one you will ask them if you have concern of it in the future and ask them to please tell them if they do begin to have thoughts of hurting themselves or thoughts of suicide or death. A person can have no thoughts and then as other symptoms progress or stressful situations arise, they may begin to struggle with suicidal thoughts, intention, or plans. We must get comfortable with talking about the topic so our loved one can also be encouraged to overcome telling someone in a moment of crisis and emergency in order to get help. We both must learn how to safely talk about difficult topics. Chapters 6 and 10 go into more detail on suicide risk.

A Pivotal Night

Yes, it was a pivotal night. I knew it marked a new chapter. I had no idea the path we were headed on or how long we would face this issue. I didn't know what the future would look like.

All I knew was my husband wasn't in the fight alone, anymore. I was beside him.

We were facing trauma and PTSD.

PTSD is its own giant. The trauma responses, the adrenaline rush to fight or flee. The revving up without an actual danger present. The body feeling on edge, hypervigilant, anticipating danger. Never knowing when your body will feel on edge or with impending doom all of a sudden from something that occurs in your day to bring the trauma right back (known as a trigger). For my husband, there was also dreading the terror at night overtaking him without any ability to get away or escape and stop the nightmares from occurring.

As I mentioned, he had tried to handle the issue by himself as an independent, resourceful guy since the previous year, not wanting it to affect our family. Affect us. The problem is it already *had* affected us.

Regardless of whether he fought it in secret or openly, it was torturing him and affected how he could show up in his life and in his most important relationships, his relationship with me and with his children.

Being alone and isolated in his battle caused him to begin to cope in unhealthy ways.

Fighting a battle alone and isolated is what the enemy of your soul (Satan) would like you to do. *If he can keep you alone and isolated,* *he can take you down a path you may have never gone down if you had other people in the fight with you.*

The insidious, isolated fight for my husband meant he didn't access the mental health care he needed when he began having nightmares and full-blown PTSD. It kept getting worse and more struggles were added as he numbed the pain and self-medicated his symptoms, thinking he was taking care of it.

Negative Coping Strategies

Many who find themselves in a similar situation may resort to similar methods thinking it will help, not realizing the severity of the struggle they are facing. They, like my husband, will use one or more negative coping strategies to numb out the pain.[1]

A negative coping strategy is anything a person turns to in order to numb their emotional pain or bring comfort, distraction, or soothe dysregulation, emotional pain, uncomfortable thoughts, memories, or feelings, or other mental health symptoms they are experiencing.[1]

My husband self-medicated with alcohol and Ambien. Many resort to alcohol since it is widely available and socially acceptable. Going to a doctor for help with sleep can also be a conceivable strategy like he did in order to be prescribed Ambien.

There are many other negative coping strategies people use to try to numb their pain, soothe dysregulation, or give comfort to include turning to: food and binge eating or restrictive eating, sex, pornography, exercise, drugs, money, shopping, perfectionism, people-pleasing, workaholism, busy-ness, control, show or screen watching, or any other behavior or choice used to distract from or numb emotional pain or distressing feelings, thoughts, memories, or in order to face difficult situations.[1] Some people do the opposite and seek out sensation seeking to feel again which can include cutting and self-harm, bungee jumping, gambling, or other high-risk activities.[1]

Identifying negative coping strategies in your loved one's life and in your own life is incredibly important in order to begin to shift towards positive coping strategies (discussed in Chapter 3 and Chapter 9).

When any of these negative coping strategies are used in excess a person enters into a relationship of dependence and toys with the realm of addiction. Addiction is its own difficult beast to overcome.

The problem at its core, however, with any of these negative coping strategies and decisions is this:

They don't fix the underlying problem.

They don't help you get better but add additional problems on top of an underlying issue.

Numbing the Pain is Like a Band-aid Over a Gaping Wound

Numbing doesn't make the pain go away.

Numbing the pain is like placing a band-aid over a gaping wound. When you put the figurative band-aid over the gaping wound, the wound is still there and must be dealt with, must be cleaned out and sewn up. There must be healing work done through mental health therapy to carefully support and guide the person through the struggle they are facing and the underlying emotional pain, symptoms, trauma, or other issue present.

Don't mistakenly believe you or your loved one can "cope" for a little while or longer by exercising it away, eating it away, taking drugs and substances to silence it away, taking alcohol to numb it, using sex or pornography to numb and distract from it, drowning it in perfectionism or workaholism, packing your schedule full so there is no time to think, or any other negative coping strategy.

Numbing emotional pain, difficult memories, or other struggles won't make them go away. They will be there waiting to be dealt with when the negative activity wears off. For more discussion on negative coping strategies, head over to the beginning of the introduction also.

Give Empathy, Validation, and Kindness.

If your loved one is trying to use a negative coping strategy, come alongside them with empathy, validating their pain, and kindly sharing that the choice they are making isn't going to help their struggle get better. Share with them you are there for them and want to support them in receiving mental health therapy to help work through what they are dealing with.

Supportive words you could use are:

"This is bigger than you or me."

"We need help to get through this."

"I'm here to support you."

I will talk later in this chapter about how to talk to your loved one who is resistant to seeking professional mental health therapy or behavioral health care. In that case, seeing a medical provider first will be helpful. Medications are often needed for short-term or long-term for symptom management, depending on the person's needs. These medications can help the person with their symptoms while they are going through mental health therapy to address the underlying issues and conditions.

This is likely the first time you or your loved one have faced this type of issue before. Offering empathy, validation, and kindness can help counteract uncomfortable feelings or thoughts your loved one may have associated with processing and accepting the reality of their mental health struggle.

Let's Focus on Your Story. How Did You Find Out?

Now, friend, let's talk about you and how you found out about your loved one's mental illness. I'm sure you also have a story or pivotal moment when you knew in your gut your life would be different from there on out.

What is your story?

How did you discover you were in the midst of caregiving for a mental health condition or mental crisis? How did you find out you were facing depression, severe anxiety, PTSD, trauma, bipolar disorder, alcohol abuse, substance/drug abuse, schizophrenia, or any of the many mental health conditions our loved ones may find themselves being diagnosed with? While I mention a number of different mental health conditions in the previous sentence, I know I did not state all mental health conditions.

My story as a caregiver involved caring for my loved one specifically through trauma, PTSD, then self-medicating, alcohol use disorder, and the addition of major depression and also suicidality (including suicidal ideation, intention, plan, and attempt). These are the conditions I focus on in this book—the conditions I had 'lived experience' caregiving for.

The resources, tools, and approaches shared here may be applicable to other situations also, but my focus is directly on the issues I interacted with on a daily basis and what our life revolved around. Some may not apply to you, but a lot of it probably still will.

I pray what I share still helps you and blesses you if the conditions you care for are different.

Each story is different in how co-morbidities present and are added (A co-morbidity is an additional diagnosis that is connected to and occurs after an initial first diagnosis.).

I have empathy for all the significant battles you face but will not speak beyond my own lived experience or knowledge I have gained through training, research, and extensive reading and study.

Your loved one's mental health condition may not have begun with PTSD and trauma, but it may have begun instead with insidious depression or bipolar disorder. You may have discovered your loved one had an alcohol or drug problem first—before it turned into suicidal ideation and even suicide attempts.

There can be many paths that wind up in the battle for life and the battle against suicidality and death.

Processing & Accepting the Battle Being Faced

Wherever you find yourself on the journey of mental health caregiving, please acknowledge the truth of it, the reality of it.

Name it—what you are dealing with. Write it down or tell yourself.

Name the mental health condition you are suspecting or worried about if you aren't fully sure and haven't received a diagnosis yet for your loved one.

Coming to terms with the fact that there is a mental health struggle present, and validating that reality is very important.

The reason naming what you are possibly facing is so important is to help yourself begin to *accept there is a new reality to your life.*

The reason this is important is because—

When we acknowledge the new struggle, the new reality we are facing, we can begin to do something about it.

We may not do anything proactive with talking or action yet, but we can begin to work on our own mindset and process the news.

Our loved one needs us. They need our support. They need our advocacy. They need our ability to educate ourselves and research the issue from websites and resources that are trustworthy and from hospitals and professional organizations that will equip us with new knowledge.

We need new knowledge for a new reality. We need new knowledge for a new battle. Our loved ones need us.

They will need us to support them in seeking mental health therapy and likely in seeking out the right behavioral health medications also. There will be a learning curve. We don't have to have all the answers, but we do have to begin to equip ourselves with the knowledge, education, and resources needed to support our loved one with their mental health struggles.

I will stress it again, friend. **Your role in your loved one's life is vital. *They need you.***

As my husband needed me.

How Did I Make It Through?

I didn't know everything.

I did, however, look for the answers I didn't know. I researched and read. I found a book written by a medical doctor to help me understand my husband's war PTSD and how to support him and understand more fully what was going on inside of him.

You don't have to have all the answers either.

But.

You *DO* have to go in search of the answers you need.

That's why you picked up my book. That's why you, in fact, are here right now sitting down with me having this conversation. That's why you are reading my words...

Because you need a friend who's gone through it and learned some stuff along the way.

Stuff that will help you.

In the midst of where you are at right now.

In the midst of chaos, uncertainty, and fear.

Fear? Yes.

Fear is there too because *we fear what we do not know and what is bigger than us, and we fear we will miss something.* I know I did, at least. Our loved one needs us, and there can be fear or worry present for the prognosis and how this diagnosis will affect our loved one and our life. It's okay to name those feelings, too. It's even healthy to name them.

Naming your feelings only acknowledges their reality and validity. It's okay to be honest with yourself, friend. You don't need to share all these thoughts with your loved one who is struggling though presently. Acknowledge them to yourself for now and make sure to read further in Chapter 14.

I won't tell you I know all the answers. I certainly don't know every right answer for every situation that will be faced, but I will encourage you to do what I did in order to learn further.

- Learn all that you can from trusted sources about the mental health condition your loved one has. You can search for the organizations

AFSP, NAMI, and SAMHSA to educate yourself on suicide and other mental health conditions. I share about these organizations in Chapter 6.

- Seek out a professional diagnosis from a medical provider for your loved one if they are willing to be seen.

- Learn what you can from me and other trusted resources. I share many of these resources in Chapter 6 and in the Appendix at the end of the book so you have access and connection to the support and education you need to help your loved one and yourself. I didn't know about all the resources available as I was caregiving through our lengthy ongoing mental crisis.

In Chapters 6 and 7, I share how I approached each day, moment by moment, as I continued caregiving for my husband. Stay tuned.

How to Bring Up the Struggle to Your Loved One

If you suspect your loved one is facing a certain mental health struggle or notice something that indicates the need for mental health support, be careful how you bring it up to your loved one.

Your loved one who is struggling may not be ready to seek professional care. They may be worried and unwilling to consider the idea of seeking a diagnosis or talking with anyone about their mental health symptoms.

Let's be honest. It is hard to talk about our struggles, to talk about our pain, our trauma, our inner world.

Validate the Difficult. Validate the Hard.

The first step to make it a little easier is to:

Validate the hard.

It's okay to tell them: *"That is difficult."* or *"That is hard."*

Try to start a conversation gently about what you have noticed. Give one observation possibly and test the waters out, see how they respond. Are they receptive to what you are sharing?

Are they argumentative?

Are they combative and defensive?

Do they shut down and refuse to talk?

Be patient. Be kind. Share the one observation. Tell them you care about them. Tell them you are there for them and think it would be good to talk to someone about what they are struggling with.

Ask them if they'd be willing to be seen by a doctor about it?

If they are willing, take the next step and tell them you want to support them.

"Can we look at what appointments are available?"

Do it together if they are willing.

You could also find out what appointments are available from their doctor if you have your loved one's permission to call for them.

This approach gives support, choice, and accountability to your loved one which are important.

Your Loved One Needs Support, Choice, & Accountability.

Your loved one may struggle to make an appointment on their own. They may be worried and unsure about going to a mental health appointment for the first time, which is understandable. If they are willing to allow you to make the appointment for them or help them make it, this offers accountability and shared decision making in the process.

They will likely feel safe and heard. They may feel like they had choice and a voice in the decision when you make it together. Working to not be pushy but also encouraging them in getting an appointment made can be a delicate balance. Keep at it.

It may be wise for your loved one to first see a medical provider first as they are aware of what to expect at a doctor's office. It may not feel as scary or "different" as seeing a mental health therapist or counselor. There can be less resistance to making an appointment at a regular doctor's office because they have done it before.

Tell your loved one you would like to be with them at the appointment to support them. Ask if they are okay with you being in the appointment with them so you can help share any additional symptoms you have noticed that may help the provider. Discuss what those symptoms are so your loved one is not surprised in the room when you share additional observations. Offering to go with them to the appointment and acknowledging the importance of it provides support and accountability to your loved one as they go to their first difficult appointment.

If your loved one doesn't want you in the room, ask them what they plan on sharing with the provider. Encourage them to write those symptoms down to not forget any. If you feel there are a few additional symptoms or observations that are important to mention, share those with them also and write them down. Ask your loved one if they'd be willing to share those observations with their provider in the appointment also. Try to communicate these symptoms as observations *(I have noticed 'this.')* rather than accusations or 'you' statements *(You do 'this.')*.

Another way to phrase it is: *"I have noticed 'this' occurring."*

By giving your loved one choice but also providing support, they will hopefully be more receptive to your words and the idea of going to see a medical provider and then after that, a mental health therapist.

Empathy, Compassion, & Trust

As you share with your loved one what you are concerned about for them, be gentle and kind with your words, non-combative and not aggressive. They likely haven't faced or processed what they may be dealing with. They are probably worried themselves and uncertain about talking about it. They need empathy and compassion from you, not a fight of words to convince them about their issue or what they need.

"I think you may be dealing with some depression." comes across kinder and softer than the direct statement of: *"You have depression."*

You could also ask a question in the conversation:

"You've seemed kind of down recently. Why do you think that is?"

Then after they've answered you may share your thoughts also: *"I've been wondering if depression could possibly be present. What do you think?"*

It isn't an accusation but a coming alongside in conversation and support. It helps your loved one feel more okay (safer) with what you are sharing because of how you choose to communicate it. If you are going to be their support person/their primary caregiver, they must be able to trust you.

Building trust as a caregiver is key to keeping trust long-term as you continue to care for your loved one through the ups and downs of their mental health struggle.

Focus on being in it for the long-haul. Be careful with your words. When your loved one trusts you, they will feel more able to tell you when they are struggling mental health wise.

When Your Loved One is Defensive and Resistant to Talking About It

Let's talk about if your loved one is defensive to the observations you've noticed. They may struggle with naming and accepting what they are struggling with. They may be in denial or get angry at you or attack you personally when you lovingly share what you've noticed and observed and what you are concerned may be occurring.

"I'm concerned about you."

"I care about you."

"I have noticed _____."

"I am wondering if you could be struggling with _____."

Remember observations are helpful. Stay away from 'you' statements or ones that could feel accusatory. Communicate your care and concern for them.

The types of phrases in quotations can help the conversation. You may have other statements you use that convey a similar message. These supportive and wondering out loud statements can help your loved know you care about them, are concerned for their wellbeing, and are thinking they may be struggling with depression, PTSD, too much alcohol use, or whatever struggle you are concerned about.

It also welcomes them into considering it for themselves if they haven't yet.

Be aware and discerning with how you word your statements.

If Your Loved One Gets Upset or Angry About the Observations

Your loved one may get angry with you or deny and dismiss your observations completely. Don't push the issue.

You can reply with—*"I'm sharing my thoughts with you because I love you and am concerned about you. I'm not wanting to upset you."*

If you mentioned a specific issue like depression or PTSD you could say: *"Would you be willing to think on what I said and consider the possibility of it? I'm not saying you have it but am wondering if it could be. I'd like to talk more later about it after you've had time to think about what I shared."*

If they immediately become upset about what you've shared, it isn't the time to keep sharing observations and thoughts. It won't go well.

Don't tell them more of what you've observed right then. If they are defensive and upset, they won't be receptive to your words and observations. In the first conversation, try to diffuse the anger, *"I apologize that bringing this up was upsetting to you. Can we talk about it later after you've had time to think about what I shared?"*

Reiterate that you care about them and change the subject.

Don't belabor the point, yet.

If they said they were willing to think about it and consider it, know it is a big win. For someone who was resistant and closed to a subject to the point of being argumentative, to now acquiesce and lower their defenses to say they are willing to consider it, willing to think on it—is a positive.

Be patient and bring the topic up again in the next week to talk about it with them.

"Have you had time to think about what I said the other day about what you might be struggling with?"

They'll answer with yes or no.

Ask them what their thoughts were. If they think there could be validity to it and why.

Once they share, tell them, *"I'd like to share with you why I came to that possibility in the first place. May I share with you so we can talk about it?"*

Get their permission. This shows respect for them as a person and instills trust into the relationship.

Then, share observations that are tangible. Share what you have noticed, specifically.

If it was depression, you may say words such as:

"I've noticed you not wanting to do 'such and such' which you used to love doing."

"I've noticed you spending a lot more time alone in your room away from people."

"I've noticed you saying you are really tired all the time."

"These are symptoms that can sometimes be related to depression." Showing them a list of depression symptoms would help them with clarity and beginning to recognize symptoms that might be attributed to depression.

You could ask them if they have ever experienced any other serious mental health symptoms. *"Have you ever thought about hurting yourself or of being gone? Know that I care about you and am here to come alongside you in support."*

Another question to ask: *"Would you be willing to talk to someone professionally about what we've been talking about? About the observations and symptoms we've noticed?"*

Be patient. Depending on your person, the 2nd conversation may not be able to occur in 1 session. It may take a few conversations as they process the ideas, the observations, and symptoms. It may take a little time for them to come to a place of being open to accepting the idea of the symptoms, the issue, or the diagnosis you are presenting as possible.

Avoid Declarative Statements

Again, avoid making declarative statements about them such as, *"You have depression." "You have PTSD." You have an alcohol problem."* This can put someone on the defensive, and they will be less likely to get the professional help they need.

Your goal is to build trust while encouraging them forward so they can get better and your relationship can stay intact.

Even if you know they have a specific issue, don't be declarative.

Be gracious and gentle with your wording to invite them safely into considering the scary possibility of that reality. Don't allow their pushback to dissuade you.

Here are three sentences for us to consider using instead.

"I think you may have depression."

"This is what I've been noticing. I'm not here to judge you but to come alongside you."

"I think you may need help."

Now, remember, your loved one may get spooked and recoil from just hearing what might be true about them. They will be more likely to consider and accept what you have to say with the last three sentences.

The 'you' statements come across strongly and will likely be immediately rejected and not even considered because the sentences may feel forceful and attacking. *"You have depression." "You have an alcohol problem."*

These statements don't invite the person into conversation or allow the listener to have an opinion on the subject.

The bold declaration can be off-putting. Be aware of that and change your approach.

Friend, I know you care about your loved one and want them to receive the help they need. It is a difficult dance as you respect them as an individual while at the same time coming alongside and coaxing them towards the professional care they need to get better. Keep at it.

Remember, you are in this for the long haul. Your loved one may need time to process the conversations and concerns you are discussing together.

Don't be afraid to bring up the conversations again, with discernment if previous conversations haven't gone well.

"Have you had time to think about what I said before?"

"I care about you and want to support you."

Sharing these types of statements is powerful and will hopefully help your loved one be willing to consider what you are saying. Keep persevering, friend. Support. Care for. Come alongside. Encourage the right help to get better.

Validate their feelings while supporting and encouraging medical and mental health support continuously. Don't give up.

In Chapter 4, we are going to add some knowledge and understanding to your repertoire. We are going to discuss important definitions of potentially underlying trauma symptoms and diagnoses present.

Lastly, ***you also need time to process this news.*** I know it is overwhelming to discover your loved one is struggling with a significant mental health condition. It is life-changing. Acknowledge the truth and reality of that. Work to process through that knowledge. Realize you will need resources and new information to help you in this significant battle you are facing.

Begin researching and learning from trusted and professional sources on your loved one's mental health condition. Encourage your loved one to see a medical provider for their symptoms. Begin talking about psychotherapy and looking for someone to help them process what they are struggling with. If they are resistant to professional help, starting the conversation is the first step to breaking down that barrier.

If your loved one is choosing negative coping strategies to numb or distract from their underlying pain, trauma, or symptoms, *don't only focus on the behavioral choices they are making and distract yourself fully from seeking out the why.*

Why are they numbing with alcohol? Why are they using [insert here what their go-to negative substance or coping strategy is]? They need help healing from something underlying in their mind or emotions in order to begin to learn and choose healthier coping strategies.

You are a mental health caregiver now, and as such, you have a powerful role to encourage, support, and advocate for health and wellness for your loved one. They will likely fight against it at times, but keep persevering, encouraging them toward health and healing. Remember, the healing journey is a long-term focus.

REFERENCES

1   van der Kolk, B. A. (2014). *The Body Keeps the Score: Brain, Mind, and Body In the Healing of Trauma.* Penguin Books, 268.

Chapter 3

CAREGIVER BURDEN & PROTECTING AGAINST BURNOUT

Song: "In the Room" by: Maverick City Music, Naomi Raine, & Chandler Moore (feat. Tasha Cobbs Leonard)

In order to keep going as a caregiver, you will need some care yourself, especially if you are deep in the trenches of mental crisis caregiving. We are going to shift gears and focus on you right now and caring for yourself, the caregiver. If you don't need this yet, that's wonderful. You will soon. It is incredibly important to understand caregiver burden and signs of burnout. Research is finally focusing on this crucial issue—the impact on the caregiver themselves.

The caregiver of mental crisis carries a heavy unseen weight, known as caregiver burden.

Caregiver burden is a term used to describe the emotional, mental, and physical responsibility and weight a caregiver has in caring for their loved one struggling with mental illness.

Research has shown that caregiver burden is increased when the caregiver and ill loved one live in the same house (ex: parent caring for child (or adult child) living in same household or vice versa), and the burden is even further increased if it is a spouse caring for a spouse.[1][2] One study on caregivers found the highest caregiver burden is on the female spouse caring for their spouse living in the same household.[3]

Caregiving can have a negative effect on the caregiver's psychological and physical health as well as on finances.[1][3] Caregiving following a suicide attempt can have objective burden present including: "financial strain, household disruption, increased physical responsibilities, and impaired inter-personal relationships within the family and social network".[1]

Caregiving following a suicide attempt can also have subjective burden on the caregiver which can include the emotional stress from caregiving with difficult feelings of "shame, stigma, grief, worry, and resentment" present for the caregiver.[1] Those who caregive for any aspect of suicidality could have some or all of the types of burden mentioned above.[1][2]

I am not surprised by these findings. While in the past I didn't label the weight and exhaustion and responsibility I had as "caregiver burden", it makes sense. There is a burden, and those who live in the same household do not have a "break" from caregiving.

My experience as a caregiver was as a spouse, the female spouse, caring for her husband in the same household with young children to also care for. There are many similar and also different dynamics present for a parent caring for a child, especially an adult child struggling with mental crisis in the same household. Whether it is a spousal relationship, parent/child relationship, or a different relationship, *there is a significant burden and responsibility present as a caregiver.* Living in the same household means being constantly "on the clock." One research study identified not having time away or time off from caregiving as a factor which could increase caregiver burden.[3] Having no respite.

It makes sense for those who get little to no respite or "time off" from caregiving to have the highest caregiver burden. **Burden can lead to burnout.**

We'll discuss burnout later in this chapter.

The Truth About Caregiving

Here's the truth about caregiving that no one tells you—

Your capacity to juggle as much as you used to will likely diminish.

Your pace may slow some also. This is because you are now taking on a large and impactful new role of caregiver. Give yourself time to learn it and go slow, carefully, with discernment and educate yourself along the way. Give yourself grace as you grow in your new abilities.

Educating yourself with the new knowledge you need helps in moments of overwhelm and moments of urgency or emergency.

Researching and learning about the condition your loved one has will *empower you* to ask better questions of medical professionals, *advocate better* for your loved one's needs, *share truth* with them, and *make wiser, more informed decisions together* as you navigate the difficulties and complexities of your loved one's symptoms and struggles.

Realize you are one person—*Be realistic with yourself about what you are able to accomplish in a given time period.*

Give yourself permission without guilt to decrease the number of scheduled to-do's, activities, and commitments for yourself or your family. It's reasonable and appropriate for a shift in your time and commitment priorities to occur presently as you caregive for your loved one.

Your present priority is supporting your loved one getting better and actively protecting your and your family unit's health—not just physically, but mentally, emotionally, and spiritually as well. Protect your health.

The Weightiness of Caregiving Requires Down-time & Rest

There is a weightiness that comes with constant mental health caregiving and not having time off. As a continual caregiver, it's vital to plan for rest for yourself.

You need a break. You need time "off-the-clock" from caring for and supporting your loved one.

You can only be hypervigilant for so long before your body crashes in exhaustion.

Give yourself down-time. Create space in your life and schedule for downtime, rest, and rejuvenation for yourself. It doesn't have to be lengthy, just intentional. Set aside small moments or larger blocks of time and commit to keeping them.

If you have children and are able to *receive supportive help* from others, you can accept it without feeling guilty for not being able to "do it all yourself".

In Part 3, we'll address how to navigate and determine when to accept offers of help from others and when it's wise to decline help offered. We need support, but we also need to protect and conserve our emotional, mental, and physical health.

It is imperative to consider if an offer of help would be emotionally draining or emotionally supportive when considering the physical, tangible offer of help. We have limited reserves and must protect our energy in order to caregive and care for our other life responsibilities.

Do not accept an offer out of obligation or to not "hurt someone's feelings". Be grateful and always show appreciation in your words for the care and concern if you do decline an offer of help. Again, protect all aspects of your health, to include your emotional health, as you balance your life demands and caregiving.

Rest and rejuvenation are necessary for your continued health and wellbeing. Again, it is wise to be intentional and plan moments of self-care into your life or they will easily get pushed out of the schedule by other demands. Value your needs as important.

Do not try to push yourself too hard through Herculean efforts in your caregiving. Your body has limits. Your energy has limits. Rest is necessary to function well.

Remember, you are in it for the long-haul, not a short sprint. You don't know how long you will caregive in crisis with your loved one. Look at it as a marathon you are on. Fueling your body in all ways, to include rest, is necessary.

Self-care & Physical, Emotional, Spiritual, and Mental Health

Self-care can often have the negative connotation of selfish choices or unnecessary "hope-to" items on a to-do list. This may be our own voice talking in our head that says to care for self is selfish. Let's dispel that lie right now.

Your health matters. Your physical health. Your emotional health. Your spiritual health. Your mental health.

If you are taking care of someone who is ill on a continual basis, you likely have sacrificed and given up activities that would help support your health in one or more of the health categories I listed above.

If you continue to deplete your own resources and sacrifice "your needs" for the higher priority of another's care, you will begin to suffer yourself and head toward burnout.

Many mental health battles are lengthy ones, not just ones better in a week or two. Identifying where you might be struggling and assessing where you are beginning to feel weary and drained is incredibly important. Why? It's because you can't pour from an empty cup.

You have heard the phrase flight attendants say at the beginning of a flight in case of an emergency *"Put on your own oxygen mask before helping put on the oxygen mask for another person."* The idea is self-explanatory. You would stop being useful and pass out and potentially die if you didn't put your oxygen mask on.

In the same way, taking time to consider what vital activities and needs you have to continue doing well (*your oxygen mask as it were*) is very important so you can continue to caregive (*help your loved one put their oxygen mask on*) for your loved one struggling with suicidality. It's also so you can stay healthy yourself.

Let's identify ways to care for yourself and focus on your own self-care.

Your physical, emotional, spiritual, and mental health are connected to each other. Choosing to be intentional and eat food that is healthy for you and nutritious can be a way to fuel your physical health. Making sure you take time to eat throughout your day is also important. Caregiving can require so much of your focus that you may forget to do something as simple and necessary as eating.

Sometimes an activity can help many of the health categories at once.

Exercising is a wonderful form of self-care that can help physically, mentally, and even emotionally. Going for a run, going on a walk, or going to an exercise class is important.

Doing a hobby you enjoy is another wonderful activity. Do you enjoy painting, knitting/crocheting, sewing, pickleball, shuffleboard, running, hiking, chess, board games, a variety of crafts, or another hobby? If you are able to do the activity with people you enjoy being with, that can be very helpful as well and bring a community element in as well.

Being a part of a Bible study and having discussion and support of each other can bring support spiritually, emotionally, and mentally.

Caring for your mental health can mean meeting with a mental health therapist or counselor.

My experience of seeing a mental health therapist and doing EMDR therapy to process caregiving, as well as trauma, was life-giving. I was already working on my spiritual health, emotional health, and physical health, and it was incredibly impactful to prioritize healing for my mental health as well.

Additional examples of self-care are prioritizing a need of yours to include: scheduling a medical appt, therapy appt, or dentist appt, going to a medical, dental, or therapy appt, getting a haircut, getting a massage, or even as basic and important as taking a shower.

I think you get the picture and can begin to brainstorm ways on your own for you to prioritize and care for your health. They don't have to be big activities or be large time commitments to have a big impact on your health and wellbeing.

Positive Coping Strategies

In times of stress, we, the caregivers, *can also turn to negative coping strategies* to help relieve distress, cope with stress or emotional pain,

or numb or distract. In caring for ourselves and our loved one, though, it is important to learn positive coping strategies to counteract moments of stress and overwhelm. These moments will come, and we want to be ready with techniques to aid us in healthy ways. This will be further discussed in Chapter 9, but I will share a short explanation here and my favorite coping strategy. I hope you will try it out yourself. Make sure to read the full section in Chapter 9.

Positive coping strategies use various healthy techniques to help regulate yourself and your nervous system and calm emotional distress or upset.

Positive coping strategies are healthy outlets and activities to manage emotional pain, mental health symptoms, or regulate your nervous system. Examples of positive coping strategies include: breathing techniques, grounding techniques, cardio exercise (including running, dancing, group exercise classes, cycling), yoga, activities that engage your body and movement (including walking), art and creative expression, woodworking, and many other hobbies and activities. Read further on these in Chapter 9.

I will share my favorite coping strategy with you here though as it has helped me significantly at moments of increased stress and tension. You can start using it right away too.

Boxed Breathing & Exercise

My favorite positive coping strategy is boxed breathing which helps decrease stress and tension the moment it starts. My mental health therapist introduced me to it, and I have found it works well.

You can try it right now with me.

This is how to do boxed breathing:

Breathe in for a count of 3 seconds, hold your breath for a count of 3, and lastly, exhale for a count of 3.

Repeat.

I usually repeat this simple technique 3 times if I'm stressed or feeling upset, tense, or dysregulated by something. If you feel lightheaded, make sure to pause between sets for at least 10 to 20 seconds.

If you focus on the exhale portion, you activate your rest and relax system, your parasympathetic system. It will help calm you and decrease your stress a little quicker. To do this, repeat the exercise with a 3-4-5 count.

Inhale for a count of 3 seconds, hold your breath for 4 seconds, exhale for 5 seconds. Again, focusing on your exhale for a longer count pushes your parasympathetic system to help the body rest and relax more quickly. I can usually feel less tension in my shoulders after doing 3 rounds of boxed breathing.

What I love about boxed breathing is I can benefit from it anywhere I am, and no one will likely notice I am breathing slightly differently. It is as simple as breathing and choosing how to breathe.

Exercise is also a wonderful stress reliever. Being active and going for a walk or doing cardio and sweating can help manage stress. Running is one of my go-to stress relievers. You don't have to run though. You can try any activity that moves your body and affords some exercise in order to counteract the stress you have as a caregiver.

Find the positive coping strategies that work well for you. Use them. They are powerful tools in staying mentally well and counteracting stress, difficult emotions, or challenging situations.

We must first take care of ourselves in order to have anything to offer someone else.

Ignoring Caregiver Burden Can Lead to Negative Emotions & Burnout

Caring for yourself as the caregiver is incredibly important to protect against burnout. Ignoring yourself and your needs continuously leads to negative outcomes. One outcome could be resentment of your caregiver role and the sacrifices you've made to caregive. This builds up over time until your ability to caregive well is extremely limited. *If not processed and worked through, resentment of the role could evolve into resentment toward your loved one or their condition.* I know you don't desire to feel resentment towards them if you are feeling that presently.

Thoughts or feelings like this are not ones to feel ashamed of though. **Any negative emotions or feelings that come up are ones to acknowledge and bring into the open in a safe space with a therapist or counselor.** *These feelings and emotions need to be validated and processed in a safe space.*

I will caution you and say, ***don't share these feelings or thoughts with your loved one who is ill.*** It would not be good for either of you at this point to talk about this. Your loved one likely won't have the capacity to interact with your negative feelings, and it could worsen their mental health symptoms and potentially increase their suicide risk (due to feeling bad about how they are affecting you). You need an unbiased professional third party such as your therapist or possibly a mental health caregiver support group to help you process through your negative emotions to be in a healthier place.

I don't recommend sharing these feelings with a friend or family member who is connected to you both either. They will not be unbiased and may feel conflicted, feeling the need to "choose a side" between you and the ill loved one. It is difficult to be a middleman and stay unbiased or give the full support the caregiver needs. They may not understand how to offer support with what you are sharing or may feel the urge to "fix", rather than listen and validate. It can cause more harm to you and leave you confused on how to proceed or feel guilty and condemned for how you feel.

Someone who doesn't understand how to support your negative emotions won't be able to validate your feelings and experiences. They will more likely cause harm to you by dismissing your emotions, placating you, changing the subject, or shaming or judging you for having the thoughts or emotions in the first place.

The person you've been close to "forever" or "since you were kids", etc. will likely be too emotionally invested in you to be able to support you in all the ways you need right now also. It is not a betrayal of friendship for you to need additional support people in your life who "get it". It's normal.

Your close family members will also likely be too emotionally invested to support you in the way you need in processing these emotions and thoughts. Neither the forever friend or close family member will likely be the right person to confide in unless they have walked a very similar story and path to you and have experiential knowledge of this specific experience. This is through no fault of their own. We learn and grow through the processes we have been through and how we respond to them.

You need someone who can validate you and help you process your emotions and thoughts in a healthy way, without bias.

New, Safe People Are Needed—Ones Who Experientially Understand

For a new and difficult challenge, you will need to add new, safe people to your life too. You can still keep your friends you've had "forever", but they will likely not be able to support you in all the ways you need presently. That is okay. It is no one's fault. They can support you in other ways. It is important to realize you need specific individuals who understand the specific struggle you are walking through—ones who experientially get it because they have walked through it themselves.

You need people in your life right now who *experientially understand* the specific struggle you are facing of suicidality caregiving and who can come alongside and support you in that nuanced struggle.

You can keep the other people in your life also, but they won't be able to support you in all the ways you need presently.

Remember—*Share your experiences, emotions, and thoughts in safe spaces with trustworthy, safe, authentic people who will validate and support you.*

Caregiver Burnout

The caregiver often gets pushed to the back and forgotten by everyone, *including themselves*.

Ignoring yourself can lead to burnout and resentment of your role and your sacrifice, thereby limiting your ability to caregive well for your loved one.

Now, you may not deal with resentment, but resentment and other emotions like it (including irritability, anger, and a sense of unfairness) can be signs of heading toward caregiver burnout. Extend compassion to yourself if you are feeling any of these ways. Acknowledge their presence and begin to look for ways to care for yourself as well.

Regardless of the way one gets to burnout, burnout can be difficult to overcome.

Burnout is when you have *nothing left to give*. Your reserves are empty. You are worn-out, overworked, and overtired.

You care about your loved one, but you yourself can't take care of them effectively anymore because you are depleted. When you have reached the place of burnout, you, yourself, need care to restore your health and energy.

If you find yourself completely spent, you have ignored your body's warning signs of depletion long before you got to this point. All hope is not lost though.

You will need to change your habits and intentionally caregive for yourself to begin to restore your own health.

Be patient with yourself, and be gracious.

You likely are used to going full-speed ahead and getting as much done as possible. You can't keep that speed up now. You need to make yourself a priority and take your needs and care off the back-burner and back to front and center. This is not selfish, remember, but a very important focus so you will continue to have the capacity and energy to pursue the tasks and priorities you value, such as supporting your loved one's life and wellbeing.

You matter too, friend. It takes time and patience and you valuing yourself.

You can get back to a place of health, but it's going to take you intentionally choosing to care for yourself and be patient with yourself and your capacity.

The Caregiver Check-In Quiz

Here is a quiz I put together to help you on your caregiver journey.

I want you to take this caregiver check-in quiz and assess how you are doing in caring for yourself.

See how many of these answers you can say yes to indicating if you are taking care of yourself at a present moment or heading toward increased burden and burnout.

Where are you on the continuum?

Give yourself 1 point for each one you can say yes to in the last 7 days.

Caregiver Check-in Quiz

Score yourself by giving 1 point for each Yes answer below.

In the last 7 days, have I:

1. Intentionally gone on a walk or exercised in some way
2. Read a devotional, the Bible, an inspiring blog, book chapter, or encouraging words
3. Talked with someone who was validating, encouraging, and uplifting
4. Been in community with others in a Bible study, hobby group, or support group
5. Eaten a nutritious sit-down meal on 3 different days
6. Written down my thoughts or feelings in a journal, book, phone app, or computer to process them
7. Listened to uplifting, inspiring music
8. Intentionally chose a self-care activity (a hobby or activity you love, can include pedicure, massage, extra workout, or time at a coffee shop or place you enjoy)
9. Scheduled or planned an uplifting, self-care, or friendship-focused activity for the following week
10. Considered my emotions in a given moment and been validating and kind to myself

11. Accomplished a task I felt proud of (if you are in survival mode, it could be a household chore)

12. Prioritized a health need of mine (scheduled a medical appt or therapy appt or had a medical or therapy appt, taken a shower when really didn't feel like it, etc.)

Scoring Directions: Add up your yes answers.

The closer you are to 12, the better you are doing with your caregiver self-care. There is still room for improvement. See below.

- *If you scored a 12-* You are focusing on making yourself a priority in your life. You should feel proud of that. It doesn't mean you aren't still carrying caregiver burden. We all are, which is why we need to take inventory of how we are doing in a given week.

- *If your score is 9 or above-* You are pro-actively working to balance your care also right now.

- *If your score is 4 to 8-* You are heading toward doing better, but you may need to prioritize additional ways to care for yourself.

- *If your score is 3 or below-* You are dealing with more burden right now and don't have the support you need. If you keep going, you are likely going to burnout and run out of energy and the ability to give care as you want to and need to. Remember, you also need care too for your own health and wellbeing. Take time for rest and to take care of yourself. Look at the different categories and write down ideas of something you could do to begin to support yourself better.

Now, if you scored high on the quiz (9 or above): **I would like you to go back to the quiz and take it again, but this time answer the questions for only the last 3 days.**

For item no. 9, answer it for the next 3 days.

The score you now receive for only 3 days will reveal interesting data for you to reflect on as these caregiver needs are needed much more frequently than 1 time every 7 days.

Keep pursuing your own health and needs and identifying ways to care for yourself as well as your loved one.

Identifying areas of self-care in which we can improve or have a need can help us to intentionally consider our week and focus on adding one of them into the next week to try out. **Our focus is to grow and slowly improve in caring for ourselves just like we care for our loved one.** *The intention is not to add further burden or a feeling of failure but to identify areas of growth and ways to support ourselves.*

Put this list up somewhere you can see it.

Carry a copy in your wallet or purse.

*If you begin to notice signs of burnout or overwhelm, exhaustion or weariness—**take the quiz for the last week and see what score you get.** It's likely you began to put yourself and your needs on the back-burner.*

Re-focus and prioritize the self-care item you feel you need right now.

Intentionally, plan a couple other self-care items into the next week (as simple as plan a simple and nutritious meal two days in a row, take a shower, and spend time with a safe, trusted person) If you are faith-based, ask yourself the last time you read the Bible intentionally and connected with God and the last time you had fellowship with other believers. These activities matter significantly.

Choose to intentionally care for yourself (and your loved one).

I can't stress the importance of that idea too much.

Remember—**Choosing to care for your own health allows you the capacity to care for the needs of others more fully as well.**

I want to also give you additional truths to remember and a quick reminder caregiver support check-list to help you along your way.

Caregiver Truths to Remember

These are truths for you—the caregiver. Read them. Speak them over yourself. Internalize them. Do them.

As you actively pursue these truths in your life, you will find your burden feel a little lighter, and you will feel a little more grounded and able to keep persevering. Remember, you are a caregiver warrior. You are mighty. You are important.

Caregiver Truths to Remember

- Advocate for yourself too.
- Small changes create big impact.
- Let go of some to-do's, activities, and commitments.
- It is not selfish to care for yourself; it is necessary.
- Give yourself grace.
- Slowing your pace is needed for this season. Without guilt.
- Protect & Reserve your energy.
- Speak positive truths to yourself.
- Be gracious to yourself.
- You are human too.
- You matter too.
- You are not alone.
- Your loved one still loves you; they are just hurting.
- You are going to make it.
- Keep learning.
- Educate yourself.
- Don't try to do everything.
- Lay down your pride. Ask for or accept help when you need it.
- Write down your to-dos to decrease your mental fatigue.
- Don't be so hard on yourself.

Your pace may slow and your capacity to juggle as much as you used to will likely diminish. This is because you are now taking on a large and impactful new role of caregiver.

Give yourself time to learn it and go slow, with discernment.

Realize you are one person—Be realistic with yourself.

Caregiver Support Checklist

Here's a checklist for you to use as you determine if you are caring for yourself.

You can reference this checklist and the caregiver check-in quiz to identify how you are doing in a given week. If one of these resources is more helpful to you than another, use the one most helpful.

The purpose of these resources are to be simple and quick supports for you as you navigate your caregiver journey.

As you use this caregiver support checklist, checkmark the items you can say yes to right now and over the last week. Identify moments in the last week that one of the bullet points occurred for you. You may have to think a little bit for some of them.

Come back to it weekly or bi-weekly and check-in with yourself and how you are doing at that moment in time.

As you read this checklist, you may have forgotten or not been able to prioritize one of the items or been putting it off. If so, you can choose to go forward with that item, without guilt or judgment of yourself, but grace. Some of the items may require support from other people such as planning respite/rest or spending time in community with others. Consider ways to schedule or plan those times in also if you can.

Caregiver Support Checklist:

You need:

- Respite/rest— time away from caregiving (mental & emotional also) to recharge and regroup
- Self-care— exercise, a hobby, an enjoyable activity, pampering, time with safe friends
- Your own mental health therapist— to help process and heal
  - Do you have an upcoming appointment scheduled with them?
- Support— from your community—mentally, emotionally, spiritually, physically
- Grace— to give yourself and give and receive from others

- God— to give you strength and sustainment to persevere and keep going
- Community— to lift you up and help you know you aren't alone
- Connection— with others who have walked through a similar battle as yourself

Caring for Your Loved One List

This next list is a little different and is focused on your loved one. As caregivers we desire for our loved one to be doing well, and as such, we need them to have quality care and for us to be connected to their care. You don't have to answer any of these with a yes or no but keep them in mind. Which are you needing right now for your loved one? Which one(s) do you need support in presently?

Caring for Your Loved One Checklist:

In caring for your loved one you need:

- Knowledge/researching about your loved one's condition and treatments
  - Education on signs/symptoms of crisis including: signs of increased suicide risk and suicidal intent and information on when to seek emergency care.
- Tools and strategies for navigating different aspects of their care
- Mental health therapist for them
  - The right medical professionals which may include a primary provider and psychiatrist
- Behavioral health (psychotropic) medications may be needed
- Access to your loved one's Suicide Safety Plan (developed with their therapist)
- Understanding their plan of care

Considering these needs for your loved one will help as you navigate their care, trying to determine what aspect of care is needed to help them improve and heal. It will help improve your own sense of wellbeing as their care is more well managed also.

Before we close, I want to shift back to focusing on you, the caregiver, and your needs again. Take time and be intentional in trying out an aspect of caring for yourself and then try another.

As you begin to practice caring for yourself, it will become an increasingly normal and prioritized aspect of your life. You will also start to notice when you are beginning to feel weary and weighed down and in need of being refreshed and cared for. You will begin to proactively make time to care for yourself and realize the importance it has for your health and wellbeing. I know I found this to be the case in my own life. I hope it is for you as well.

REFERENCES

[1] Wayland, S., Coker, S., and Maple, M. (2021). The human approach to supportive interventions: The lived experience of people who care for others who suicide attempt. *International Journal of Mental Health Nursing*, **30** (3), June 2021, 667-682. https://doi.org/10.1111/inm.12829 .

[2] Souza, A. L. R, Guimaraes, R. A., Vilela, D. A., Assis, R. M., Oliveira, L. M, Souza, M. R., Nogueira, D. J., and Barbosa, M. A. (2017). Factors associated with the burden of family caregivers of patients with mental disorders: a cross-sectional study. *BMC Psychiatry*, **17**, 353 (2017). https://doi.org/10.1186/s12888-017-1501-1 .

[3] Phillips, R., Durkin, M., Engward, H., Cable, G., and Iancu, M. (2023). The impact of caring for family members with mental illnesses on the caregiver: A scoping review. *Health Promotion International*, **38** (3), June 2023, 1-23. https://doi.org/10.1093/heapro/daac049 .

Chapter 4

CIVILIAN & COMBAT TRAUMA, PTSD, & THE AMYGDALA

Song: "Yet" by: Maverick City Music (feat. Ashley Hess & the King will come)

I believe when we understand why and how something occurs, we begin to take power and control back for ourselves.

By understanding how trauma responses occur in our body, we can find a way forward toward overcoming them through therapies aimed at the underlying causes. By delving into exploring the way the brain works and how memories are stored, we unlock agency for ourselves.

We take back power for ourselves over something *we once felt powerless against*—trauma and the ensuing triggered responses that come at unsuspecting times and in unsuspecting ways.

I have experienced this in my own life, with my own trauma and the trauma responses that overwhelmed—unsuspecting, powerful, and unwelcome. As I have begun to understand what is going on inside of me with them, I have been able to decrease my responses and take back my life, my choices, my presence in a moment.

By researching and understanding the neuroscience and the way the brain works, I was able to seek out the best treatment, EMDR therapy, for my husband for his PTSD when I was desperate and in the middle of caring for him in crisis. I later used EMDR therapy for myself too, with powerful results. I was also able to learn techniques in therapy to help me in the middle of a response.

Understanding the why brings power and control back. I want that for you also.

Let's dive into these important topics together. Stick with me and reference these descriptions later too.

Trauma To PTSD (Post Traumatic Stress Disorder)

In discussing combat veterans: **"Anyone who has witnessed or been confronted by extremely frightening or horrific events that involved death or serious injury of someone they loved, and who felt helpless or powerless to intervene effectively, are going to be at very high risk for developing PTSD."**[1]

This is an incredibly important explanation for the type of experience that could be trauma in a person's life and later develop into PTSD as a result of trauma responses and additional PTSD symptoms. There is potential inference for how PTSD could develop for civilians also. PTSD is a diagnosis based on specific criteria present in the DSM-5 for the disorder (The DSM-5 and updated DSM-5-TR is the American Psychiatric Association's manual on mental health diagnoses.), and the diagnosis of PTSD is determined by a medical provider.

"Unit members who are likely to be most at risk to develop serious PTSD symptoms are those with the closest personal connection or friendship to the injured individual, those who felt directly responsible in some way for the health and welfare of the injured individual, or those who felt most helpless to intervene in preventing the tragedy."[1]

"...the more personal the trauma is –the higher the likelihood of developing PTSD."[1]

These statements help shape the focus of the discussion of trauma, PTSD, and the intricacies of how it develops, especially for the war fighter, the combat veteran.

No person has control over an experience becoming trauma in their life.

Later in this chapter, we will discuss the amygdala's important role in the brain for cataloging an experience as trauma. Let's first talk about the difference between combat and civilian trauma, though.

Civilian Trauma vs. Combat Trauma

PTSD can result from either: civilian trauma or war/combat trauma.[2] The symptoms must be present for at least a month.

For civilian trauma, typically, the event is a single overwhelming event where the individual felt *powerless and helpless.*[1] [2]

For individuals who have experienced repeated events, such as is the case often for childhood abuse of any form, each traumatic event was a time the person felt powerless or helpless. Bessel van der Kolk has researched the long-lasting impact of ACEs (Adverse Childhood Experiences), including childhood abuse, with impact stretching far into adulthood. I refer you to his book, *The Body Keeps the Score*, for more detailed focus on the long-term impact of Adverse Childhood Experiences.[3]

An adult also can experience a single overwhelming event or multiple events where they felt powerless and helpless. A civilian is not planning for or preparing for trauma to occur, for an accident to happen, or an emergency to take place.[2] The event often takes them unaware; whereas war fighters are trained and prepared to respond to intense and dangerous scenarios.[2]

"Warriors are professionals trained to deal with trauma; most civilians are not and often feel like victims when they experience trauma."[4]

A military member who has been in combat or deployed to a war zone is trained to be tactically ready or on alert.[2] They fall back on their training during combat or when faced with significantly dangerous or potentially traumatic events.[4] This level of alertness keeps them safe and ready for action at any time, ready to assess danger and respond to threat.

There is always a low 'hum' in the background when risk increases, in situations where the potential for danger is higher. To be watchful, more aware. This level of alertness is vital and important in handling any dangerous and potentially life-threatening situation.

Law enforcement, fire fighters, emergency medical personnel, security personnel, military combat veterans (encompassing all active duty, guard or reserve, separated, or retired), and others who put their life in harm's way for duty and/or their job understand the continual present state of being 'ready' and 'on-alert.' It is a crucial aspect of these roles in order to conduct their roles well. Caregiving for a life-threatening diagnosis is another role with a continual present state of 'readiness'. The 'on-alert' term can be vigilance or even hypervigilance.[5]

When a person is trained for a job where they will be in harm's way or directly responsible for life and death situations for themselves or others, they have prepared and trained to anticipate stressful situations, as well as emergent or life-threatening situations. Emergency disaster relief, medical units responding to trauma, and medical personnel interacting with emergencies in their field of training (or responsible for caregiving for life and death conditions for a patient) all can relate to the low hum (readiness) of being aware, alert, and responding with their training.

They utilize this same low hum of adrenaline to execute their job well. They must be alert and ready, with focused energy and clarity, to complete the job before them well. While adrenaline and the fight or flight response is activated in these individuals, this does not mean PTSD is automatically present for these individuals. Accessing their body's natural stress response helps them execute their crucial job with excellence and focused intent.

With continual exposure to these types of emergency and extreme stress situations, there is a higher potential for these individuals to

experience an event at some point in their role which impacts them in a traumatic way.[2]

When a casualty involving death or serious injury occurs, military members at increased risk of developing serious PTSD symptoms are ones with *"the closest personal connection or friendship to the injured individual, those who felt directly responsible in some way for the health and welfare of the injured individual, or those who felt most helpless to intervene in preventing the tragedy"* as quoted in the previous section also.[1]

Feeling "powerless to intervene effectively" in a military combat scenario can have risk for an event being traumatic and ensuing PTSD symptoms developing later.[1]

If an experience was a traumatic event, the person does not have control or choice over whether their experience was, in fact, traumatic or not.[1]

Trauma is determined subconsciously.

For trauma to occur, ***a person does not make a cognitive, rational choice that an experience is traumatic.***

On the contrary, the person's body and limbic system respond to an experience where they felt powerless and helpless, and their amygdala subconsciously catalogs that memory and event as traumatic.[1][4] The limbic system is not controlled by what you may think of as your thoughts or cognition, your conscious thinking.[6][7]

In the limbic system, the amygdala (which processes emotions), the hippocampus, and additional parts of the limbic system are involved in the subconscious memory storing of an event, attaching emotion to that event.[6][7][8] If the amygdala catalogs an experience as trauma, there will be subconscious responses to something called triggers in the future. [8]

The person won't consciously know they went through a traumatic event until later when they begin to experience post-trauma responses to sensory stimuli/triggers connected to the traumatic event.

Triggers and Sensory Information

A trigger is a sensory input that reminds the brain of the trauma that occurred.

A significant discovery by the neuropsychologist, Donald Hebb, is: **neurons that "fire together, wire together."**[7] [9] This is because when two or more pieces of information enter the brain at the same time, they become connected with neural circuitry.[9]

At the time of trauma, other sensory information that 'fired' simultaneously will remind a person of the experience and *take them back' to the moment as if it were occurring right then*. Sensory information is anything communicated by the five senses: sight, smell, touch, hearing, or taste. If something is smelled or heard (or one of the other senses) at the same time as a traumatic event, the two pieces of information can be connected together, 'wired' together.[7]

This is the idea of neuroplasticity and the adaptability/flexibility of brain cells (further discussed in Chapters 8 and 9).[7] [9]

When the information is fired at the same time, it can be wired together and activated again later together, as well.[9]

If I've lost you in that explanation, please stick with me for a little longer. Understanding what occurs during a trauma response is incredibly important to help lessen the effect and take back control during the moment a response is occurring.

Let's unpack this more fully in the next few paragraphs.

A military member experiencing combat trauma (or one of the many emergency-focused roles above) has gone through extensive training to face stressful, emergent, and life-threatening events. As explained above, there could be an event that occurs in conducting their job that their body subconsciously (via the amygdala and other parts of the limbic system) determines to be traumatic. This specific event and the triggers/sensory stimuli associated with it will then affect them traumatically even if other difficult moments and emergencies didn't affect them.

For civilian trauma or combat trauma, a person will have the reminders of the trauma, the sensory information that fired at the same time and therefore is connected to the traumatic memories. **These triggers can activate the fight or flight response when no danger is present.**

The Four Trauma Responses: Fight, Flight, Freeze, Fawn

There are four trauma responses which can occur: fight, flight, freeze, or fawn.[10] [11]

The amygdala activates the stress response to protect the individual from danger.[6] There is the revving up of the adrenaline (fight response) or the need to flee (flight response).[10]

Two other trauma responses are the freeze response and the fawn response.[11] The freeze response is a "shutdown" response where a person is not able to take action even if they desire to or want to, or a person could also freeze or shut down emotionally.[11] Dissociating or passing out can also be connected to the freeze response.[11]

The fawn response is the least known of the trauma responses but necessary to understand as the fawn response can be mistakenly 'praised' in society as a good interaction. The fawn response is to appease or please in order to avoid further trauma or negative action against oneself from another person (from the perpetrator of harm).[10] [11]

"People-pleasing" can be a fawning trauma response learned to protect self from further harm.[10] [11]

By praising people-pleasing behavior, we can unknowingly encourage denial of self and an unhealthy response in others.

Stephen Porges, the creator of the Polyvagal Theory (focuses on the sense of safety or threat), states the most significant takeaway from his and Seth Porges' book *Our Polyvagal World* is to understand: "To freeze, shut down, dissociate, or even pass out is a natural (and often inescapable) response to moments of severe duress".[11] To freeze, dissociate, or shutdown is a survival reflex and outside of conscious control.[11]

The fight, flight, freeze, and fawn trauma responses are all *trauma responses activated 'automatically'* (by the Autonomic Nervous System) in order to protect the individual from danger and harm.[11]

When we understand the different types of trauma responses, we can begin to recognize when they occur for us or a loved one, bringing understanding, agency, and a sense of choice or control back which is incredibly important for a person who has gone through trauma. The choice or control can be finding coping skills to help decrease responses and also choosing to seek healing through mental health therapy.

Brief Overview of the Neural Circuitry of the Brain & the Five Senses

In order to discuss how trauma responses occur, it is important to understand the neural circuitry of the brain upon receiving sensory information. When the body receives sensory information (from the five senses: sight, smell, touch, hearing, or taste), the information is sent to the thalamus in the brain which has connections to both the emotional brain (brainstem and also limbic system, including amygdala; subconscious thought) and rational brain (includes dorsolateral prefrontal cortex; conscious thought).[7][8]

When sensory information is sent to the thalamus, it immediately passes that information to the amygdala in the limbic system more quickly than to the area controlling conscious thought (dorsolateral prefrontal cortex).[7][8] The amygdala interprets the sensory information's "emotional significance" and acts on a threat immediately by alerting the body (via the hypothalamus) to activate stress hormones.[7] It takes microseconds longer for the rational brain to consciously interpret the sensory information and take action.[7]

This is why if you come around a corner quickly and someone jumps out at you, you will likely "start", scream, or respond in some way immediately (the amygdala reacting to potential danger) and then may immediately after laugh or be upset at the person, etc. as your rational brain (dorsolateral prefrontal cortex) has processed and informed you that you are not in danger.[8]

The amygdala receives information and responds first (subconscious thought), while the dorsolateral prefrontal cortex (conscious thought) interprets and responds microseconds later, after cognitively processing.[8] The amygdala's immediate response mechanism is a protective mechanism wired in to protect a person from danger and respond immediately to potential danger rather than waiting to consciously think about and process the information first.[7][8]

The amygdala can activate the entire body subconsciously in order to protect the person.[6] The amygdala is instinctive and can cause immediate action to take place to keep the body out of danger.[7] When the amygdala identifies danger, the fight or flight response or stress response (I'll use these terms interchangeably) is activated by the sympathetic nervous system, thereby causing adrenaline and other stress hormones to be released.[6][7][8]

The physiological changes on the body from the fight or flight response (sympathetic nervous system) include: increased heart rate and blood pressure, increased rate of breathing, and decreased blood supply to the GI system, among other changes.[7][8] This helps the body be ready to respond and react quickly to danger. [6][7]

The issue that occurs with trauma responses is when this system is activated, but no danger is present.

In PTSD, Post-Traumatic Stress Disorder, a person will struggle with the phenomenon of a trauma trigger activating their stress response (fight or flight response), making them instinctively and subconsciously enter one of the four trauma responses (fight, flight, freeze, or fawn) in response to the perceived danger.[10][11] As the trauma response takes over, their body experiences the sensations of the negative event *as if it's happening right now*. This can be extremely jarring and overwhelming, to not have control of the sensations or stop a response from occurring, even when rationally you tell yourself you are safe.

By understanding what occurs in the brain and body when a trauma response is activated, a person can understand why they feel the way they do and seek ways to address the underlying trauma in order to find healing.

In order to change post-traumatic reactions, Bessel van der Kolk, a leading trauma expert and author of *The Body Keeps the Score,* says we must *"access the emotional brain and do 'limbic system therapy'."*[12] He identifies "physical movement, breathing, and meditation" as important ways to "befriend the emotional brain."[12] He mentions yoga, breath work, emotional-regulation techniques, and "purposeful movement and being centered in the present" as important in assisting with this self-awareness.[12]

The medial prefrontal cortex assists with self-awareness and interoception and is the only way to actually "consciously access the emotional brain".[12]

One therapy which can access the limbic system and help to integrate emotional memories and traumatic memories is EMDR therapy.[13][14] How it works is continuing to be discovered.

Ways to Counteract Trauma Responses

Learning positive coping strategies such as grounding techniques or specific breathing techniques focused on decreasing and de-escalating the intensity of a response are ways to help in the moment of a trauma response and also when accessing difficult memories during therapy.[12][15] Using these techniques gives control back to the person after their amygdala and limbic system unnecessarily activate the stress response when no danger is present.

Coping techniques are only one part of the arsenal used to combat these symptoms. Seeking out a professional mental health therapist trained in therapies which can target the amygdala and limbic system (where the trauma response is activated) can begin to heal the trauma memory itself.

EMDR therapy (Eye Movement Desensitization and Reprocessing therapy) accesses traumatic memories and helps re-process and integrate them, thereby decreasing the intensity of the trauma responses.[13][14]

My husband used EMDR therapy to treat his combat trauma and PTSD with great results. I also used EMDR to treat my trauma and PTSD with great results as well.

EMDR therapy works using bilateral stimulation (both sides of the body) while the person briefly focuses on the traumatic memory at the same time. The EMDR process accesses the emotional memories and trauma stored in the limbic system and begins to process and integrate the emotional memories of the traumatic event(s).[13][14] It helps create new neural connections for these memories which decreases their emotional impact.

The processing done in EMDR allows these events to not be "stuck" anymore but instead be integrated into the autobiographical memory (memories from the past), fluid and neuroplastic, as they should be.[12][16]

The memory becomes an experience to learn from, rather than a moment frozen in time.[13][16]

When a 'stuck' memory becomes 'unstuck', the emotional impact of it can lessen and not impact the person as strongly as before.[16]

EMDR therapy helps the traumatic stuck memory become a memory of the past rather than a continual, relived moment of the present.[13][16]

Cognitive elements are incorporated into an EMDR session. After EMDR, the end of the session can be used to cognitively process what occurred during the EMDR portion which may activate the medial prefrontal cortex (center of self-awareness and interoception).[12]

Activating the medial prefrontal cortex would allow the rational brain (via the medial prefrontal cortex) to be connected to the limbic system (where the amygdala and hippocampus are located) and assist in therapeutic results being more effective longterm.[8][12]

Identifying trauma responses and addressing them in therapy can help decrease the intensity of those responses. The trauma responses are usually connected to specific events and memories which haven't been processed appropriately. Someone with combat trauma (or a person in one of the jobs trained for emergencies) who plan to be deployed again or continue in their emergency-focused job would still need to have reliance on their fight or flight response to execute their job effectively. Focusing on only the trauma-related triggers/responses would be important, rather than communicating a belief of all stress responses occurring being negative.

It is in fact the overactive response of the amygdala identifying danger when no danger is present and the corresponding memories which need addressed through limbic-focused therapy (which can access the amygdala), like EMDR.

When the overactive stress response is diminished, the person begins to have improved capacity to respond to stressful situations in a healthier way, with a more appropriate level of response to a situation at hand.

Complex PTSD

While the DSM-V and DSM-5-TR have not formally identified complex PTSD (cPTSD) as a diagnosis, cPTSD is recognized in the World Health Organization's (WHO's) ICD-11 as a diagnosis.[17] Complex PTSD is often the result of "chronic repeated interpersonal traumatic events" on an individual though research has also shown it could occur from any trauma.[17] It has specific criteria for diagnosis that are in addition to a PTSD diagnosis.

I myself have experienced multiple traumas. Whether PTSD or cPTSD, each trauma a person has can have different sensory stimuli/triggers associated with the specific trauma that occurred. This is important to recognize as each trigger can set off the amygdala's fight or flight response in the body.

I believe the triggers can have a synergistic and potentiating effect, increasing the intensity of trauma responses. They can be additive in nature and cause the individual to have an increased struggle to function when one or more triggers are activated in response to something that reminds them and takes them directly back to one of their traumas.

Focused EMDR therapy on each specific trauma, separately, is important to help decrease the intensity of the person's trauma responses and thereby improve their capacity to respond to life stressors and the roles they function in more effectively.

The Amygdala—Your Emotional Processing Center

I named the amygdala: **the emotional processing center.**

I think it is a fitting name for such an important structure. It also makes sense.

The amygdala processes your emotions.[18] **All of your emotional memories, including the emotions of traumatic events, are processed and categorized by your amygdala.**[18] The hippocampus is also involved with interpreting new sensory input from the thalamus and offering feedback to the amygdala.[7] Both the amygdala and hippocampus are in the limbic system.[7]

In *Rewire Your Anxious Brain,* the authors state:

"The role of the amygdala is to attach emotional significance to situations or objects and to form emotional memories."[18]

"The amygdala both forms and recalls emotional memories," whether positive or negative.[8][18] This is significant.

The amygdala, therefore, subconsciously connects your emotions to details in your life—the good and bad of your emotions—to the situations and items of your life.[8][18]

Warm cookies, special memories, and positive feelings from childhood may come flooding back at the smell of fresh baked cookies.[8] You may be amazed at memories you suddenly remember which you haven't thought of in years.

You may see an item and it bothers you or prompts you to feel a certain negative way, but you don't know why. The reason is likely because the item is tied to, or 'wired' to, an emotional memory—a memory from your past which was negative. It may not be the same exact item from that event or time period but similar. That item may have been present when your parents were fighting when you were a little child—an item during a stressful and emotionally negative event. The item and memory (with corresponding emotions) were wired together when formed and still wired together when recalled later.

Through limbic-focused therapy, such as EMDR therapy, you would be able to access that emotional memory.[13][14] In so doing, you could interact with that memory using EMDR and afterwards cognitively process it further with your therapist. During EMDR, it could be connected to other moments of feeling similarly during other moments in your life. The memory and corresponding emotion and physical sensations could be integrated with other past memories as it is processed and the imprint of trauma resolved.[12][13] This helps decrease the impact it has on the present and decrease the intensity of the response to that trigger and memory in the future.

When a traumatic memory can make new neural pathways or connections with other past memory, it can be integrated into the autobiographical memory, where it should be located.[12] [14]

It is difficult and quite likely impossible to effectively access these connections through cognitively focused therapy because the rational, analytical brain (as van der Kolk calls it), specifically the dorsolateral prefrontal cortex, has "no direct connections with the emotional brain, where most imprints of trauma reside."[12] The medial prefrontal cortex does have connections to the emotional brain.[12] Emotional memory is not able to be accessed by the cerebral cortex (dorsolateral prefrontal cortex is a part of it), but emotional memory is accessed by the amygdala because it is processed and stored there.[18] [19]

There are two different memory systems: the emotional memory system (in limbic system with the amygdala) and the cortex-based (dorsolateral prefrontal cortex) memory system.[19]

If there are no direct connections between the two areas, then cognitively thinking and talking about a trauma will be difficult to access the traumatic memory to effectively treat it and decrease the symptoms from the imprinted trauma and the post-trauma responses the individual experiences.[14] [19] [20] The caveat to this is the work of Joseph LeDoux, a neuroscientist, who has shown the medial prefrontal cortex, the center of self-awareness and interoception, to be the only way to cognitively access and connect to the "emotional brain", within limits however.[12] I brought this up in a previous section, and it is incredibly important.

Self-awareness, emotional regulation techniques, mindfulness, breathing techniques, and other body focused awareness techniques such as yoga allow for some of this self-aware connection to take place.[12] [13] Neurofeedback or Vagus nerve focused techniques can also help.[12]

Cognitively focusing on how one is feeling (interoception) and what is occurring physiologically and emotionally in one's body is important and does assist with healing and recovery.[12]

A Brief Look at Ways to Relax and Positively Cope

In the category of trauma and trauma responses, it is incredibly empowering to have the ability to identify a trauma response occurring, understand what is going on in your body, and tell yourself there will be a stopping point to how you are feeling.

A therapist once told us the hormones released from a trauma response can take around 15 minutes to diminish.

Having tools to rely on and implement at the moment of a response is incredibly empowering and gives agency and ownership back to a person who felt helpless and powerless in the past.[20]

To implement breathing techniques which activate the parasympathetic system (the system to bring relaxation hormones), the intensity of the response can be decreased and lessened.[12] [15]

Stimulating the Vagus nerve through certain learned techniques can also be a way to relax and calm the body, counteracting the stress hormones of the fight or flight response.[12] It is wise and good to learn positive coping strategies to counteract trauma responses and also to learn how to respond to stressful moments in one's life as well.

A Powerful Groundwork

By the end of this chapter, you should now have a powerful groundwork understanding of trauma, emotional memory, and the importance of the amygdala in trauma responses. Having this knowledge about the brain is so important in pursuing the right trauma treatment for your loved one or for yourself.

Identifying triggers and learning ways to counteract trauma responses in the moment allows you to take back power and control over your body and life.

You don't feel helpless anymore, but empowered.

If you aren't technical and science oriented, thanks for sticking with this chapter. I know understanding the why and how of trauma and how the brain works will help you in your journey. Reference this chapter as you continue in this book.

When we understand why something is occurring, we begin to take power and control back for ourselves which is very important in the healing from trauma and PTSD.

REFERENCES

[1] Hoge, C. W. (2010). *Once A Warrior Always A Warrior: Navigating the Transition from Combat to Home—Including Combat Stress, PTSD, and mTBI.* Lyon Press, 27-28.

[2] Hoge, 20-21.

[3] van der Kolk, B. A. (2014). *The Body Keeps the Score: Brain, Mind, and Body In the Healing of Trauma.* Penguin Books, 145-149.

[4] Hoge, 23-24.

[5] van der Kolk, 21.

[6] van der Kolk, 42.

[7] van der Kolk, 56, 60-61.

[8] Pittman, C. M., Karle, E. M. (2015). *Rewire Your Anxious Brain: how to use the neuroscience of fear to end anxiety, panic, and worry.* New Harbinger Publications, 21-24.

[9] Thompson, C. (2015) *The Soul of Shame: Retelling the Stories We Believe About Ourselves.* InterVarsity Press, 46-47.

[10] Cook, A. (2023). *The Best of You: Break Free From Painful Patterns, Mend Your Past, and Discover Your True Self in God.* Thomas Nelson, 26-29.

[11] Porges, S., Porges, S. (2023). *Our Polyvagal World: How Safety and Trauma Change Us.* W.W. Norton and Company, 8-10, 14-17.

[12] van der Kolk, 207-210, 238.

[13] van der Kolk, 222, 230.

[14] Brayer, R. (2023). *The Art and Science of EMDR: Helping Clinicians Bridge the Path from Protocol to Practice.* PESI Publishing, Inc., 2-13.

[15] Pittman, 96-100.

[16] Shapiro, F. (2012). *Getting Past Your Past: Take Control of Your Life with Self-Help Techniques from EMDR Therapy.* Rodale, 74.

[17] "Complex PTSD: Assessment and Treatment" https://www.ptsd.va.gov/professional/treat/txessentials/complex_ptsd_assessment.asp - :~:text=The concept of complex post-traumatic. Accessed 25 March 2025.

[18] Pittman, 5.

[19] Pittman, 32.

[20] van der Kolk, 205.

Chapter 5

MILITARY & VETERAN MENTAL HEALTH BARRIERS & PREVENTIVE STRATEGIES

Song: "I Just Need U" by: TobyMac

In the military and veteran community, there is a disparity between the battle in combat and the battle when home. Significant focus is given to training the war fighter, and appropriately so. When they return home from battle, though, they are ill-prepared to recognize, much less know what to do, when mental health struggles knock on their door or *ram it down.*

The struggles begin to take over their life—with potential flashbacks, nightmares, fits of rage, emotional numbing, and/or the feeling of being *an observer to their life* rather than *an active participant* anymore.

Most combat veterans are not interested in talking about mental health.

As my husband told me: *"Whether it's due to a posture of bravado, or a fear of being medically disqualified from supporting their brothers in arm on the next trip downrange, the topic is shunned as many turn away from acknowledging the presence of mental health symptoms in themselves or those around them."*

Mental health isn't a topic desired to be talked of and will likely be shunned and turned away from by anyone in combat ready units and most, if not all, military units or veteran groups. There can be shame or a perceived weakness associated with not having their 'sh*t' together. As we learned in the last chapter though, no one has control of or conscious choice in whether an event impacts their body and their amygdala as trauma. They can't choose what subconsciously is determined to be trauma by their body's protective center, the amygdala.

There is no shame in having mental health struggles.

It is not weakness but extreme bravery to face the demons inside.

This is important for the war fighter to understand as they begin to battle one of the most difficult fights they may ever face. They will likely need a loved one or person they greatly admire to validate that truth to them.

They weren't trained on how to combat trauma responses, not prepared to identify what to do in the face of unrelenting PTSD symptoms. Even if they did have mandated training on PTSD or suicide awareness, they likely clicked as quickly as they could through it or didn't pay attention because they *knew* that would never be their fate. They would never succumb to trauma or PTSD.

The thing is, **they don't have control over what affects them and becomes trauma within them.** *They don't have control or choice* over whether they fight the demon of PTSD or not.

They do have choice in seeking healing and treatment, though.

This is why it's so vital for conversations to be had within the military and veteran communities.

It takes significant courage to muster up the words, *"I'm struggling."*

To say out loud—

"I hear that noise. I smell that smell, and I'm right back there."

"I have hellish nightmares I can't get away from unless I drink alcohol to oblivion."

"I need help."

"I keep feeling like I'm back over there, and it's happening right now."

It takes the same courage that led them into battle to voice the words of the silent battle they are fighting on the inside—the one raging and insidiously consuming them and their life bit by bit.

It may even take *more courage* to stand alone and share their silent battle, one likely entangled with feelings of guilt or shame.

Rising up and speaking out to those who will not shun, condescend, ridicule, or judge you is incredibly necessary. Choosing people to tell who will support and validate your inner battle is crucial for your continued wellbeing and ability to pursue healing—**healing which is in fact possible**.

It may take a while to realize the struggle or fess up to it. Many drown their emotional pain and intrusive, unrelenting PTSD symptoms in one or many negative coping strategies including binge drinking, alcohol abuse, controlled substances (prescribed or illegal) to take the edge off, sexual conquests, fights, or even thrill seeking and adventure-finding to get an adrenaline high, etc.[1]

Even compartmentalizing their pain and only letting the flashbacks, emotions, and nightmares 'access' them at night or when they are off-duty is difficult to do long-term. It may have become 'normal' for them and just how life is. Numbing or dulling the memories and emotional pain may allow them to *get through* their life, not at full function, but at least checking the boxes in some respect in their family life while still bringing their full force and effort to their military role. Or maybe that's slipping too.

What they don't realize, and what my husband didn't realize, about trauma and PTSD is this— **You can't out-run, out-drink, out-compartmentalize, or out-cope trauma or PTSD.**

It will come back continuously to haunt them and force them to pay attention to it.

Their mental health needs must be dealt with and can't be ignored, numbed, or run away from. It already has affected their home life, their closest relationships, and if they do not seek out help, all they have fought for on the battlefield will implode at home and may culminate in taking their very life.

Veteran Suicide Statistics

6,407 Veterans died by suicide in 2022.[2]

An average of 17.6 Veterans died by suicide each day in 2022. [2]

These statistics are sobering and significant. The urgency of need in the Veteran population is even further highlighted when suicide statistics are compared with the non-Veteran adult U.S. population. In 2022, the unadjusted suicide rate for Veteran suicide was 34.7 per 100,000 and the unadjusted suicide rate for non-Veteran U.S. adults was 17.1 per 100,000.[2]

While the Veteran population is smaller than the general population—

The unadjusted rate of Veteran suicide is more than twice the rate of non-Veteran (U.S. adult) suicide per 100,000 in 2022.[2]

We have a suicide epidemic on our hands across the country.

These statistics come from the 2024 National Veteran Suicide Prevention Annual Report discussing data through 2022.[2]

There is an urgent need for this heartbreaking pattern to shift. Many combat veterans turn to negative coping strategies to deal with negative emotions or memories, flashbacks from war, and any other unrelenting symptom. When these coping strategies add exponentially to the struggles and difficulties in their life, or when their 'demons' become too much to bear, suicidality can also enter the picture. The rate at which Veterans are dying by suicide daily is heartbreaking. We must find a way to do more for these warriors, these men and women who served our country.

Of note, there is a link between Substance Use Disorders (SUDs) and suicide risk.[3] "SUDs, such as opioid use disorder, alcohol use disorder, cannabis use disorder, and sedative use disorder, are closely linked to an increased risk of suicide."[3] The 2024 report identified the increased risk was likely connected to factors of "increased impulsivity, impaired coping mechanisms, and brain changes associated with chronic substance use."[3]

The SUDS identified in the report were Alcohol use disorder, Cannabis use disorder, Cocaine use disorder, Opioid use disorder, Sedative use disorder, and Stimulant use disorder with a chart showing rates of suicide deaths in 2022 connected to specific SUDs of recent Veteran VHA users.[2] The chart also identified rates of suicide deaths in 2022 connected to specific mental health diagnoses of recent VHA users who died by suicide. Please see the full 2024 National Veteran Suicide Prevention Annual Report, Part 1 and Part 2, for specific statistics. The links are in the References at the end of this chapter and in the Appendix at the end of the book.

Negative coping strategies can add additional problems, and SUDs can increase suicide risk.

Additional considerations from the report are a history of military sexual trauma (MST) greatly increases suicide risk.[2] Also, the highest percentage of Veteran suicide deaths in 2022 occurred in the 18-34 age range, followed by the 35-54 age range, and then the 55-74, and 75+ age ranges.[2] Increasing awareness of those with increased suicide risk is extremely important.

In supporting all Veterans, it is important to find ways to increase mental health and SUDs treatment and intervention, assist with providing needed housing, and improve lethal means safety.

Firearms are the leading means of death by suicide in the Veteran population and non-Veteran U.S. adult population.[2] 73.5% of Veteran suicide deaths in 2022 involved firearms.[3]

The VA promotes lethal means safety to increase time and space between an individual in suicide crisis and a lethal means object (firearm or any other object used for lethal means).[3] Secure firearm safety is a preventive measure being promoted through the *Keep It Secure* campaign and by offering free cable gun locks at VA medical centers, local law enforcement agencies, and community organizations.[3]

Research has shown increasing time and space between an individual in suicidal crisis and an object of lethal means can aid in suicide prevention due to intervention occurring and/or accessing crisis care.[3] We'll discuss lethal means safety further in the next chapter.

We must do better by our veterans. We must help them to access the mental health services they desperately need. We must find ways to help decrease barriers to seeking mental health care.

Moral Injury

An additional consideration in the military and veteran populations is 'moral injury.' Moral injury is: "the distress experienced when one is required to violate deeply held personal values and morals".[4]

Moral injury and the "associated guilt and shame are highly associated with military PTSD, MDD (Major Depressive Disorder), and suicidality".[4] Trauma and PTSD in military and veteran populations could also have moral injury present or not present.

It is important for the professional clinical team to identify if a patient has moral injury as they continue forward with treatment and implement an appropriate therapeutic plan for the individual patient.

A Different Approach

"Military-related PTSD has increased risk for comorbid mood disorders, anxiety, emotional dysregulation, substance abuse, and suicidality."[4] Multiple comorbidities being present can complicate treatment; however, they are often co-occurring in military-related PTSD. Negative coping strategies such as substance use and abuse are ways of numbing emotional pain. Its presence with PTSD, along with other potential diagnoses above, is not surprising.[1]

I believe there is a different approach that may help decrease the impact of combat trauma on those returning from deployments. I share my plan later in this chapter.

One Veteran I spoke with shared how some units had de-briefs immediately following missions during deployments to talk with a mental health specialist about the mission they just completed. This type of immediate processing of stressful events is beneficial.

The plan I share later is for mass EMDR post-deployment for processing and pro-actively taking steps to mitigate or lessen potential PTSD symptoms. While PTSD cannot be diagnosed until at least 30 days following an event, pro-active steps such as EMDR being utilized post-deployment would be extremely beneficial.

We must do more to change the narrative for these brave men and women to know—

There is no shame or weakness in seeking mental health therapy.

We must help decrease the barriers to mental healthcare access.

Facing their pain, rather than numbing it, is one of the most courageous endeavors a Veteran will ever embark upon.

Look Out For Your Battle Buddy or Wingman—Change the Narrative

The term wingman is used in flying squadrons.

As a military wife, I heard it often, as my husband went through pilot training.

'Look out for your wingman' was a charge to check in and look out for their fellow airmen.

A more widely used and recognizable term across units and military branches though is: battle buddy.

'Look out for your battle buddy.'

The underlying charge is to check in, to care about, fight for, and support your fellow military member or Veteran. It is crucial.

One of the first steps in changing the narrative surrounding mental health is the military and veteran community beginning to more overtly look out for the mental health of their battle buddies. Getting over the awkward or weird nature of talking about how they are impacted by combat events is one of the first steps towards change.

Being willing to talk about it and show care for a fellow military member is significant in changing the culture surrounding mental health in the military community.

It is no different than having their buddy's back on the battlefield or in the air.

It doesn't feel as comfortable or as second-nature, of course, because, likely, the right way to approach mental health topics has never been modeled by others, even if there's been copious suicide prevention training mandated... training done quickly to check a box but not for retention or to apply in real life situations.

That needs to change.

Check in With Your Battle Buddy

For veterans and military members, the culture must shift to allow for the taking a risk to ask about mental health. Choosing to check in with your 'battle buddy' may help them overcome the resistance to seeking mental health care finally.

Checking in looks as easy as a question asked with friendship and support offered.

"Hey, what was that you just said?"

"Hey, how are you really doing? I'm here for you."

"Hey- what did you mean when you said, 'Maybe they're better off without me?"

"What did you mean when you said, 'Maybe I'll just end it all'?"

These statements can be made off-hand or in the midst of joking, but often have truth present, reflecting underlying feelings and sentiments—hence the importance of checking in and asking uncomfortable questions, and showing care.

Checking in can include responding to any number of concerning, dangerous, or self-deprecating statements a person struggling with significant mental health issues could make while *acting like the statements were jokes.* These statements are cries for help.

They may be the only indicator of suicidal intent that a person makes before ending their life and dying by suicide. The people in their units must be aware of warning signs of suicide and mental health struggles in order to help save their buddy's life and get them the help they need to get better.

(Flip over to Chapter 6 to the section: Suicide Risk Factors and Increased Suicidal Behavior for suicidal risk factors to watch out for. The Appendix at the end of the book also has the NAMI and AFSP links for suicide risk factors.)

If you yourself are the military member— You have a front row seat to saving the life of your buddy. Saving the life of your friend—someone you care deeply about.

You have to overcome your feelings of discomfort when treading in the waters of emotions, feelings, and statements said against oneself.

Never assume or dismiss saying *"Oh, they were just joking. They're fine."* Making that type of assumption could mean it's the last time you see your buddy alive. Don't make that mistake. Take the words said seriously. Be a support to your friend.

Tell them to call you or 988 (the Suicide and Crisis Lifeline) or go to the nearest emergency center if they are having thoughts of suicide or a plan. Be a support to the person in your unit or in your veteran group who has made statements like this.

Don't allow yourself to believe the lie that a person is okay who jokes about ending their life.

No negative word stated about oneself is unfounded or doesn't have a possible reality based in actual narrative in one's own mind.

For the Veterans who made it back from war and yet fight a battle in their mind at home, they feel completely unprepared and unable to do so—because they don't have the tools to fight back yet. We have to do better. We must connect them to the professionals who can help them pursue healing and overcome PTSD symptoms and trauma responses in healthy ways. There is hope.

Coming home from war, many still think they must hide all that occurred over there, all that bothered them, all that was hard. And *this* is where the breakdown occurs.

No one tells them that **by facing their demons from war, *they can actually become stronger.*** By working through the intense experiences, they will have improved capacity to live and face their present life as well.

Additional Barriers to Seeking Mental Health Care

There are additional barriers for military members in seeking mental health care. One such barrier is the fear and concern they will lose their position or job. Another is they will be deemed non-combat ready. Another concern is they will fail their unit or team if they can't do their job. A thread running through each of these is the importance of duty and of identity for the service member. The connection of themselves to the job and role they have in the military. Their job defines them and is who they are. They have worked long and hard to get to the place they are. They don't want to fail. They don't want to let their team down.

And if they have deployed before and are in a combat ready unit, they don't want to be left home when their comrades are deployed. They want to fight. They want to do their job they've been trained to do. They are proud of the part they play and proud of serving their country. They don't want to be grounded. These are valid thoughts and concerns and must be addressed. Their wellbeing is at stake, and if they need mental health care, there must be a way forward to overcome this barrier.

This is a difficult barrier to navigate, since a military member who struggles from trauma and PTSD may be grounded for a short period of time or a lengthier period of time, depending on symptoms and length of treatment and response to treatment. They may be "DNIFed" if they are part of a flight unit. It is a significant impact to them as they consider seeking the care they need and also weighing having their livelihood, identity, and community 'threatened'. It is a valid struggle in seeking mental health care and one to be addressed carefully. It is not one that can be ignored.

If the community they are a part of is supportive of seeking mental health care and getting better, it can help in overcoming this barrier to seeking care. Identifying ways to have community and still be connected to their identity can also help decrease this barrier to pursuing mental health care.

An additional barrier to seeking mental health care can be lack of choice in care or needing to pay out-of-pocket expenses if using civilian services not covered by insurance. Money can be a significant barrier for anyone in seeking appropriate mental health care. The stress of increasing financial burden can negatively impact mental health symptoms also.

The Barrier of Worrying About One's Job

When an active-duty military member seeks mental health care, it is important for them to understand the improved symptoms needed or protocols followed to be cleared to return to regular duties. They can discuss these with their medical provider or behavioral health provider. This knowledge can help them feel more comfortable in accessing care. Discussing mental health conditions in a similar way to physical limitations or ailments can improve service members' willingness to access needed mental health care. This can also decrease stigma surrounding mental health treatment.

If a military member hides their symptoms or avoids treatment because they fear unknown job 'repercussions', their condition could worsen because they aren't receiving the medical or psychological care they desperately need. Both physical ailments and mental health conditions have the potential to temporarily or permanently disqualify a service member from certain duties, including deployment.

Getting treatment to get better is the most important focus while it is still important to identify and validate the barriers and concerns present for service members in seeking mental health care. Understanding the steps or protocol to regain limited duties or be fully cleared from a mental health perspective would help alleviate some concern. Being fully cleared depends on the diagnosis and prognosis of the mental health condition.

Sometimes a service member's medical or mental health condition must be evaluated by a medical board and a decision is made regarding retention, discharge, or retirement of the individual from the military due to the severity of the condition. This process can be lengthy. Being aware of this potential is wise.

In the same way a physical ailment could improve or could disqualify a member from returning to their previous job, a mental health condition could also improve or could disqualify a person from their previous job. The condition could be the catalyst to being discharged or retired from the military or (if retained) transitioning to a different role in the military. It can be difficult to come to terms with these types of decisions, but it is wise to be aware of the potential and mentally prepare for the different scenarios that could occur.

The Barrier of Not Wanting to Talk About What Occurred

Another barrier to seeking therapy is not wanting to talk about the events which occurred. Veterans especially can be resistant to talking about specific distressing moments in combat, moments which could in fact be combat trauma. In Chapter 11 on mental health therapy, we will discuss a therapy (EMDR) which helps decrease the need to talk while still providing healing.

Bessel van der Kolk, a leading trauma therapist, found that people may be able to heal with EMDR, without even talking about the details.[5] He states, *"EMDR enables them to observe their experiences in a new way, without verbal give-and-take with another person."*[5] The person can then *"stay fully focused on their internal experience"* which may assist with the results from EMDR.[5] For Veterans, this is an extremely beneficial aspect of this therapy.

Processing stressful events right after they occurred or soon after post-deployment would be beneficial. We'll now focus on potential PTSD prevention strategies to help in processing trauma and intense memories, specifically in coming home from combat.

Post-deployment Mass EMDR Initiative- My PTSD Prevention Strategy

I believe a powerful prevention strategy to decrease PTSD and trauma responses following deployments would be to implement EMDR into post-deployment assessments and re-integration efforts. There is research that shows promising results for EMDR therapy to heal and treat trauma in Veterans.[6] As already mentioned, the incredibly wonderful aspect of EMDR therapy is that even for the people who don't want to talk about what they went through or experienced, they can still find healing and be treated with EMDR therapy because of how it works.[5] [6] Not having to talk about intensely difficult combat moments but still get help processing them with EMDR is wonderful news as it overcomes a barrier Veterans can have to traditional talk-therapy or cognitively-based therapies.[5] [6]

EMDR helps the brain begin to heal itself by accessing stuck memories and integrating them to decrease the intensity of symptoms a person experienced.[7] [8] It can be used for difficult circumstances or memories, an emotionally charged event, or a different issue needing processed. It can take fewer sessions of EMDR therapy to obtain desired results than with other trauma-focused therapies used for military and veteran populations.[6] Because EMDR therapy accesses emotional memory stored in the amygdala, many stressful events experienced by combat veterans (events which were distressing but not traumatic) could still be processed by EMDR and receive benefit.[7] [9] [10]

If there was uncertainty as to the diagnosis of PTSD or trauma versus the individual having gone through stressful events, having acute stress disorder, or just stress-related symptoms, that technicality wouldn't be necessary in order for the individual to process memories and still benefit from EMDR therapy.

I worked as a primary care provider at a military base. I am a Veteran's wife. I have lived through deployments as a spouse while my loved one was in harm's way.

My desire as I envision what would occur in a perfect world for military families would be for the service member coming home to receive a certain number of EMDR sessions regardless of their PTSD score.

Every deployed military member coming home from deployment would have four mandatory EMDR sessions (one hour each) with additional follow-on sessions at the discretion of the therapist. These sessions would focus on the most intense events for them from their deployment and any emotional memories that were connected to the events. This would be done alongside scoring for PTSD and other screening. It would be part of mandatory post-deployment assessments and treatment.

In an ideal world, the spouses and potentially the children would also receive their own EMDR sessions as well. The spouse of the deployed member would receive four EMDR sessions (one hour each) with additional follow-on sessions at the discretion of the therapist. To walk through a deployment as a spouse is a stressful season.

Military spouses are incredibly resilient, strong, and amazing individuals, and they undergo many stressful transitions and situations which impact them. I went through many PCSs (moving), job changes, and other transitions as a military spouse. It would be wonderful to offer spouses the opportunity of processing through those experiences and supporting them in their own individual EMDR sessions.

Again, **seeking therapy is a brave step toward further wholeness and healing. It is not weakness to seek therapy.** It takes courage and strength to do so.

When past experiences become unstuck, an individual can become even more resilient.

I believe there need to be more services available to military spouses to support them in processing their experiences and all the many hats they wear during deployments, PCSs, etc.

During one of our deployments, I had a young toddler and was very pregnant. Navigating life without my spouse was not easy. You do what you must do. You keep at it. And you count down the days, one by one, hopeful for your loved one to return.

While there are questionnaires that are done to screen the spouses and the combat veteran, these only screen for those who may be struggling significantly at the end of a deployment. Typically, when your deployed spouse returns, there is a lot of transition to doing life together again after you have been the sole person 'holding down the fort' throughout a deployment. Learning how to be a team in-person again takes time.

Often the difficult and negative emotions and trying events during the deployment are 'forgotten' and pushed down with the excitement and relief of your loved one's return. Those deployment memories and emotions are not processed.

Wouldn't it make sense to give both the spouse and the combat veteran the opportunity to process through what they just went through—without anyone having to 'choose' or feel odd or somehow weak by needing to go 'process their experiences?'

By including the spouse in their own EMDR sessions to process their deployment experiences, it would strengthen the family unit and could help a family cohesively and resiliently continue forward in military life, stronger and better for it.

I am fully aware this strategy would be an immense undertaking, but I believe it would begin a significant transformation towards improved health in the lives of military members and their spouses.

I also recognize the immense burden of procuring that many mental health clinicians for that many sessions. A DoD contract for those sessions done by mental health professionals experienced with combat PTSD and EMDR therapy would be immensely beneficial.

I believe even on a small scale this could be implemented with advantageous results. It would also *decrease the stigma* of accessing mental health services.

If everyone was required to do EMDR sessions in the post-deployment phase, just like all needing to get their vaccines in their pre-deployment phase, **it would become standard of care. This initiative would normalize mental health services being needed to process stressful events.**

Then, if a combat veteran or a spouse began to struggle with mental health symptoms down the road, their likelihood and openness to accessing mental health services and seeking therapy or counseling would be improved. **It would *normalize the experience* of sitting down and doing mental health therapy.**

Group EMDR Model

There is precedence for mass EMDR sessions being conducted after traumatic events or incredibly stressful events. Mass EMDR therapy has been utilized in the immediate aftermath following natural disasters in disaster relief efforts.[6] A group EMDR intervention was done for child flood victims in Argentina who had experienced trauma related to a flood disaster.[6]

This same type of group EMDR model could be implemented post-deployment for combat Veterans if individual treatment was too burdensome. Four to six individuals could be guided through an EMDR protocol to help them in processing their most stressful combat moments (some potentially being trauma). Four or more group sessions could be accomplished with screening questionnaires completed by each service member before leaving the session. Those needing additional individualized EMDR sessions depending on their scores and answers could then continue with further care at that time.

Inputting this preventive strategy into the post-deployment construct already present makes sense. Because EMDR therapy is revolutionary in its ability to improve symptoms even without the individual talking and sharing their difficult stories, the service members can receive benefit without their buddies knowing (if in group therapy) and without having to verbalize extremely overwhelming memories.[5]

In the military and Veteran population, this especially decreases the significant hurdle present for military members seeking mental health care—the desire to not talk about the experiences they went through. My hope and desire in implementing a mass post-deployment EMDR initiative is for combat Veterans to process their war experiences immediately. I believe this has the potential to decrease the risk of PTSD developing due to proactively processing the stressful events of the most recent deployment through EMDR. I see significant benefit to this strategy being implemented into post-deployment re-integration efforts.

Why not begin to change the tide for our Veterans?

Why not proactively offer them stress care through EMDR therapy to process their experiences and continue forward in their life?

Be the One—A Ripple Effect

Let us support the military and veteran population in overcoming barriers to seeking mental health care. Let us find strategies together with the military members to overcome these barriers so those who desperately need care can get care before they become a suicide statistic. Every single one of their lives matters.

More than 17 veterans dying by suicide each day is too many.[2]

One death is too many.

6,407 veterans dying by suicide in a 12-month span is significant (in 2022).[2]

Those numbers don't account for the active-duty members who also died by suicide in 2022.[2]

These statistics are sobering and must compel us towards action.

We must learn to recognize warning signs of suicide and risk factors before it's too late for a person.

We must remember the number 988, the Suicide and Crisis Lifeline, to contact for guidance in crisis.

We must get uncomfortable ourselves and choose to speak up, to ask if someone is okay, to ask if someone is having thoughts of harming themselves, thoughts of being dead, or a plan for suicide.

We must help others know we care and they are not alone in their silent battle.

The change starts with each of us choosing to be aware of those around us and check in on our 'battle buddy.'

Saving one life matters.

One life saved—one life changed and healed—changes the trajectory of their future, which changes the trajectory of those around them.

It is a ripple effect where one life saved and changed affects another and another life until many lives can be changed for good.

And now, friend, I ask—Will you commit to being that one? Will you be the one to notice and to be brave to ask the person near you how they are doing and how you can support them?

And if they are not doing well—help them get the professional help they need.

You can change a life.

REFERENCES

1   van der Kolk, B. A. (2014). *The Body Keeps the Score: Brain, Mind, and Body In the Healing of Trauma.* Penguin Books, 268.

2   2024 National Veteran Suicide Prevention Annual Report Part 2 of 2: Report Findings. https://www.mentalhealth.va.gov/docs/data-sheets/2024/2024-Annual-Report-Part-2-of-2_508.pdf Accessed 9 July 2025.

3   2024 National Veteran Suicide Prevention Annual Report Part 1 of 2: In Depth Reviews. https://www.mentalhealth.va.gov/docs/data-sheets/2024/2024-Annual-Report-Part-1-of-2_508.pdf Accessed 9 July 2025.

4   Burback, L., Dhaliwal, R., Reeson, M., Erick, T., Hartle, K., Chow, E., Vouronikos, G., Antumes, N., Marshall, T., Kennedy, M., Dennett, L., Greenshaw, A., Smith-MacDonald, L., and Winkler, O. (2023) Trauma focused psychotherapy in patients with suicidal ideation: A scoping review. *Current Research in Behavioral Sciences 4*, 100102. 1-13.

5   van der Kolk, 255.

6   "Research Overview." EMDR Institute, Inc. https://www.emdr.com/research-overview/. Accessed 17 February 2025.

7   van der Kolk, 222, 230.

8   Shapiro, F. (2012). *Getting Past Your Past: Take Control of Your Life with Self-Help Techniques from EMDR Therapy.* Rodale, 74.

9   van der Kolk, 207-210.

10 Pittman, C. M., Karle, E. M. (2015). *Rewire Your Anxious Brain: how to use the neuroscience of fear to end anxiety, panic, and worry.* New Harbinger Publications, 21-24.

PART 2: CARING FOR YOUR LOVED ONE'S SUICIDALITY AND COMORBIDITIES

Ch. 6—12

Chapter 6

HIDING ALL THE GUNS & SUICIDE RISK

Song: "Outnumbered" by: Lakewood Music [feat. Tauren Wells]

I did not inform my husband when I removed the guns from our home. I did it quietly and intentionally with the help of a trustworthy and discreet friend.

During a time when my husband was out of the house, my friend came over, and we transferred all of the guns to my friend's vehicle and ultimately their home for safekeeping. It was a somber but sacred moment in the dark, transferring these items and protecting my husband's life.

Removing items that are a threat to your suicidal loved one is an incredibly difficult but brave act.

Friend, I urge you—Remove all the guns from your home in order to protect your loved one's life. Guns/firearms are not the only lethal means that increase suicidal risk for your loved one. Removing any item from the environment that you have reasonable suspicion to be a dangerous item for your loved one and you suspect to be lethal means for your loved one is justifiable and necessary. Removing excess pills from the home and environment is important. The next section will address lethal means safety more fully.

Remove the items with trust and respect present. This doesn't mean you will come right out and tell your loved one the moment you have removed them from the home, but when you discern the moment is right, you can share with them your care for them and support of them and how you did remove a certain type of item to help support them.

Trust and respect are key tenets to hold onto in the relationship, throughout the battle.

To respect your loved one's wishes and desires even in the face of mental illness is to walk a tenuous but important line.

It is important to treat your loved one the way you would desire to be treated in the same instance, *with dignity and honor. And with love.*

Love will make the hard decision to remove the guns and other threatening lethal means.

This is a necessary step to remove easy access to quick and deadly items and is one step in protecting your loved one in future moments of significant emotional overwhelm and distress.

In our situation, I removed the guns from our home because they were a threat to his life. I did not, however, sell the firearms or permanently get rid of them. I did make them inaccessible to him, did not disclose where they were, and asked him to trust me. I respected him while at the same time took steps to come alongside and protect him.

If you are facing a similar type of decision and trying to determine what dangerous lethal means' threats are present in your own life, know that I empathize with you. It is a difficult and stressful place to be in. Be brave and take the steps to protect and care for your loved one. Remove lethal means from their environment, while treating them with respect and dignity.

2022 U.S. Suicide Statistics

In 2022, a total of 47,891 U.S. adults died by suicide which included 6,407 Veterans who died by suicide and 41,484 non-Veteran U.S. adults who died by suicide.[1] These numbers are out of 18.5 million Veterans and 242.4 million non-Veteran U.S. adults, respectively.[1]

An average of 131.2 U.S. adults died by suicide each day in 2022.[1] On average, 17.6 Veterans died by suicide a day in 2022 and 113.7 non-Veteran U.S. adults died by suicide each day in 2022.[1]

As shared in the last chapter, the unadjusted rate of suicide deaths for Veterans was more than twice the rate of suicide deaths in the non-Veteran U.S. adult population per 100,000 in 2022. The exact unadjusted suicide rate statistics were: 34.7 per 100,000 Veterans and 17.1 per 100,000 non-Veteran U.S adults in 2022.[1]

This is sobering and highlights the urgent need to make strides in preventing suicide for Veterans and non-Veterans alike. One death is too many.

Implementing lethal means safety and other supportive and preventive interventions can begin to change the tide. Educating the general population on mental health crisis, symptoms of increased suicide risk, as well as increasing awareness of the 988 Suicide and Crisis Lifeline can help.

For further details and statistics, reference the 2024 National Veteran Suicide Prevention Annual Report. The link to the full report is in this Chapter's References and in the Appendix at the end of the book.

Lethal Means Safety

As a caregiver for a loved one struggling with suicidal thoughts, intention, attempts, or plan, it is incredibly important to decrease their access to lethal means as a loving, protective measure for the loved one.

Removing lethal means from the environment of your loved one struggling with suicidality is a loving, protective, pro-active measure.

Lethal means safety *encompasses the intentional, focused actions to remove and limit access to lethal means objects (firearms/guns, stockpiled medications, knives, other sharp instruments, etc.) in order to decrease suicide risk.*[2]

Increasing time and distance from a person with suicidal intent and their ability to access guns/firearms, medications, or other lethal means helps decrease risk of suicide and aids in suicide prevention.[3] This is a goal of the VA to reduce military and veteran suicides. According to the 2024 National Veteran Suicide Prevention Annual Report, the leading means of death by suicide was by firearms in the Veteran population and non-Veteran U.S. adult population.[1]

73.5% of Veteran suicide deaths in 2022 involved firearms.[4]

The 2024 report shares a chart with specific percentages of different lethal means involved with suicide deaths including firearms, suffocation (including strangulation), poisoning (including intentional overdose), and other means (including all other means of death) for Veterans and non-Veteran adults, with further subcategories of gender and age as well.[1] Refer to the report for further information.

Awareness and taking pro-active steps for treatment and prevention can effect change and further prevent suicide. As previously mentioned, the VA's Office of Suicide Prevention implemented the *Keep It Secure* campaign and offer free cable gun locks through VA medical centers, community groups, and law enforcement agencies. Increasing "time and space" between a person in suicidal crisis and access to a firearm by using secure firearm storage (firearm locked and ammunition stored in different location) can help decrease risk of death by suicide.[3] [4]

This same strategy can be implemented with the general population. Increasing time and space applies to any lethal means.

By applying the lethal means safety method to the general civilian population as well, it can reduce our loved one's access to lethal means and aid in continued efforts to prevent suicide and decrease suicide risk.

All who are at risk for suicide matter. The Veteran population specifically is at even higher risk of death by suicide, and we must identify strategies to help keep them alive in order to receive the mental health care and other support needed. We must identify strategies to help support every person, Veteran and non-Veteran, struggling with suicidality and at risk for death by suicide. Every single person fighting for life matters.

Implementing lethal means safety is an important step in suicide prevention and decreasing suicide risk. It is a brave and difficult act to carry out— Removing lethal items from your loved one's environment and decreasing their access to items dangerous for them. Limiting their access to lethal means is a powerful step to help protect them in their most vulnerable moments.

Discernment and Careful Decision Making is Required

Every situation is tenuous and requires discernment and careful consideration. In taking steps to remove threats from our home, I didn't remove every knife, rope, and noxious chemical. For my situation and for our story, I knew the guns were very dangerous. I also tried to remove extra pills from the house to limit the potential of him taking toxic levels of a medication such as Ibuprofen or Tylenol. For my own mental wellbeing, I didn't let my mind second guess everything in our home, viewing it as a potential threat to my husband's life. I did the best I could. I was managing so much already and had to ask the Lord for wisdom in removing the most threatening items from our home, the guns—because they were the quickest means towards death.

While I did not remove every knife, rope, and noxious chemical from our home then, I believe I would do it differently today. I wasn't reading about lethal means safety then nor did I realize there were specific guidelines to follow. I took the most necessary actions I knew to protect my husband by removing the guns and decreasing the pills. For our situation, my husband is very able and resourceful and if determined enough, he would have figured out a different solution regardless of my careful protection.

Today, as I read about the VA's strategy to increase time and space from a person in crisis and their access to lethal means as a protective measure against suicide risk, it resonates with me.[3] Reflecting back on my husband's crisis moments, increasing time and space was an instrumental and protective measure for keeping him alive with increased suicidal thoughts and a suicidal plan. My or his therapist's intervention and a subsequent hospitalization were implemented as a result.

If I had it to do differently now after reading about the guidelines on lethal means safety, I would have tried to remove the kitchen knives and use a more child safe knife in the kitchen. He would have strongly pushed against that though with cooking. It would have been a difficult battle. I would have tried to get rid of any ropes lying around also. It was difficult because I was walking on eggshells around him, trying to not upset him and cause him to go into emotional distress and increased suicidal risk already. Removing kitchen knives when he did a lot of cooking and removing ropes would have been incredibly challenging. If I had to go back to that time now though, I would fight to try and do it. Armed with the knowledge from the VA's report and the lethal means safety information, I would have felt more confident to go forward with it. I would have shared respectfully and kindly with him the why behind my actions.

Another challenge with lethal means safety for me was my husband was in the military and as such had many pocket-knives. He used these tools often. I knew he would resist me significantly and just buy more pocket-knives and hide them if I tried to remove them from his environment. I had to be discerning and careful with my decisions to not upset him but also protect him.

Friend, I pray that in your situation you will feel empowered to go forward, carefully and lovingly removing the items posing the greatest risk of harm from your loved one's environment. Remove all guns and get rid of excess pills. Decrease your medicine cabinet amounts. And yes, remove all the knives, friend, whether a pocket-knife or kitchen knife.

In addition, if an item or a means for self-harm is something they mention to you or something they have considered for committing suicide, then that item or type of items has, by very nature, stopped being innocuous. It has become a lethal means for your loved one. It should be removed.

It is now an item that poses a threat to your loved one's life. Carefully work to remove all the items like it from their environment. Discernment in what items to remove can sometimes be difficult to traverse. You can call 988 to have assistance in what steps to take or you can talk to a mental health professional who is knowledgeable concerning lethal means safety. You don't have to do it alone.

As you consider what may be unsafe, ask yourself: Are pills an area unsafe to them? Should you fully remove all prescription-controlled medications to decrease the chance of an overdose or instead significantly decrease the amount present? If you are able to remove all of it, then do it.

As time went on for us, I did remove controlled substances (prescription medications) from the home as much as possible. When I would find Ambien or later another sleep medication in hidden places later when he wasn't supposedly taking them, I found myself in a difficult dilemma. The medication was hidden, and I'd found the hiding spot. Because they were hidden, I had to think through the difficult determination of disposing of all of them, getting rid of some of them (to decrease the quantity of pills), or leaving them there (in order for him to keep using that hiding place, me keep tabs on it, and also not potentially decrease his trust of me). He was hiding the medication from me which affected my trust of him, but because suicidal ideation was an issue, I often chose not to confront him about the pills. I decreased the number of pills or got rid of them all together when I would find them. Confronting him would have blown up and had a high potential for him proceeding down a suicide pathway and possibly losing him. I had to keep my mind on the whole game, not the one moment. It was intensely difficult, not always knowing what the *right* decision was for a given moment.

Would you, in your situation, need to remove all Tylenol and Ibuprofen from your home so they wouldn't take too many of those pills? It's possible. I would encourage you to decrease the amount of any medications in the home, to include Tylenol and Ibuprofen.

If one type of suicide means is removed (firearms/guns), a person who is significantly struggling with suicide intention could turn to a different means. Be aware and discerning. Be wise as you remove items posing harm for your loved one.

You can't control their decisions, *just like I couldn't control my husband's choices.* However, **you *can* support your loved one by limiting their access to ways to harm themselves and end their life.**

Additionally, I would check in with my husband over the course of a day (just a text or phone call saying hi) and have increased awareness of our interactions or job or other stressors he had. **This was important in being aware of** *potential suicide pathway triggers or increased suicide risk while caregiving for him.*

Having A Therapist and Suicide Safety Plan

In addition to removing lethal means from your loved one's environment, it is also imperative your loved one has a therapist they are actively discussing their suicidal thoughts and mental health struggles with. Working in therapy on suicidal ideation and having a suicide prevention plan (suicide safety plan) in place with their therapist is a significant step toward prevention. It is also a proactive step towards life.

A suicide safety plan is a step-by-step plan agreed upon by the client and therapist of what the client will do if they have increased suicidal risk to include increased thoughts, intention, or plan. The one struggling with suicidality often signs the plan alongside their therapist, forming an agreement. The plan details the specific steps the person will take if they begin to notice signs or symptoms of emotional distress and increased suicidal thoughts. Their caregiver/support person should also have a copy of this plan and be aware of the steps in order to help support their loved one in a crisis moment, to get them the emergency care they need.

If you do not have a mental health therapist or counselor, I wrote a resource that is yours free.

Here is the link to download and access my "How to Find a Mental Health Therapist" E-book Guide:

amberjparker.com/theforgottencaregiver/gifts

This Free E-book Guide has the steps I took when we were in crisis. I have used the steps multiple times since as well in finding a mental health therapist.

When Your Loved One Finds the Items Missing

You may be asking or having anxiety over what to do when your loved one finds items missing which you previously removed. That is understandable. Expect it to occur so you are not taken aback when it does. Be prepared to give a kind and caring answer, whilst not disclosing certain details at that time. You can also be proactive in sharing how you removed an item or items from the home in order to support them and share that information in a moment when they seem receptive and calm. Regardless, they may feel upset or accuse you of violating a personal boundary in their life by going through their things, taking away an item belonging to them, or taking away some of their autonomy, by removing an item or multiple items from their environment.

How I Told Him the Guns Were Gone

As I said earlier, I did not inform my husband when I removed the guns with a trusted friend. We did it quietly and discreetly. I knew he may ask at some point where they were, and I was ready to give an answer.

An answer based in truth without disclosing their location. An answer also founded on the message that I cared about him deeply and was there to support him in his fight against suicide.

I actively supported him, advocated for him, and championed him. I had no intention to control him but instead to keep him alive.

I would lovingly tell him "I know you shared with me in the past that you held that gun in your hand and considered ending your life. It is not safe to have guns available in our home for easy access. I would be doing you a disservice as your wife and friend, if I allowed them to be present and available right now. A trusted friend has them in safekeeping."

Additional words could also be "I hope what I did does not upset you, and I hope you will understand this is a step I am taking to support you and care for you. We need you. Your children need you. I need you. You matter."

You could also share "I am removing from our home the items that are lethal means, items that increase suicide risk. I'm removing items that would make it easier to end your life. I'm doing this because I love you and care about you."

Thankfully, when the topic did come up for us, it was not a blow-up moment or a severe crisis moment. He acknowledged their danger and accepted my decision as a protective and loving gesture. He recognized it was an important action step in fighting for his life alongside him.

That may not be the same reaction and conversation you have when your loved one finds out the step you took in removing an item that was life-threatening to them. Again, it's okay to proactively share once it is done and to share in a calm and receptive moment for your loved one.

When Your Loved One is Upset You Removed Lethal Means From Their Environment

Lovingly hold your ground in the difficult conversation if your loved one is upset you removed items of lethal means from their environment.

- Acknowledge their feelings and validate their emotions, without agreeing with them.
- Apologize for the impact your decision had on them—that it upset them and caused negative emotions for them. This shows respect.

"I didn't desire to upset you. I'm sorry that my taking this step was upsetting. My intention was to come alongside you in your mental health fight. I believe this is a necessary and important step in keeping you alive. I hope you will not stay mad at me, and we can continue to have open and trustworthy communication with each other."

Your loved one may try to push for the items to be returned.

- Don't give the items back if they are life-threatening to the person.
- Hold your ground, lovingly.
- Don't enter into an argument or heated discussion.
- Take breaks from the conversation if emotions begin to escalate.
- Do not enable your loved one or be coerced by them.

If you feel able to share with them, let them know if you disposed of the items and threw them away or if you removed them from the environment for safekeeping for an unknown length of time. If you do throw the items away and dispose of them, do not dispose of them at your house or at your loved one's home who is struggling with mental illness.

The times I searched for and found hidden medicine, I made sure to get rid of them away from our home. You don't want the person searching through your trash and finding the items. With controlled medication, there are specific rules for where and how to dispose of them. Look the rules up to find out the appropriate way to get rid of the medication. Contact a hospital for guidance if needed.

Again, it is extremely difficult to make these decisions in real-time as you weigh the risk of your loved one harming themselves against upholding trust in the relationship so they will hopefully tell you if they are having increased thoughts of suicide or suicide intention or plan. It can feel like a catch 22 working to balance protecting their life and holding onto trust and openness in the relationship.

Evaluate each moment and situation individually and consider if there's a way to remove the concerning item from the environment. If it is an item of lethal means, it must be removed to keep your loved one safe and decrease the risk of losing them.

These decisions are weighty, friend, and I'm so sorry you must interact with these decisions and situations.

I've been in the midst of the same angst and struggle so many times, trying to discern the right decision for that specific moment. Please know I am praying for you as you make the hard decisions. Fight to keep your loved one alive. What you are doing matters. I know it feels hard.

Do what you know needs to be done in removing items of lethal means like guns/firearms, pills, knives, and any other item that poses a risk to your loved one. This can include ropes, chemicals, and so many other difficult items.

Be discerning. Reach out for professional guidance if you are unsure at any moment. 988 is the Suicide and Crisis Lifeline number to call or text in the U.S. You can call and be directed to the right person to be given guidance and assistance in your specific situation and help support your specific questions. What you are doing is of significant importance. It is vital because your loved one's life is at stake. Your role is necessary.

Keeping Trust & Rapport Present

Let's explore further the trust aspect of this relationship between yourself (the caregiver) and your loved one struggling with suicidality. Keeping rapport and trust alive and present in the relationship is a high priority as you consider any decision, carefully weighing every action, and all of your words, so if your loved one does have a plan to take their life, they will be more willing and open to telling you.

You must work to keep the channel of communication open with your loved one, so you stay a trusted lifeline of support.

This is important so they have someone they can reach out to when they are significantly struggling and need support.

You walk a difficult line as you discern which step to take and which step to wait on, in your actions and in your words with them. All the responsibility does not fall on your shoulders to get your loved one to the help they need.

You can do everything within your power and not miss any cue or sign, keeping all trust present, and being aware of every warning sign/symptom, and yet, *your struggling loved one still has a choice and responsibility that no one else can take off of their shoulders.*

Your loved one still has to make the choice to reach out or speak up and tell you or someone else if they are struggling with increased suicidal thoughts, intention, or have a plan.

Your loved one struggling with a mental crisis is the only one who has access to their inner world. We can't read their mind. They have to let others in.

We, as the caregiver, can't force our loved one to speak up in severe crisis. We don't have control over that choice, though we desperately wish we did. We can pray they will reach out and we can be present and a support to them. We can also be aware for them and notice small changes in them or identify increased risk factors for suicide to help support them to the best of our abilities.

Suicide Risk Factors and Increased Suicidal Behavior

NAMI (The National Alliance on Mental Illness) offers education on their website of **suicide warning signs** which include "increased alcohol and drug use, aggressive behavior, withdrawal from friends, family, and community, dramatic mood swings, and impulsive or reckless behavior."[5]

Call or text 988 to reach the 988 Suicide and Crisis Lifeline in the United States.[6]

Other suicidal behaviors indicating increased risk of suicide are "collecting and saving pills or buying a weapon, giving away possessions, saying goodbye to friends and family, and tying up loose ends, like organizing personal papers or paying off debts".[5] These suicidal behaviors are indicators of a mental health emergency and seeking professional assistance immediately.[5]

The AFSP (American Foundation for Suicide Prevention) identified risk factors which can increase the risk of suicide or a person dying by suicide. AFSP identifies health related, environmental, and historical risk factors.[7]

Health related risk factors for increased suicide risk include a mental health diagnosis (depression, substance use, bipolar disorder, schizophrenia, and other mental health conditions), a serious physical health condition (including pain) or even TBI (Traumatic brain injury).[7]

Environmental risk factors for increased suicide risk include access to lethal means (such as firearm or drugs), prolonged stress (relationship, bullying, harassment, unemployment), stressful life events (rejection, divorce, financial crisis, loss or other transition), exposure to another's suicide or detailed description of a suicide, or discrimination.[7]

Historical risk factors for increased risk of suicide are history of previous suicide attempts, family history of suicide, generational trauma, or childhood abuse, neglect, or trauma.[7]

When a person has a "change in behavior or the presence of entirely new behaviors" it can be a warning sign of increased risk of suicide, especially if the new or changed behavior is related to "a painful event, loss, or change" in their lives.[7]

A protective factor can help decrease risk. The protective factors AFSP shares for decreasing the risk of suicide include "access to mental health care and being proactive about mental health, feeling connected to family and community support, problem-solving and coping skills, limited access to lethal means, and cultural and religious beliefs which encourage connecting and help-seeking, discourage suicidal behavior, or create a strong sense of purpose or self-esteem."[7]

With increased awareness of suicide risk factors and symptoms, we can more easily recognize symptoms or behaviors in those around us and offer support. As this isn't a comprehensive list of suicide risk factors or symptoms, please reference the NAMI website, NIMH website, and AFSP website for further education, knowledge, and awareness concerning warning signs of increased suicide risk. Those references are at the end of this chapter and in the Appendix at the end of the book.

Mental Health Emergency

Increased suicide risk is a mental health emergency and must be treated in the same emergent manner that other medical emergencies are treated, with focused steps of action to help the person receive the appropriate emergency care for their condition without delay. That is easier said than done if the person at risk refuses to be seen or tries to talk you out of taking them for care. Communicating they have symptoms that need to be seen by a mental health professional and calmly speaking with them and supporting them by driving them to an emergency room or mental health facility offering emergency care is incredibly important.

Arm Chair Advice Givers

Other people who are not in the primary caregiver role will have a lot of opinions and advice on what should be done in just about every situation. Not all of it will be good advice, and often you will receive advice from people who do not understand suicidality and the significant complex nature of crisis caregiving, some of which I have touched on already in this chapter.

They may mean well but their advice could put your loved one at risk and sever the necessary communication you must keep with your loved one to help support them. These people may say: *"You should do this." "Don't let them do that." "If I were in your position, I would just tell them such and such."*

Arm-chair advice giving can be very easy to offer, but it often doesn't take into account the long-term plan. It's usually based on their own opinions and not backed by professional suicide prevention guidelines.

The long-term plan is to stay a trusted individual in your loved one's life who is struggling with suicidal thoughts and to stay a support to them without enabling their behavior or crossing boundaries that should not be crossed, whether a boundary in your life or a boundary in their life. The purpose for this approach is to keep them alive, so they can work through mental health therapy and have stabilizing medications on board… in order to begin to have healing and improvement in the battles within their mind, healing with any trauma, or other significant mental health battle they face.

You are in it for the long-haul so consider everything through that lens.

Close friends, family, and acquaintances won't always have the right answer.

Uphold your loved one's physical safety, feeling of trust, and respect and follow professional advice.

I can't stress this enough. Do not accept advice just because of someone's close familial or relational connection to your loved one struggling with mental crisis.

Be discerning with what advice you take.

Educate yourself from the professional mental health organizations that give education, support, resources, and additional information.

Professional, Government, or Nonprofit Organizations

Some of these organizations include:

U.S. Department of Veterans Affairs

National Center for PTSD

SAMHSA- Substance Abuse and Mental Health Services Administration

NAMI- National Alliance on Mental Illness

AFSP- American Foundation for Suicide Prevention

NIH- National Institute of Health

NIMH- National Institute of Mental Health

American Psychiatric Association

American Psychological Association

AACC- American Association of Christian Counselors

AA- Alcoholics Anonymous

National Council for Behavioral Health

National Council for Mental Wellbeing

PTSD Alliance

DBSA- Depression and Bipolar Support Alliance

Community of Hope

Rethink Mental Illness

The Brain and Behavior Research Foundation

The Jed Foundation

Reboot Recovery

More information will be in the Appendix under Resources in the back of the book.

When you are reading and researching online, please make sure the information you find is from a reputable medical, educational, professional, or government website to ensure the information you are reading is accurate. Use reputable evidence-based information to inform appropriate treatment decisions.

Your role in your loved one's life is important, and your growth in understanding how to navigate suicidality is vital for both of your wellbeing.

REFERENCES

1 2024 National Veteran Suicide Prevention Annual Report Part 2 of 2: Report Findings. https://www.mentalhealth.va.gov/docs/data-sheets/2024/2024-Annual-Report-Part-2-of-2_508.pdf Accessed 9 July 2025.

2 "Lethal Means Safety." https://www.mirecc.va.gov/visn19/lethalmeanssafety/. Accessed 18 February 2025.

3 "Lethal Means Safety Evidence." https://www.mirecc.va.gov/visn19/lethalmeanssafety/evidence/. Accessed 18 February 2025.

4 2024 National Veteran Suicide Prevention Annual Report Part 1 of 2: In Depth Reviews. https://www.mentalhealth.va.gov/docs/data-sheets/2024/2024-Annual-Report-Part-1-of-2_508.pdf Accessed 9 July 2025.

5 "Risk of Suicide." NAMI, National Alliance on Mental Illness. https://www.nami.org/about-mental-illness/common-with-mental-illness/risk-of-suicide/. Accessed 14 February 2025.

6 "Suicide." NIMH, National Institute of Mental Health. https://www.nimh.nih.gov/health/statistics/suicide. Accessed 18 February 2025.

7 "Risk Factors, Protective Factors, and Warning Signs." AFSP, American Foundation for Suicide Prevention. https://afsp.org/risk-factors-protective-factors-and-warning-signs/ Accessed 5 June 2025.

Chapter 7

DAY TO DAY CHAOS & ENTERING INTO ANOTHER'S STORY

Song: "Lion" by Elevation Worship
(feat. Chris Brown & Brandon Lake)

A caregiver of mental crisis or of suicidality does not have an easy role. Being aware daily and checking in without annoying a person is a difficult balance.

For a time, keeping my husband alive was an all-consuming focus of each day and night, and the Lord used that focus to protect his life. I had to learn the touchy dance of being connected enough to know some of what he was up to without him getting suspicious and irritable, hiding or not communicating anymore via talk or text. I tried to keep a careful balance of connecting with him during the day in a normal way in order to hopefully pick up if something was off. I was more specific and intentional about it than maybe at times in the past before I knew he was 'ill'.

Chaotic, Urgent Moments

I remember a chaotic and traumatic night when he became very emotionally upset and unwilling to talk or interact. He grabbed the car keys to drive away, in a very emotionally upset state. I carefully pleaded with him to not leave the house, to stay, but he wouldn't. The risk for suicide was high. I went driving into the night with our kids in the vehicle, hoping to get to him in time before he did anything.

"Lord, let me not be too late."

That night I tried to locate him with the shared location feature showing where he was, but it led me to a desolate spot in the desert with no one around. The phone told me one truth—he was here. My eyes told me the actual truth—he was nowhere close by. Desperate to find him, I pleaded with the Lord, asking Him to help me not be too late.

The Lord guided me.

Somehow, I was led to the remote place my husband actually was—parked, out of his vehicle, shirt dirty, emotionally distraught, but physically unharmed, as of yet. I came alongside him in support. Checking in with him, he denied having a current plan to harm himself. His torrent of emotion from before had lessened enough for him to accept input and support from another person, and he was able to be supported and brought home.

Another time, I bought an emergency plane ticket and flew to a different state to support and help bring him home following a very difficult and triggering experience for him. My friend came to my rescue to care for my children as I came alongside my husband out-of-state.

There were middle of the night emergency room visits as well and either a friend or my dad coming to my aid at a moment's notice.

There were many other nuanced, chaotic moments and days and often nights of worry, concern, and careful discernment of what to say or not say, do or not do. Evaluating. Determining if he needed care right then. Discerning what the right decision was in the present moment. Moments of support, of caregiving, of advocating, of being present.

Walking On Eggshells

There were so many moments for me of living life, walking on eggshells around him, not wanting to set him off, or be the trigger in him becoming dysregulated and heading down a suicide pathway.

I put immense pressure on myself—pressure that I had to at the time.

We were in the thick of battle—in the thick of fighting for his life, and I didn't get a day off. My husband was sick, and I was there to care for him.

I couldn't let my guard down or not be on alert. If I did, the results could have been too high, losing him fully to death. It was intense. I talk more in detail on the impact it had on me in Chapter 16: My Indelible Scars & Mental Health Struggles.

Responding To Others' Stories With Compassion and Validation

When I or another person shares vulnerably about an experience or story, others may immediately judge or have opinions about the actions or choices, or how the story was told, what was communicated or intentionally left out. This can be part of processing and interacting with new information.

There can even be the temptation to be an armchair quarterback which we discussed in the last chapter. An armchair quarterback is one who offers their opinion, advice, or determination on a situation they've never experienced or found themselves actually in. In this instance, they may immediately jump to judging, dismissing, being skeptical, critical, or finding fault with parts of a story someone shares- such as with my sharing of intense difficult moments during mental crisis caregiving.

If this is your tendency, make sure to pause yourself before you go forward with sharing your opinions or advice on someone's significantly difficult moments. Try to find commonality even if you've never walked through that specific experience.

Empathy is incredibly helpful in these moments. Pause and think back to one of your most painful, overwhelming, or potentially traumatic moments in your life. Think about how you felt in it. Then, consider how you would hope someone else would respond to you if you shared your vulnerable, painful details and story...

Likely, you'd hope they'd be kind with their words, validate how difficult that experience was for you, and show appreciation for you sharing your story with them.

As you consider yourself, hopefully, you will be able to shift and treat me or my husband, or another person in front of you sharing a difficult experience, with more grace and empathy and less criticism or judgment in the moment of hearing a story.

We can all collectively do better with how we respond to difficult stories or news someone shares about their life.

Rather than responding with pat answers, platitudes, or even negativity, criticism, or immediate "kind" advice, *let us pause and honor what has been shared.*

Let us respond to another's experience and vulnerable sharing with validation, kindness, and compassionate acceptance.

Anyone can have "after the fact" ideas about how they might do something differently or how something could be done better. Please consider the impact your words will have on the other person, whether it is me or my husband, or someone else sharing vulnerably, before sharing the opinions or judgments you have.

Asking questions of another person in a kind way to have more understanding can show care and consideration.

"How was that for you?"

"That must have been very difficult."

"Did that type of experience continue to occur, or was it a few intense moments?"

"Did it begin to get better at some point, and how?"

These types of statements create connection and show validation and support of the person sharing. Let us all work to listen and show care better in our interactions.

My Purpose In Sharing Vulnerably

Also, let's consider what my purpose in sharing the painful parts of our story is. I am only sharing the details which are necessary to help validate and connect with another's difficult caregiving story. True connection with someone who has walked a similar path as ourselves is powerful.

My heart behind sharing vulnerably is for the primary caregiver to read my words and feel they are not alone in their tumultuous up and down caregiving moments fighting for their loved one's life.

My husband's desire is for others to find healing as he did which is why he is willing to be vulnerable in these pages too. I don't share all the details of our story for privacy reasons and because it's not necessary in order to get the point across.

My purpose in sharing is not to satisfy anyone's curiosity or to explain or defend a choice or action. *My purpose in sharing is simply and only to access another caregiver's pain through our own pain, with the purpose of lifting them up.*

I know you are walking through your own painful and difficult moments, trying to ascertain what the right way forward is when the situations before you are not straightforward at all. They can feel messy. They can feel overwhelming. I get it. You know I've been there.

I pray you have safe people in your life who will not add additional pain by questioning you, dismissing you, or criticizing you when you share vulnerably with them for support, validation, and understanding. It isn't easy to open up to others with the threat of being judged, criticized, or dismissed.

An armchair quarterback is not a welcome addition to these painful, jagged, sacred bits of our story. Or your story. A person who immediately jumps into, *"Why didn't you do—" "Well I would have—" "It's time you started doing—when they do—".*

Immediate assertions and strong advice can feel jarring and attacking, putting you on the defensive as you begin to question yourself and wonder if you can keep going, weary as you are, and apparently, not doing it well either.

You need the right type of support, friends.

I pray protection and blessing over your story and my own as we choose to open up in vulnerability to others.

I pray for a hedge of protection around you, myself, and our loved ones we care for from any of the uncaring, thoughtless, foolish, ignorant, condescending, or calculated words from other people who knowingly or unknowingly inflict pain or harm with their words or actions.

I pray you feel a deep sense of belonging and acceptance when you choose to be brave and share with another about your painful, vulnerable moments. There are safe, trusted, and authentic people you can share with in community, and I talk about what is needed for that type of community in Chapter 14: Safe, Trusted, Authentic Community.

Sharing Our Voice Gives Voice To Others Too

My sharing of these stories is to give a voice to all the other brave caregivers who are fighting the same silent and scary battles for their loved one's lives, trying to determine the right path forward in the moment, discerning how to care for their loved one well.

If you are presently or have been the primary caregiver of suicidality, it's likely your day in and day out of caregiving looks a little different from mine as each of us are unique and different from one another. Our journeys will look different as well.

Let us give grace to each other in the midst of our caregiving journeys. Let us be supportive and encourage toward self-care and seeking professional medical and mental health support as needed for our loved ones and for ourselves. Let us give validation, kindness, and understanding rather than pass judgment which can be easy to jump to. Let us be honest with ourselves about the struggles we and our loved ones are facing.

Statements For Everyone to Avoid

We must be discerning and wise with our words toward each other.

Statements and even thoughts to avoid are ones starting with:

"If I was her, I would have—"

"If it had been me, I never would have—"

"She should have—"

"I never would have put up with—"

"Why didn't she just—"

"How could they never have told me—"

"I had a right to know 'that'—"

Any statements like these miss the point. They don't have a message of support or empathy for the person caregiving but instead over-simplify a complex issue. They also communicate a message of knowing what's best and having one 'right' opinion about specific experiences they likely have never walked through themselves.

The last two statements even move the viewpoint and focus onto themselves, rather than focusing the priority and focus on the person with suicidality and their primary caregiver.

It is incredibly important for the focus to stay on supporting the primary caregiver and their loved one struggling and what both of them need from a mental, emotional, spiritual, and physical aspect.

Other people in their life may shift the focus onto themselves as they process information and the desire to 'have known', but it's important for them to re-focus on supporting the primary caregiver and the loved one struggling.

We can all find ourselves thinking these types of statements if we are caught off guard or surprised... Hopefully we will catch ourselves before saying them out-loud if we are not the exact person who walked through those exact experiences.

Again—**Armchair quarterbacks are not a helpful addition to the landscape of suicide and mental crisis caregiving.**

Casual observations and hypothetical judgments can be dangerous and negatively impact those who are in constant day in and day out caregiving. We must all be careful and discerning with how we interact and respond to finding out about "details" of another person's life.

Let us respond with compassionate acceptance, thanking the person for sharing, validating the difficult, and asking how best to support them.

Changed Person Through Experiences

As we grow and change in life, what's interesting is we can look back on the person we were before differently. Who I am now would do things somewhat differently, but that is because of the experiences I have walked through and lessons I have learned along the way. I am not the same person now that I was then, in the midst of crisis caregiving. I have gone through so much since then. I have learned a great deal. I have walked through significant pain. I have experienced multiple traumas and grown and been transformed through the many healing decisions I have made since. I have walked through intensive EMDR therapy to work through trauma and emotional pain in all of this. I have been guided and taught by wise therapists, Biblical spiritual leaders, and God has shown me so much too.

I can look back and have compassion on the person I was throughout this specific time period of crisis caregiving. You may also feel similarly as you look back and may consider "doing something differently". It is a natural inclination but only because you have grown and learned since that moment.

May you also extend grace to your younger self.

When I reflect, I know that how I responded and what I did during the intense crisis caregiving season, the Lord allowed for me to do to keep my husband alive. I don't judge or find fault with that person from years ago because I know what I was facing and the tools I had at my disposal. I know what I learned along the way and how God sustained me.

Caregiving with all that I had kept my husband alive and also took a great toll on me. What I did needed to be done in each of those moments and experiences, and I am grateful. I didn't walk it alone. God was with me, helping me discern what to do when the way forward was murky. I am thankful to have grown and healed some of my trauma (we can always do more healing work) and thankful to be in a different, more healed place now. I'll talk on that though in a future chapter.

Compassion For Your Fellow Caregiver

Now, for the ones who have also walked through suicidal caregiving, I urge them also to have the utmost of empathy and compassion with a fellow caregiver. From their own experiences, I am sure they have wisdom and insight to share. This should always be done carefully, with discernment, making sure to also point the caregiver and the person struggling with suicidality to professional support also.

To be an ear to listen saying *"Me too" "You are not alone" "You aren't the only person to have dealt with that."* is incredibly powerful and helpful to the person walking through it for the first time, desperate, feeling alone, scared, and overwhelmed by the sheer magnitude of the battle before them.

Validating someone else's feelings and experience without shame, judgment, or condescension is a beautiful gift.

We can know we would do things differently because we are uniquely different from another person, but a different perspective does not negate validation of another person's feelings or experiences.

The purpose of my sharing is to bring commonality, to be vulnerable and go first with my raw painful bits, so other caregivers and those suffering in the suicidality battle can come out of the shadows and feel permission to share vulnerably too.

Both the caregiver and the person struggling with suicidality need to know they are not alone. There must be support for both of them, separately, and collectively, for their own unique journey and struggles.

Safe Spaces to Share

Friend, as the primary caregiver of suicidality, I desire for you to have safe spaces to share in and not be censured or put down by well-meaning or possibly thoughtless or ignorant comments made by "friends, family, or church family."

You should instead be embraced, held, and sat with by those around you. There shouldn't be rejection over the battle you have walked through or are currently walking through. You need a safe space to share your experiences, to process them, and to have community. Not everyone you encounter will be safe to share with, unfortunately.

I have discovered some people don't feel comfortable interacting with such serious topics or hearing your emotions and worries about it. You may run into pat answers or hurtful, dismissive statements that do nothing to ease the ache and burden you feel.

Some people may invalidate your feelings or experiences by trying to *"look on the bright side"* or twist something you share into a positive. Often this is done due to an uncomfortableness on their part to acknowledge and accept the difficult. Take note and keep looking for the people who will provide a safe space to share.

Safer people will respond with statements such as *"That is really hard."* Those who validate your feelings and experiences are priceless treasures. They get it. They may be going through entirely different battles in their own life. They don't need all the answers or advice—just to offer their presence, empathy, willingness to listen, and validation.

Sometimes you may need "a second set of eyes" on the situation from a wise, discerning person. If you are in need of their take on it, letting them know you need their wise counsel is important. This allows for trust and for you to build your own support system with others around you.

Hopefully others won't assume permission to share advice.

Focused Caregiving

You may understand what I've said up until now but aren't sure why it's imperative to be so vigilant, so focused with a mental health battle.

All caregiving for serious diagnoses have similar approaches. Mental health crisis caregiving is not different.

Those who are the primary caregiver of suicidal ideation and suicide attempts, day in and day out, must care for and be aware of the details and ins and outs of the illness, know the nuance of the trauma and triggers.

This is honestly no different to knowing all the nuanced detailed ins and outs of a different life-threatening illness and battle. One with a different diagnosis, dealing with a significant issue with the brain, the heart, the kidneys, or a specific cancer.

You, as the primary caregiver, are the one championing your loved one, caring for, advocating for, nurturing, and loving. It is imperative for you to know the minute details of the disease and the specific nuances of your loved one's illness and presenting symptoms. No one else cares as greatly as you for your loved one's best care. There are specific details that won't be the same as someone else's similar battle.

Your role is extremely important in getting your loved one the care they need. It is extremely necessary and life-giving. Constant caregiving is also exhausting, bone-wearying work.

Both truths can be acknowledged—the importance of the work and the exhaustion that it brings.

Your work as the caregiver is not unseen though you may feel unseen, forgotten, and fully alone often. It is crucial. It is front-lines' work, on behalf of your loved one, fighting for life, goodness, and healing for your loved one.

This same intentional nuanced focus must be present in mental health caregiving. It is no different on the battlefield of mental health crisis. A person may look physically well, and be in a fight for their life at every moment of every day. It is no different in the battle for life in mental health crisis, in suicide prevention. The steps for caregiving for a mental health crisis are going to look different than the steps for caregiving for one with heart disease or a loved one with lung cancer.

Let us not judge the steps taken in love, discernment, and careful consideration of the nuanced illness our loved one has.

Let us normalize the chaotic and detrimentally silent battle against suicide, the unseen battle, the battle that so many are walking through, and have no one they feel they can share with.

Let us be the first voice to speak out on the struggle and the fight for life.

May those caregiving share and receive validation of their feelings and emotions from others without judgment, unsolicited advice giving, or pity.

May they be welcomed and given space to process without others minimizing or dismissing what they say. May they find community and a safe space to be heard and seen.

You Are Not Alone; So Many People are Fighting the Same Battle.

I am honored to be a voice allowed to speak on the subject of caregiving for mental health crisis, specifically on trauma, PTSD, and suicidality (both suicidal ideation and suicide attempts). Let me normalize this battle because I have found that as I go about my daily life and am open to opportunities to share and be vulnerable with others when prompted to, I have been amazed by how many other people have a person one-removed from them who also struggle with suicide, either suicidal ideation or also self-harm and suicide attempts.

By my willingness to go first, it has opened up the conversation to allow others to share. It takes down the barrier that is up, the hush-hush quality of the painful and significantly dangerous battle they are walking through. It allows for community.

It decreases the stigma of mental health. If we as a society began to choose to be more open about struggles many of us have with mental health illness, I can promise we would be shocked by the solidarity that would come out of speaking these struggles out loud, and into a space that is safe and accepting, empathetic and supportive. To not be afraid of judgment, dismissal by others, or to be viewed "differently," whatever that means, would be incredibly important.

To be validated, heard, and empowered would be the start to the road to healing, in and of itself.

To be seen. To be validated. To be heard. To feel understood. To be fought for.

We all want that in our life.

Chapter 8

NEGATIVE SELF-TALK, SHAME, & OUR GOD-GIVEN IDENTITY

Song: "Same God" by: Elevation Worship (feat. Jonsal Barrientes)

Most of us struggle with sharing vulnerably with others about our inner world. Most of us feel nervous or down-right scared to let anyone know, truly, our inner world, our inner struggle.

One factor in this can be shame.

"Shame is being exposed—the flawed parts of yourself that you want to hide from everyone are revealed. You want to hide or die."[1]

For Josh, his inner struggle wasn't safe to hide anymore, and it became necessary to share with a mental health therapist in order to heal. I also needed to know his symptoms and issues as the primary caregiver supporting him. As time continued, more people were shared with about his mental health struggles.

In the beginning though, he couldn't have anyone know.

If others had known of his inner mental health battle in the beginning, he would have felt too exposed. If he felt too exposed, his risk for suicide would have increased. The shame would have been overwhelming if others found out his inner hell, initially.

Even though he'd said at the beginning he didn't have self-harm or suicidal thoughts, I knew they could easily begin. Suicide. If that occurred, there wouldn't be any chance at healing or help. It was a thin line to walk.

He needed to feel safe and supported.

I supported his need for privacy and not telling anyone initially and focused on the long game to continue to be a trusted, safe person in his life. My focus had to be on the long game.

Shame & Guilt

Shame and guilt were both prevalent for my husband. They are likely present for your loved one also. It is important to understand the difference between them.

Shame and guilt are close cousins but incredibly different in how they affect a person's life.

Brene Brown, a shame researcher, well-known for her TEDTalk, differentiates shame and guilt as "I am bad" (shame) versus "I did something bad" (guilt).[2]

Guilt focuses on a person's behavior; whereas shame focuses on who a person is.[2]

At the core of shame is an attack against our very identity.

Our identity and who we are is constructed only by what God says about us, but in life we unconsciously and consciously take on labels and identities based on how we desire to be or how we view ourselves, whether good or bad.

Shame says I am unworthy, unlovable, and my personhood (who I am) is wrong, is flawed.[1]

Guilt, on the other hand, separates the boundary of the person from the action or decision. A person is not bad, but a behavior or choice can be.

Guilt is conviction over something done wrong, and it can sometimes positively motivate someone toward good choices.[2] Shame often leads to more negative behavior or the inability to take action.[2]

I am a mistake' is an incredibly different message from '*I made a mistake*'.[3] The difference between shame versus guilt is profound. With guilt, there is room for growth and positive change.

Shame keeps a person stuck because when they begin to take on the identity or label that shame places upon them, then they begin to live out that label and do not try to rise above it.[3] They believe they are and so cannot change or work to overcome it.

"Shame is being exposed—the flawed parts of yourself that you want to hide from everyone are revealed. You want to hide or die."[1] This description was so powerful, I shared it again.

For my husband, he couldn't let anyone know the parts he saw as flawed. I only happened upon it (thankfully) by God orchestrating the events leading to my finding out about his nightmares, self-medicating, and depression as I shared in chapter two.

It is difficult to enter into vulnerability when you are used to hiding for so long, and shame tells you to keep hiding.

Shame is Universal.

When discussing shame, it is important to focus on a person's inner world of beliefs, thoughts, and self-focused talk. Negative self-talk and negative self-beliefs are rooted in shame. Understanding this connection is crucial.

Shame is the belief that 'I am bad' or any other variation of a negative identity or statement about oneself. Shame statements create a place of bondage and staying stuck in those statements and beliefs about oneself.

Stephen Porges, a trauma expert and the founder of the Polyvagal Theory, found a connection between trauma, shame, and guilt.[4] He found that many people who have experienced trauma struggle with shame and guilt connected to their trauma and due to not understanding what occurs in their body after trauma and the physiological changes.[4]

For my husband, and many other Veterans, there can be shame and guilt surrounding the events of a combat trauma experience, along with a sense of responsibility. The shame can be debilitating.

For those facing civilian trauma, there also can be shame and guilt present.

This topic is multi-faceted as the shame and guilt a person experiences can stem from the traumatic events, beliefs surrounding the events, or due to the new and concerning tension, emotions, or maladies that can occur afterwards.

The source of shame can be different, but shame is, in fact, universal, according to Brene Brown, the renowned shame researcher.[5] She says: "Shame is universal—no one is exempt".[5]

Curt Thompson, a psychiatrist and author of *The Soul of Shame*, corroborates this truth further stating, "To be human is to be infected with this phenomenon we call shame".[6]

If it is universal, then we all interact with shame on some level in our own lives.

Shame has been identified as the "dominant emotion experienced by mental health clients, exceeding anger, fear, grief, and anxiety".[5] Shame is being studied and researched with regards to its role in suicide, depression, addiction, anxiety disorders, and many other mental health and public health issues.[7]

Shame is, thereby, a significant and powerful negative force and negative emotion that cannot be ignored.

The Self-talk—Shame—Suicide Continuum

I see shame as part of a continuum. I invite you to consider my continuum as it relates to suicide, specifically. I believe it is beneficial to understand and identify precursors to shame (ex: negative self-talk) which can turn into shame and later suicidality. When we can address earlier issues, prevention may be able to occur for suicidality and the negative and dangerous behaviors and thought patterns present with it.

Negative Self-talk ⟶ Shame ⟶ Suicide

The self-talk—shame—suicide line continuum has negative self-talk (including negative self-beliefs or thoughts about oneself) on the left side of the continuum with the line representing worsening and repeated negative thoughts about oneself as the line goes to the right towards the middle. The symptoms increase in severity from left to right. Shame (negative identity about oneself) is in the middle of the continuum and beyond that potential self-harm, suicidal ideation, and suicide attempts/plans as the line continues towards the right side. At the far-right side of the continuum is suicide. Halting the continuum at any point along it is imperative.

The precursor of shame, in my estimation, is a strong negative belief or thought about oneself that has been fed over and over until it turns into a negative identity (which is, by definition—shame). Shame can be a catalyst to self-harm and suicidality.

We can begin to effect change and break the continuum if we see a negative belief or thought about ourselves for what it is (by using self-awareness) and begin to combat it with truth about ourselves. We have the power to effect change in our very minds and mindsets by being attuned to ourselves and willing to analyze our beliefs and thoughts about ourselves. This, in fact, uses the power of neuroplasticity, the brain's ability to adapt and change.[8]

Analyzing our thoughts and beliefs about ourselves to determine if there is validity and truth present in them is a powerful practice.

This is a very simple continuum with many additional factors and complex issues present and I am not addressing those here. I will leave that analysis to the researchers. I do, however, believe strongly there is an important connection between our thoughts, repeated negative thoughts turning into negative identity (shame) which can then have a role in suicidality occurring.

Not all shame turns into self-harm or suicidal ideation/risk as shame can have a role in many other harmful behaviors and choices as well.[7] For the purposes of this book and looking specifically at suicide and suicidality, I believe this continuum has merit. If we do not work on the precursor problems that seem harmless like negative thoughts or statements about oneself, shame can ultimately occur, and possibly turn into thoughts of harming oneself or ending life.

When we don't combat lies with truths about oneself, they can continue down the continuum to become statements of identity. Statements of identity are often "I am" statements such as: "I am a failure." "I am worthless." "I am un-loveable." "I am terrible." and these could turn into statements of "I am better off dead." or similar ideas.

Only we ourselves know our inner world. When we begin to become aware of the statements and beliefs we use attacking or labeling our identity, we must stop and realize it. This shift is not easy if we or those around us are accustomed to using negative identity statements about themselves or others.

Alison Cook, a psychotherapist who integrates faith and psychology, refers to this as "naming" in *I Shouldn't Feel This Way*.[9] Naming is the bringing awareness of a feeling, emotion, thought, or belief.[9] Naming it can be powerful. She goes onto framing and braving in her book helping the reader learn what to do with what has been named in order to shift, process, and grow.[9]

This next section has questions I constructed to be answered for yourself and/or your loved one also. Your loved one would have to answer the questions as they apply to themselves if they are willing.

Questions to Ask Yourself and Consider

I put together these questions to help us consider where on this negative Self-talk—Shame—Suicide Continuum we or our loved one falls.

Is negative self-talk a part of your life?

Do you view yourself in negative ways?

Do you potentially have negative viewpoints or beliefs about yourself?

If so, what are they?

Are there any negative "I am" statements about yourself you can think of that you've had recently or in the past? Write them down.

Have you ever struggled with thoughts of self-harm, death for yourself, or thoughts, attempt, or plan of suicide?

Please accept that those negative thoughts and viewpoints about yourself are not innocuous. If we do not address and fight back against negative self-thoughts or negative self-beliefs in our life, it can begin to take center stage and become the lens we see life with. It can take on more sinister aspects when difficult life circumstances occur.

Negative self-talk and negative beliefs about oneself can morph into a temptation to take action against yourself, to harm oneself. It can be a slippery slope that catches a person unawares. One moment you think badly about yourself, and the next moment, those negative self-thoughts pave a way to increasingly detrimental thoughts and beliefs, ones entrenched in shame (negative identity about oneself). These thoughts and beliefs could toy and tempt you further into thoughts of harming yourself. Unless we halt those thoughts before they go down the continuum. Unless we combat the lies with truth.

The Impact of Others' Thoughts & Words

The thoughts we think matter. The beliefs about ourselves we hold onto deep within us matter. The statements others made to us in our past can also have long-lasting impact, whether positive or negative. Words stick with us and settle deep within us for our encouragement and rising up or for our pulling down and potential demise. We cannot afford to ignore hurtful words said to us or negative beliefs we hold about ourselves. To process through them takes time but offers the hope of healing and resiliency on the other side.

Pay attention and don't dismiss the words and statements you hold onto and the thoughts you think towards yourself. They are powerful.

Your thoughts are the bedrock and foundation for the choices and decisions that you make in your life.

Your thoughts impact how you will act based on your beliefs and viewpoints. In times of extreme stress and when shame potentially enters into the picture and consumes, these negative beliefs and negative self-talk can give birth to self-harm and lead down a pathway towards suicidal ideation and suicide attempts. Attempts to take life, to harm forever a person, yes that person being you, but a person made in the image of God.

How Can We Have a Positive Identity?

We are going to shift gears and jump into the Creation story in the Bible to get a clearer picture on positive identity. Let me assure you, God is the one who gives life and the one who orders everyone's life. He is the sovereign One who knows how many days each person will live. When He created the world in creation as well as the first man and the first woman, Adam and Eve, respectively, He made them in His own image. He gave them attributes that reflected Himself. No other living creature was formed to reflect God's image. He made each person with uniqueness and bestowed on each one attributes of His character.

He made us eternal beings as He is eternal. He made us relational beings.

He gave humans autonomy and free choice—the choice to decide to follow God or to take for themselves their own knowledge (You can read more in Genesis 3 on the account of the tree of the knowledge of good and evil and how sin entered the world through Eve's and Adam's decision to disobey God).

The detail I want us to hone in on though is the distinct truth of man and woman being made in the image of God.

Made in God's Image

Each one of us are made in God's image—Each one of us matters and are uniquely made.

When we study the scripture for what it says about us as people, as humans, we naturally obtain a better view of how God sees us. We begin to understand what His perspective is towards us. We start to have fuel to fight against the negative beliefs in order to trade them for the positive beliefs found in scripture and grounded in truth.

This truth is absolute—it doesn't change regardless of what occurs in your life, regardless of the choices you make, the past you have, or any circumstance you are facing.

You are made in the image of God. You are an image bearer of God, whether you believe in God or don't believe in God. This fact doesn't change because God doesn't change. No matter if you are walking in relationship with Him or you don't believe He exists, you still are inextricably tied to God due to being created in His image.

Some additional truths are that God loves you, He accepts you as you are right now, without you doing anything or proving anything to Him. He doesn't want you to stay the exact way you are right now though. He wants better for you. He wants to do a new work in you, to kindly and graciously encourage you toward something better, towards a better life, a better viewpoint, based in knowledge grounded in Him. He doesn't push it on you though. He waits for you to choose.

God's truth can dispel the lies we believe about ourselves or dispel the harmful words told to us by another, words we haven't been able to shake. Jesus himself dealt with many negative circumstances and harmful actions done to him and words spoken at Him and about Him. He was betrayed, rejected, beaten, and ultimately murdered without rightful cause when he was taken to be crucified.

I don't know what your story is or what you've faced in your life, but God does. God is all-knowing, omniscient. He understands the temptation to believe harmful messages. He suffered an excruciating death on the cross. He was reviled. He felt lonely as He walked through all that He endured.

And yet for the joy set before him he endured the cross. He knew there could be a better way on the other side of the cross. He knew there could be hope, because He knew He was in the business of conquering sin and death, right then. Three days later He rose from the grave, having paid the penalty for our sin, conquering sin and death, and making a way for us to have a right relationship with Him and the ability to have eternal life in heaven.

We have hope. Hope through Jesus. There is hope in your situation because Jesus is in the business of resurrecting that which seemed dead and gone. He brings newness of life. He is the life-giver. He is the hope-giver. Lift up your head, friend. You are not alone though you may feel lonely. Jesus offers life to those who welcome Him into their heart and life.

"Because, if you confess with your mouth that Jesus is Lord and believe in your heart that God raised Him from the dead, you will be saved" (Romans 10:9, ESV).

If you don't already have a relationship with Jesus, now is the time. Believe and be saved. Tell Him about your life and situation. He hears. He cares. And He understands deep suffering too.

A Different Way—A Path Toward Healing from Negative Self-talk and Shame

You may be holding so much pain right now from hurtful moments and past experiences, but there can be a different way, a way toward healing. There are ways to fight back against negative thoughts and negative beliefs about yourself. There are ways to begin to dismantle shame's hold in your life.

Through God, therapy, medication, and communal support, you can find a new way.

You can bury those struggles that are pulling you down once and for all, bit by bit. You can do this in a healthy way of overcoming them, rather than hiding or ignoring them.

Cognitive Behavioral Therapy (CBT) is a type of mental health therapy (psychotherapy) which helps break down negative beliefs and change one's thinking to healthier thinking.[10][11]

Eye Movement Desensitization & Reprocessing (EMDR) is also a therapy which can be used. EMDR helps one interact with subconscious memories and process and integrate them which then can positively impact the emotions and thoughts attached to those memories.[11][12]

It is vital to heal from wounding words or moments that occurred causing you to feel a negative way, which may have led to thinking a negative way, and affected your decisions as well. We will discuss these and other types of mental health therapies in Chapter 11. When a person works through what is holding them back using powerful therapies, they can become free from what hinders them.

You can walk more freely, not as burdened as you have been. It is possible, friend. It's possible because I have seen it occur with my own eyes. I have seen it with my husband and have seen it with myself—the life-changing improvements that mental health therapy can make.

When we become aware of negative self-talk and negative beliefs and how they turn into shame, we can combat them with truth-filled tools, from the Bible and also from mental health therapy, to help change our thinking. There is hope.

REFERENCES

1 Brown, B. (2007) *I Thought It was Just Me (But It Isn't): Making the Journey from What Will People Think? To I Am Enough.* Avery, 5.

2 Brown, 13.

3 Brown, 14.

4 Porges, S. W. and Porges, S. (2023). *Our Polyvagal World: How Safety and Trauma Change Us.* W. W. Norton and Company, Inc. 24.

5 Brown, 3-4.

6 Thompson, C. (2015) *The Soul of Shame: Retelling the Stories We Believe About Ourselves.* InterVarsity Press, 21.

7 Brown, Introduction.

8 Thompson, 46-48.

9 Cook, A. (2024) *I Shouldn't Feel This Way: Name What's Hard, Tame Your Guilt, and Transform Self-Sabotage into Brave Action.* Nelson Books, 15-16.

10 van der Kolk, B. A. (2014). *The Body Keeps the Score: Brain, Mind, and Body In the Healing of Trauma.* Penguin Books, 222-224.

11 "PTSD Treatments" APA Clinical Practice Guideline for the Treatment of Posttraumatic Stress Disorder. https://www.apa.org/ptsd-guideline/treatments . Accessed 5 June 2025.

12 van der Kolk, 230, 256-258.

Chapter 9

ALCOHOL, ADDICTION, & USING NEUROPLASTICITY TO OVERCOME

Song: "No Longer Bound" by: Forrest Frank and Hulvey

Self-medicating with substances can quickly morph into full-blown addiction.

Here is my poetic offering on the insidious path to addiction.

May it pave the way to new insight for you.

The Insidious Path to Addiction

The path to addiction often starts small with just trying to cope with life's struggles and stresses by pouring a little more alcohol, and then a little more, to help take the edge off of life.

For some, it's trying a different substance other than alcohol.

Whatever the type of substance used, the path to addiction is insidious, unrealized until one is fully there, entrapped by the desire for more, to keep numbing, to self-medicate and self-soothe whatever is too much to handle, and to feel the feeling that goes with the substance.

The thing with addiction is it grabs ahold of you and won't let go.

It begins to have you act in ways you never would have prior, because you must at all costs go after that substance.

Your loved ones and support people can't control or stop your desire or the choices you make in seeking out more of what your brain now tells you it must have.

Addiction begins to own your life.

The choices and behaviors you make and ways you treat the closest to you are what you may regret in sober moments, but the desire and demand returns again.

To wreak havoc on a home already harmed by its pain, its lies, its breaking of relationships, breaking of trust, and harming of oneself.

The path to addiction is rarely consciously chosen but rather decided in a multitude of miniscule moments of temptation—taken and grabbed ahold of again. And again.

Until… Its control locks one in fully, unable to escape.

Important Questions to Ask About Alcohol Use

A substance use disorder of any kind can be damaging to one's life.

If what I shared resonated with you or hit a little too close to home, I understand. It's painful. It's okay to face the reality of life right now.

There are questions below that help identify if someone may have a problem with alcohol.

It is difficult, this walking through life, bit by painful bit, while your loved one makes destructive choices that don't just affect themselves but also those closest to them. Affecting you.

Answer these questions for your loved one if they aren't willing or ready to face the questions themselves. I'd encourage you to answer the questions for yourself too. It's always good to check in with ourselves as well, making sure we aren't entering into a negative interaction with alcohol. Let's be honest and brave as we consider the potential of increased alcohol use or abuse for our loved one or ourselves.

Here is the alcohol screening questionnaire, also known as the CAGE Questionnaire.[1]

The CAGE acronym stands for: cut down, annoyed, guilty, and eye-opener.[1]

- Have you ever felt you should *cut down* on your drinking? Answer: No (0), Yes (1)

- Have people *annoyed* you by criticizing your drinking? Answer: No (0), Yes (1)

- Have you ever felt bad or *guilty* about your drinking? Answer: No (0), Yes (1)

- Have you ever had a drink first thing in the morning (*eye-opener*) to steady your nerves or to get rid of a hangover? Answer: No (0), Yes (1)

The person is scored with a 0 to 4 based on the no or yes answers to each question.

Scoring 2 or higher can indicate an issue with excessive drinking. It's important to talk with a medical professional concerning any increased to excessive drinking.

Even if only the eye-opener question is answered yes, it could indicate an unhealthy drinking behavior.

Again, you can try to guess at your loved one's answers on the CAGE screening if they aren't willing to answer them or you know bringing up the topic would cause significant conflict. I am sharing these with you to bring awareness.

Please reach out for professional medical assistance and guidance. These questions are intended to be asked in a medical office setting to screen for potentially unhealthy drinking patterns and allow for further discussion and support with a medical professional. Excessive drinking and using alcohol to cope can easily lead to alcoholism and addiction. Reach out for the help your loved one needs or you yourself need.

Many may need inpatient detoxification to stop their alcohol use and be monitored during detox for dangerous physical withdrawal symptoms from alcohol. Reach out and ask for professional and medical advice on the path forward.

Alcoholics Anonymous (AA) has wonderful resources and support for those struggling with alcohol use or abuse. AA is supportive and welcoming, without judgment. It is free to go to a group, anonymously. It is a significantly brave step for someone to take. It is extremely hard to stop drinking by oneself when addicted or drinking excessively. Having others who experientially understand (because they too have dealt with alcoholism and addiction to alcohol) is powerful. They can come alongside in the fight for a better life. Go to **www.aa.org** for support and to find a group.

If your loved one won't even talk to you about their problematic drinking, much less seek out help from others, you can still have assistance and support for yourself.

Al-Anon is the anonymous support group for anyone who is worried about someone with a drinking problem. Go to **al-anon.org** for support. You don't have to face it alone.

Words for Your Loved One Struggling

It is, in fact, possible to be freed from alcohol because we have walked that road and are continuing to walk toward freedom for my husband from his turning away from alcohol and breaking free from addiction to alcohol. He is over two years sober, and I am grateful.

There is hope, friend—for the person struggling with alcohol and for the person who loves them. There is a way forward.

Here are my words for your loved one who is struggling with alcohol use or another substance.

If they are open to listening, please read these words to them:

You Can Be Brave

Don't say you have it figured out or you've got it taken care of. I know you are tempted to dismiss this issue (of alcohol) and say you can handle it.

The truth is what you are up against is incredibly powerful and difficult to overcome.

It is not weak to say you need help with a struggle. It is instead, incredibly brave.

We all need help at different times.

Being brave is not numbing or drinking into oblivion.

Being brave is not drowning the pain, memories, or feelings in a sea of alcohol. It's not drinking to be able to 'face something.'

Being brave looks like taking the first step and saying, 'I don't have power over alcohol, it has power over me.'

Being brave looks like acknowledging the pain, the fear, the memories, the struggle and bringing those issues to someone who is trained to know how to help you overcome the struggle and fight for freedom from substance's grip.

Take the first step and be honest with yourself and a trusted person. Begin considering what it would be like to not have to hide it anymore, what it would be like for it not to have power over your life anymore, for you to not be controlled by it anymore.

It has control of you, but it doesn't have to anymore. There is a better way—a brave way—and you are brave enough to take that small step toward freedom from it.

Reach out and get help.

You can be brave.

If you are willing to be brave right now, go back to the last section and answer the CAGE alcohol screening questions if you haven't yet.

Be willing to see the response and be honest with yourself.

If you are able to right now, try to not dismiss or justify anything but be open and look at it with fresh eyes desiring freedom. Once you see the number and consider the questions' implications, be brave to reach out for help towards freedom and accountability. You can do this.

It is not the weak, but the strong who face their own demons.

Don't face them alone, though, or they may overwhelm you. You deserve to get better. There is hope, and you don't have to walk this journey alone. You need others in it.

There are detox centers and professional groups who can help.

Alcoholics Anonymous can come alongside in the fight against alcohol. Narcotics Anonymous can come alongside in the fight against drugs. Search for a group near you. Choose to be brave. Take the first step.

Reach out for professional support and help to overcome dependence on alcohol or addiction to alcohol or drugs. Find an AA group to try out. You can do brave things, friend.

One of the worst lies you can believe is you can fight the beast of addiction alone.

Community accountability and professional support is incredibly important for lasting change in the fight to stay sober. Alcoholics Anonymous uses peer-led support with great results, and through it, people find community, accountability, and support in the fight against alcoholism. My husband has experienced AA's support, accountability, and community.

I believe you can do this because I have seen Josh walk this path as I've supported him.

You can do brave things too, friend.

If you read that whole last section to your loved one, I'm proud of you and hope these words spark hope and foster healthy conversations as you both consider the possibility of life being different and freer without being under the grip of alcohol or drugs.

Other Substances

If alcohol is not your go-to substance for numbing pain, but rather you turn to a controlled prescription drug or illicit drug, it is important to ask yourself questions to identify if there may be dependence or abuse present.

Addiction is a slippery slope and will entrap you in a "must-have" focus. Questionnaires help point us to what may be going on and identify any issues we or a loved one may need help with.

Again, let's face these questions with openness and bravery. You are strong and there is help for those who want a change in their life. Let's answer these questions too, friend, if this might be an issue for your loved one or for yourself.

There are self-screening questions on this website to help you screen for alcohol and drug use: https://nida.nih.gov/nidamed-medical-health-professionals/screening-tools-resources/chart-screening-tools

Head over to it and choose a screening questionnaire to answer. Always reach out to your mental health professional or medical provider about your loved one's or your own substance use, to include using drugs or excessive alcohol.

In the fight for health and wellness, we can use the brain's ability to change and adapt, the topic of these next sections.

Neuroplasticity—the Pathway Towards Change

Numbing the pain is not the way.

Medication with psychotherapy, and God by your side, is the only way to go forward toward healing and wholeness.

The pathway toward change is complex and takes time, but in the same way that the path to addiction is made up of many small decisions, the path toward healing and wholeness is made up of small, everyday choices. Healthy choices.

The brain, in fact, has the ability to overcome old patterns of thinking and beliefs and slowly trade them out for positive thinking patterns. This is studied in the field of neuroscience. Neuroplasticity refers to the brain's ability to change and adapt. The brain can change its structure and create new neural pathways and connections. It is "plastic" meaning it has the ability to change its own structure rather than remaining "static."[2]

The brain's plasticity can assist in rewiring pathways leading to suicidal thoughts and in the realm of addiction as well. New neural roads can be formed towards healthier thoughts and behavior choices.

EMDR therapy can assist with integrating and rewiring neural pathways and help to neutralize or resolve the negative memories.[3]

Brain Pathways Change With Suicidal Ideation

When the brain has gone down that road of thinking before, that pathway, thinking of suicide, it actually will begin to see suicide as a positive, an answer, to the pain. A way out. The brain can begin to see it as positive, rather than negative.

With further considering and thinking on suicide and allowing one's mind to settle on that idea, the mind begins to create positive feelings around that very negative thing. The thought begins to be comforting, odd as it sounds. The pain is so strong for the person struggling with their mental health that they want a solution.

For those of us caregiving for this person, hearing this idea is incredibly difficult and can feel defeating. How can you combat against such a flipflopped idea, where the very thing so dangerous is now considered and viewed in the ill mind as positive and a comfortable option?

Quite a ways into our mental crisis battle was when my husband's therapist shared this concept with him. My husband then shared it with me. It wasn't easy to hear, but it helped us profoundly in understanding what was occurring. The more thinking someone does on a specific topic, the easier it is to go down that pathway again. My husband's thoughts about suicide were reinforcing his suicidal thinking again and again, making it easier to head down that familiar path.

The hope in receiving this knowledge was knowing this pathway could be broken. There was a way to break this road in his mind, with the wheel tracks having made such a riveted mark imprinted on his brain. There were ways he could combat the suicide pathway when it popped in his brain at a random moment or became glaring in his face, pressing into his mind for attention. He could begin to create new pathways of thought.[2] He could actively fight to replace the old, suicidal thoughts with new thoughts again and again, counteracting the path to suicidal thoughts.[4]

New ruts in his mind could be formed, to shift his mind, when of its own accord it would head down the familiar and oddly comforting road of suicidal thinking. EMDR therapy plus Neurofeedback and IFS (Internal Family Systems) was instrumental in helping dismantle and break the old, suicidal thinking pathway for him and begin to create new pathways.

His first powerful step towards change was identifying and being aware of heading down the path when it happened. Having awareness that his mind had all of a sudden turned to suicide was key. He then had to stop the thought by retraining his mind using strategies he learned in his therapy sessions.

New Thoughts Begat New Neural Pathways.

In the moment, he would have a choice to make. Once he was aware of thoughts of suicide, he would have to consciously decide to turn his mind toward something else.

The strategies he learned in therapy were integral to his success. To implement the strategies was the only way to begin to create new neural pathways.[2] New neural roads in his brain.[2] The old neural roads to suicidal ideation and suicidal contemplation had to go. New thoughts and new thinking had to take their place.

Whenever you remove something negative from your life, it is important to replace it with something good and positive.

To only remove the bad can create almost what seems like a vacuum, and bad may come back into that place, maybe a different type of 'bad', or a different type of negative coping, but bad nonetheless. We don't want to go back to our old way of thinking, our old way of doing something, when we have, in fact, pivoted and changed our trajectory, changed our thinking. We have the power to transform and move forward to new and better things once we are aware of what needs to change.

This is easier said than done, obviously. To change one's way of thinking is a continual renewing of one's mind.

There is a verse in the Bible (Romans 12:2) that talks about the renewing of your mind and transforming of yourself through that practice. The verse's focus is on changing one's thinking in order to be more in tune with God's will. It is speaking of the spiritual life and renewing your thinking to set your mind on pursuits of godliness and discerning what is best. It is a Biblical reference to the powerful ability of the brain for regenerating and adapting through neuroplasticity.[2][4]

The same idea can be applied to the thinking pathway toward suicide and death in renewing one's mind. Curt Thompson, a psychiatrist who focuses on interpersonal neurobiology, speaks of focusing one's attention on renewing or changing our thoughts in order to allow the brain's natural neuroplasticity to work, strengthening new and different neural pathways.[4] This attention or intentional attunement is the use of the medial prefrontal cortex discussed earlier in this book (which allows the emotional brain and rational brain to connect).[4] Creating clarity of thought and mind and body is important in overcoming the suicidal thoughts. Allowing yourself to enter into a space that is aware and intentionally focused is also necessary.

For the one struggling with suicidality, it takes courage to pursue this kind of change. It takes resolution and a will to live. It takes support from others, including your therapist and care team, and most definitely your primary support person (primary caregiver) and additional friends and family members. It takes accountability.

Accountability with yourself is needed to admit when you allow your mind to go down that road. Accountability to choose to be honest with your closest supporter when you are having thoughts about suicide.

It also takes accountability to be fully honest with your therapist and be willing to follow your suicide safety plan if you are in danger and are beginning to think of how to end your life and are creating a plan.

Don't go down that road. Stop. Tell your therapist. Tell your loved one you are struggling. Reach out for help.

Using positive coping strategies can help to interact with difficult emotions and thoughts too (discussed below).

It is hard, but it is so important. Your life matters.

In this new pursuit of positive, healthier thinking, it is important for your loved one and yourself to be connected with and interact with emotionally safe and trusted people.

I know it can be hard to take that first step toward change and fighting against old patterns of thinking or behavior. You can do it, though. You can choose to create new healthier patterns in your brain and in your thinking. You can create new neural pathways.

Like with anything new, it takes intentional choices and focus.

Positive coping strategies can help counteract the temptation and pull to turn to learned negative coping methods that have been habits in the past. Positive coping strategies can also help with stabilizing yourself if you are feeling emotionally upset or dysregulated.

Positive Coping Strategies

It is important to have healthy ways to counteract stress, triggers, dysregulation, and even suicidal thinking. **Positive coping strategies use various healthy techniques to help regulate yourself and your nervous system and calm emotional distress or upset.**

Positive coping strategies are healthy outlets and activities to manage emotional pain, mental health symptoms, or negative memories.

Some different types of positive coping strategies include: breathing techniques, grounding techniques, cardio exercise (including running, dancing, group exercise classes, cycling), yoga, activities that engage your body and movement (walking also), art and creative expression, woodworking, other hobbies, and many other activities. We will talk about a few of these strategies below.

Boxed Breathing

One of my favorite positive coping strategies is using boxed breathing to regulate my stress and tension. You can try it right now with me.

This is how to go about it:

Breathe in for a count of 3 seconds, hold your breath for a count of 3, and lastly, exhale for a count of 3.

Repeat.

I usually repeat this simple technique 3 times if I'm stressed or feeling upset, tense, or dysregulated by something. If you feel lightheaded, make sure to pause between sets for at least 10 to 20 seconds.

If you focus on the exhale portion, you activate your rest and relax system, your parasympathetic system. It will help calm you and decrease your stress a little quicker. To do this, repeat the exercise with a 3-4-5 count.

Inhale for a count of 3 seconds, hold your breath for 4 seconds, exhale for 5 seconds. Again, focusing on your exhale for a longer count causes your parasympathetic system to help the body rest and relax more quickly.

I can usually feel less tension in my shoulders after doing 3 rounds of boxed breathing.

What I love about boxed breathing is I can benefit from it anywhere I am, and no one may even be aware I am breathing slightly differently. It is as simple as breathing and choosing how to breathe.

Grounding and Other Positive Coping Strategies

Grounding techniques can focus on sensation and being present in your current moment. This is especially helpful for those who have had trauma as a person can feel disconnected from their present moment at times.

One grounding technique has a person focus on all 5 senses. Focusing on sensation and what they feel, focusing on smell and what smells are present right then, focusing on what they see in specific detail, focusing on what they hear at that moment, focusing on any taste present right then. This grounds a person in their present moment and connects them more fully with what is occurring right then.

Another wonderful positive coping strategy uses art and creative outlets. Art is therapeutic. There are so many different types of art for creative expression. Painting is a wonderful way to have an outlet for the emotions and feelings bottled up inside. To allow oneself to enjoy and create, whether it is for the murky and difficult negative feelings you have, or if it is simply to find joy and relax and create beautiful paintings or mold pottery, it is good.

If one creative outlet does not sound enjoyable, allow yourself the freedom to learn something new. It is not about mastery, necessarily, but being present in the moment.

I find there is something about picking up a paint brush and beginning to apply color to a canvas that is extremely satisfying and deeply rewarding, especially when I do not place expectations on myself of perfection as I paint. My husband has also found painting to be quite enjoyable and my children as well.

There are so many different forms of art. Choose one to try out and learn a new skill, without expectations of doing it well. If you don't like it, try a different one. You can see which one resonates with yourself.

Exercise is also a wonderful stress reliever. Being active and going for a walk or doing cardio and sweating can help improve a person's mood. Running is one of my go-to stress relievers. You can try yoga or a kickboxing class. Pilates, barre, weightlifting, bicycling, swimming, etc. If it helps to move your body and get some exercise, it can help counteract stress and is a positive coping strategy for mental health struggles.

Find the positive coping strategies that work well for you. Use them. They are powerful tools in staying mentally well and managing stress and difficulties that will arise in life for us.

I shared some of these same positive coping strategies in Chapter 3 on caregiver burden and burnout. Implementing these helpful tools is incredibly important for the caregiver and the loved one struggling, but they can also be used by all of us to counteract stress, difficult emotions, or challenging situations.

In closing, when we can begin to identify negative or unhealthy patterns in our life or identify addiction and reach out for help, we can have hope to get better.

There is hope for the future.

We can find a path toward healing and have support from professionals and also people close to us. We can replace negative patterns of thinking and behavior with new thoughts and new coping strategies and pursue a healthier way of life overall.

REFERENCES

[1] "CAGE Questionnaire Assessment" https://americanaddictioncenters.org/alcohol/rehab-treatment/cage-questionnaire-assessment. Accessed 22 February 2025.

[2] Thompson, C. (2015) *The Soul of Shame: Retelling the Stories We Believe About Ourselves.* InterVarsity Press, 46- 47.

[3] van der Kolk, B. A. (2014). *The Body Keeps the Score: Brain, Mind, and Body In the Healing of Trauma.* Penguin Books, 302.

[4] Thompson, 48.

Chapter 10

RESPONDING IN CRISIS- SELF-HARM WORDS, RISK, AND EMERGENCY CARE

Song: "I Am Not Alone" by Kari Jobe

If you have never interacted with someone who has struggled with suicidal ideation or thoughts of harming themselves, it can be surprising the first time. You may not know what to say or what to do in the situation.

I want to stress this point—

Always take a person's self-harm words seriously.

As we discuss this further, I hope you will feel a little better equipped after reading my words here and know additional resources to access also. Hopefully, I can share some bits of wisdom or insight to help you that I learned through our scary, up and down battle with suicidal ideation, intent, plan, and attempts.

You may be asking yourself—

- Where does one (thoughts) start and the other (plan/attempts) begin?
- How can I know if we are in an emergency and have to take immediate steps right then to protect life?
- How can I determine we are facing urgent needs for support with self-harm thoughts or suicidal ideation/thoughts?
- How do I know to reach out to my loved one's therapist versus taking my loved one to the emergency room right then?

The delineation between these questions is not straightforward.

My word of advice—

- Always reach out to a professional for assistance and support when there are increased symptoms and you aren't sure. You can call 988 at any point for support.

It can be difficult in the moment to know what to do. As the support person and caregiver, you are at a disadvantage when discussing suicidality with your loved one because you cannot get inside their head, their mental space, and know beyond a shadow of a doubt or test that yes, it's their regular level of ideation, or no- it's increased suicidal ideation, intent… Or, there is, in fact, a suicide emergency with a plan.

You are at the mercy of your loved one's word. Will they be forthcoming and honest in telling you about their suicide plan?

Everyone would like to say yes, of course, but quite frankly, through the path my husband and I walked, it was never cut and dry in discerning the level of suicidal ideation he typically would have versus increased ideation, suicide intention, or having an active suicide plan.

I couldn't trust that what he said was actually the reality of the moment because of our past history with his self-medicating behaviors, not sharing honestly about suicidal thoughts in the past, and the past experiences of increased mental turmoil for him and how those situations transpired.

How Are You Doing On the Inside?

I was not able to trust my loved one with regards to his answers about suicidal thoughts or increased suicidal risk. Not being able to rely on his answers concerning suicidality was stressful.

Not being able to trust what he said when it came to suicidality continued to be the case for us for a long time. Because he initially covered up and denied having suicidal thoughts for months at the beginning of my caregiving for him, from that point on, I knew he could lie about it in the future too.

I continued to have reasonable suspicion for suicide risk, whether or not he affirmed or denied having suicidal thoughts or a suicide plan.

I would encourage you also to keep an increased level of suspicion for suicide regardless of what your loved one says to you about how they are doing if there are increased warning signs of suicide or increased suicide risk. Stay aware.

Because my husband was adept at not giving anything away facially, with tone, or in any other nonverbal way, I began to ask him in moments of concern or duress in a different way.

I would ask him how he was doing on the inside. This became our way of checking in about having increased suicidal thoughts and/or a suicide plan. It wasn't fool proof, but it was the best I could do to have access to his inner world.

As I spoke with him, my tone was calm and welcoming, not pointed or accusatory. It was important for him to feel supported and safe in the interaction. It was imperative he knew he could trust me. I share this in case you implement my way of questioning with your own loved one.

"How are you doing on the inside?" I'd ask while having eye contact with him, if possible.

He'd reply with an answer. *"Okay." "Okay, I guess." "I've been better."* Or a similar response.

I'd ask follow up questions. *"What do you mean by 'I've been better'?"*

"What do you mean when you say 'Okay'. Can you tell me what you mean?"

Then, he'd try to expound further.

I would kindly and directly ask him (while maintaining eye contact):

"Do you have any thoughts of harming yourself?" or

"Are you having any thoughts about hurting yourself right now, or did you have any prior?"

He'd say *"No"* or something along those lines.

I would mirror his words or my interpretation of his words to verify what he said,

"So, you don't have thoughts about hurting yourself?" or something along that line.

If he gave any possible indication or I had any concern about a plan, I'd ask him also,

"Do you have any plan of harming yourself or ending your life?"

He might say *"I had thoughts about hurting myself, but no, I don't have a plan."*

I'd thank him for telling me and ask him follow up questions about the thoughts he'd had.

"Have the thoughts been increased from what you have occasionally?"

"Will you promise to tell me if anything changes and you start having increased thoughts or begin having a plan?" and I'd wait for his affirmative response.

If at any point I wasn't sure about what to do, or I wasn't sure if he had increased suicide risk or increased symptoms or not, we would contact his therapist or seek additional professional advice concerning the thoughts he was having and what he needed mental health wise (if we couldn't get ahold of his therapist).

Suicide Safety Plan

Does your loved one have a suicide safety plan?

Do you know where to access it to help support them in a moment of crisis?

I ask these questions because they are important to be able to answer yes to so that a safe-guard is in place if your loved one has increased suicide risk.

There is a plan to follow and offer guidance in a moment of emergency, and it's a plan created with a professional.

It is incredibly important for your loved one to have a suicide safety plan in place with their mental health therapist. It is an agreement and plan made by the therapist and person struggling and will have steps to take in case suicidal symptoms or risk increase.

The suicide safety plan should be easily accessible and shared with you, the caregiver, and anyone else involved in your loved one's care. A suicide safety plan allows for your loved one to have the plan to follow in the case of increased suicide risk.

By you, the caregiver, knowing the suicide safety plan and having access to it, you are not alone trying to get your loved one help, you are following the steps given by the professional in a moment of crisis. There is accountability and support beyond just the two of you.

This is also why it's incredibly important for your loved one to be under the care and treatment of a mental health therapist. You don't have to shoulder all the burden upon yourself, the caregiver. Your loved one's therapist is a strong and valuable voice in their life, and they are also someone to support your loved one in getting the help they need when they need it.

If your loved one doesn't have a suicide safety plan and know where it is and the steps to take, have them make an appointment right away with their therapist to create a suicide safety plan and ask for it to be shared with you so you are empowered to come alongside them in crisis.

If your loved one doesn't have a mental health therapist yet, that is your next step right now in order to start care and then create a suicide safety plan.

If you haven't downloaded your free E-book guide: "How To Find A Mental Health Therapist" make sure to do so now. It's free and will guide you through important steps to consider as you seek a mental health therapist.

Here is the link:

amberjparker.com/theforgottencaregiver/gifts

Once you input your information, you will receive the digital guide in your email. Check your spam mail if you don't see it.

Listening To My Gut & Assessing Suicide Risk

In considering suicide risk, I did use my loved one's answers as one point of reference.

I also listened strongly to my intuition and gut in these instances.

The careful questions I asked of him allowed for communication and opened up the opportunity for him to know he was supported.

By slowly asking one question and then a follow-up question and then a verifying type question, it gave him the chance to process his thoughts and emotions. It gave him a few opportunities to tell me if he wasn't doing well but hadn't felt brave enough to share.

The slow back and forth conversation decreased his defensiveness or denial and sometimes led to him actually telling me finally the last time that yes, he actually was struggling with suicidal thoughts and to what degree. Then, I was able to come alongside him and what he was choosing to share so we could determine the next step, consider his suicide safety plan, and what professional help was needed. The help needed may be talking to a therapist, talking to the suicide lifeline, or going straight to the ER because there wasn't a question of increased suicide risk, it was definitive.

Improvement, Getting Help Before a Full-blown Emergency

At one point later on in our suicide care journey, the slow question volley led to Josh finally communicating he wasn't doing well, though he hadn't shared that information at first.

In that particular instance, there wasn't a suicide plan, but he did have significantly increased suicidal thoughts and emotional upset/ distress. He was under duress and needed a hospital stay to help resettle his baseline, change medications, and receive additional mental health support. That particular time it took a while before he told me of his increased suicidal thoughts, but we continued to spend time together before he came around to sharing with me the degree to which he was struggling.

I stayed present with him and showed tangible support, creating emotional safety for him which encouraged him to finally tell me what he was actually struggling with.

It was progress because, instead of a suicide plan or suicide attempt landing him in the hospital, *we were able to access the help he needed a step or two before the emergency.*

Accessing care before an emergency is major progress.

Identifying the warning signs of increased suicide risk and taking steps to receive mental health care at that moment is a significant step towards health and growth.

Be Willing To Have the Uncomfortable Conversation and Be Safe, Rather Than Miss Something.

This type of back-and-forth interchange is difficult, but it is incredibly important. It is important for the caregiver to be willing to ask these specific and difficult questions of their loved ones and not take the first answer as reality.

- **Never assume** they are doing okay just because they say they are and they make it sound convincing.
- **Never brush off** a niggling worry or thought you have.

- **Check in** with your loved one.
- **Let them know** you support them.

It can be the tipping point of them living or dying that day.

I don't say that to be dramatic. What I want to emphasize is the power and impact simply checking in with your loved one can have on them. It sends the message they matter and someone cares about them which is a significant & important message for them to receive. We all want to know we significantly matter to someone else.

You are not responsible for the decisions they make, but your support and care for them is invaluable. Asking more than just one question is also important.

I have found it helpful to use the slow volley of a question, then answer, another question, and another answer.

The Power of Truth-Filled Words

Another valuable message to share with your loved one is their own inherent worth as a person and also how important they are to you and why. We all benefit from knowing how valuable we are in another's life.

For those who are struggling with thoughts of being better off dead or their loved ones being better off without them, it is incredibly impactful to be told truth about themselves such as their importance and worth. Being told their worth as a person and their importance in others' lives is invaluable and incredibly powerful to combat the lies their mind is telling them of their lack of worth and importance.

Never underestimate the power your truth-filled words can have on another person, especially on your loved one struggling with suicidal thoughts and self-harm.

Take the time to tell your loved one why they matter as a person and identify their positive and good attributes. It is also incredibly important to share why they matter to you and are important in your life and others' lives around them.

Ask them to promise they will tell you if they are struggling with thoughts of hurting themselves.

After you communicate with your loved one and ask them questions about suicidality, you accept what they told you as one data point.

Remember, it is possibly a fallible data point, not because they are fallible, but because they are hurting. Don't rely only on their words.

Rely strongly on other important factors: knowing any increased stress points in their life, anything recent that was troubling for them, and listen to your intuition or gut. Identify any warning signs of increased suicidality risk.

The Difficult Reality: I Couldn't Read His Mind or Control His Decisions

Both times Josh attempted suicide I did all the careful check-ins, and he gave all the responses telling me he was doing okay, or he was struggling but did not have a plan. He was okay. No plan.

All the while, he was planning out in his mind to end his life, at the very same time he offered reassurance he was doing okay.

A calm outside but inner turmoil.

I pray your loved one is much easier to read than my husband. My husband was trained in the military on interrogation tactics and how to not give up information during an interrogation. While that was helpful training, it was not helpful in our mental health battle for his life. Even before he went through that training, he kept a pretty calm exterior.

If you recall, he had fought on his own against this battle for almost a year before I discovered it. If he didn't want anyone to know what he was thinking or feeling, he wasn't going to allow me or anyone else to know by any possible means.

The times Josh had suicide emergencies, I leaned into my own discernment and intuition to guide me in assessing suicide risk. I'm thankful I did.

Though he reassured me he was okay those times, I knew there was a stressor, a potential suicide trigger, that increased his risk, and therefore, I was on high alert.

Suicide Attempt & the Holy Spirit's Guidance

[Suicide Attempt Trigger Warning]

I accepted what he said and also checked in with him to make sure he was still doing okay. I stayed very alert both spiritually and mentally. With his second suicide attempt, the Lord allowed me to save his life. The Holy Spirit kept prompting me. *"Go downstairs. Don't do anything else. Get down there. Don't tarry. You have to get down there. Right now."*

It was our kids' bedtime. I had just spoken to him on the phone because he had gone down ahead of me, and I was concerned. He had just told me he was chilling in the basement. And he said he was fine. And yet, the Holy Spirit prompted me urgently to hurry downstairs, to finish nursing our littlest one and get to him quickly.

And I obeyed the prompting. Another 30 seconds and my husband would have been dead. Our life story would be different.

The Holy Spirit allowed me and guided me to get to the help of my husband and save his life. To fight to get the rope off from around his neck as he was actively hanging himself.

I didn't ignore that quiet, insistent voice urgently telling me to get down there. *"Don't do anything else. Get to him. Though he told you he was okay and fine."*

I followed the Holy Spirit's insistent, quiet voice and saved my husband's life in an emergency. I got him the emergency care he needed, and the Lord led the way.

I'm grateful. Thankful. It was too close a call.

My mind said of course he was fine, but the Holy Spirit said ***"Get to him now."***

In Deep Waters, We Don't Have To Be Alone.

"When you go through deep waters, I will be with you" (Isaiah 43:2a, NLT).

Whatever deep waters I went through to caregive for my husband and save his life, God was with me in them.

God is with you in your caregiving as well.

I can't promise you the future. I can only share the moments and testimony of what God did for me, for us, in our specific story and testimony. I can't extrapolate our story's outcome onto another's story, but we can pray for healing and deliverance and miracles in each story, asking God to move on behalf of our prayers. I pray it be so in your hard story.

I can share how I leaned into God in painful, difficult moments where the way forward was hard to see and difficult to traverse, and how God never left me, left us. He was right there with us in the pain and in the traumatic moments too.

I'm sorry for the deep waters and the trauma and pain you are walking through right now, friend. Caregiving for mental crisis is not easy. It's extremely difficult.

Fighting against the elusive adversary of suicide is excruciatingly difficult and will require all you've got. All I've got. And yet, we don't have to walk it alone, praise the Lord.

The same God who led me in the moment of saving my husband's life is the same God with you also. The same Holy Spirit who guided me can guide you also, not just to care for your loved one, but to lead you, comfort you, and come alongside you in your life as well. I can't do it in my own strength. None of us can.

The same power that raised Jesus from the dead lives in you if you have asked Jesus into your heart and asked Him to save you. You can have access to that power in your life too, in order to face the battles before you in God's strength.

I saw the miracle of God in saving my husband's life and using me to do so.

God uses ordinary people for extraordinary moments, when we are willing.

Our story could have been different, and my husband could have died by suicide. God still would have been good and still would have been beside me in that too.

He, Jesus, has suffered excruciatingly, and He knows deep pain and suffering. He can minister to us in our pain and suffering because He experientially understands our experience of pain. In this world we will have trouble, but we can take heart because Jesus has overcome the world.

I don't know your story friend, but I know there's pain, struggle, and hardship, and likely fear.

God was with me in the middle of the night, and I know the same God is near you right now in the dark of your night.

He will answer and come near to you to help you and guide you in your dark night if you call to Him. You don't have to walk it alone.

Yes, There is Impact On You

Yes, I have my own trauma—as you can imagine. The moment of saving my husband's life in the basement was one of my traumas, with its own triggers associated with it.

I sought out therapy for my trauma and found healing through faith-integrated EMDR therapy.

There was wounding and also significant impacts in this battle for life—Yes, I had trauma occur for me as a direct result of my caregiving efforts. The Lord used me in mighty ways to keep my husband alive, and I am grateful. My own wounds and scars are a subject of its own chapter in this book, Chapter 16.

I am forever grateful I didn't ignore the Holy Spirit's voice guiding me, urging me in that moment to get to my husband. My mind told me one thing, he was fine, but my spirit, guided by the Holy Spirit, said another, "Get to him now."

I am forever grateful the Lord allowed me to be where I needed to be in those moments of my loved one's greatest need.

Let's delve into the data points I spoke of to help solidify the concept for you in your own circumstances and situations.

The First Data Point

1. The first data point is what my loved one tells me.

I've checked in with him, and he is telling me he is doing okay. He does not have a plan.

OR

I've checked in with him and he is telling me that he's had some random thoughts of suicide, like he usually does, but no plan. And I've checked and made sure that he will tell me if it changes.

OR

I've checked in with him, and he's telling me he's not doing well and has increased thoughts of suicide or a suicide plan. This would be an emergency and require immediate care. (I would take him to the ER or the correct emergency location for evaluation and hospital admission.)

This is the first data point—what my loved one is telling me.

The Second Data Point

2. The second data point is the circumstances surrounding the moment we are in.

Are there additional added stressors or difficult life circumstances?

What just occurred in life, and is it a trigger or something that is difficult for him? Could it be something that is a suicide pathway trigger for him?

Ask yourself about your loved one and what is occurring right now in his or her life?

What stressors are they dealing with? Are any stressors more than normal at this exact moment/day/week? Is there an upcoming one?

Did a significant interaction with someone (whether with you or another person in their life) occur that was upsetting for your loved one?

Did anything troubling for them occur just now or just recently? If so, it would be wise for them to get in with their therapist to have support working through and processing whatever stressor is currently present.

Increased stressful situations or relationships can worsen mental health symptoms significantly. Processing an issue with their therapist is important to mitigate risk and help the external factors or stressors to not escalate into a more serious mental health situation with increased suicide risk.

The Third Data Point

3. **The third data point is my intuition and degree of suspicion (of a mental health emergency or of increased suicide risk).**

I base this off of all the knowledge I have of my loved one's mental health history that I already know. I base it partially off of their past habits and history when similar situations occurred in the past.

Often, my intuition and degree of suspicion increases significantly when I have something to point to in the second series of questions— concerning any potential additional present stressors for my loved one.

Regardless of what my loved one is saying to me and answering me with, if there are increased stressors or a suicide trigger (risk factor) I am aware of for them, I am going to *more closely and actively support them* without trying to irritate them.

I will engage more with them via text, phone, or in-person interactions when my degree of suspicion of an emergent need is present. I will be just a little bit more present in their day or days, not to text about mental health necessarily, but just to interact relationally, as a friend, or as a spouse, in my instance.

If he does come to a place of emergent need, he may more easily reach out to me for help in that moment. Even if he doesn't reach out, my awareness will be increased, and I'll be ready to support or recognize something "off" hopefully. Or at the very least, maybe he will more easily reach out to his therapist or another support person because he is engaging with and communicating with someone already (me).

Having pro-active awareness when there are additional stressors or risk factors present is an important way to support our loved ones.

Additional Support People

It is important for your loved one to have additional people who they can lean on, in addition to you and their therapist. These people are secondary and tertiary caregivers as we learned in Chapter 1.

You and I cannot be the only lifeline and support people in our loved one's life. Not at all.

Your loved one needs at least a few supportive and caring people in their life who have learned symptoms of increased suicide risk and understand ways to support someone in mental crisis. The other support people should come alongside both the loved one struggling and the caregiver.

If these secondary and tertiary caregivers are truly supportive, they do not try to take control or create added conflict by focusing on their own plans or agenda but instead offer emotional and tangible support to both the primary caregiver and the loved one struggling with mental illness. You also need supportive, safe people for just you in your life (a topic addressed in Chapters 14 and 15).

Support People Need Suicide Risk Awareness Education

A dangerous situation can arise when one of the close people in the person's life doesn't understand the warning signs of suicide or how to support or interact with mental crisis or mental health symptoms. *They may be well-meaning or have good intentions, but if they do not have mental health knowledge and suicide risk awareness,* **they can cause harm with their words.**

Minimizing feelings or emotions shared, being dismissive, or even using spiritual bypassing, with a loved one struggling with mental health symptoms can be dangerous.

Validation and emotional support are needed instead, along with helping the loved one receive the professional mental health care needed.

If a person doesn't take it seriously when self-harm is mentioned or implied or self-deprecating words or jokes are made, they could miss an urgent or emergent moment. *Any references a person makes about self-harm are not idle words.* They indicate a potentially serious mental health self-view which could proceed into suicidal thoughts and risk to self.

Never dismiss self-harm or self-deprecating words a friend speaks, and never assume they are okay. We can't see the secret battles people are warring against in their inner world each day.

If self-harm words are dismissed or ignored by a friend or the friend or family member assumes the person's okay and didn't mean the self-harm words, they will have missed a vital moment to *speak up for life for their loved one.*

Each person's life matters. We all need people who speak life into us and offer validation and emotional support.

Take Self-harm Words Seriously & Respond In Emergencies

I want to emphasize that if a person has said anything regarding self-harm or you have any concern for harm, take their words very seriously. Be supportive.

Be affirming, empathetic, and validating of their feelings. *Make sure they know you hear them and you take what they say seriously.*

If they indicate having thoughts about harming themselves or that they have a plan, it will likely feel surreal to you in the moment, but stay calm.

You may think *"Are we really talking about this? Is this really happening right now?"*

Speak truth over them.

Reassure the person of how much their life matters. Tell them how God sees them and what He says about them.

Share also how much you care for them, their importance in life to you and to specific people they care about.

"I care about you. Thank you for telling me that. I know that was hard to tell me. I believe what you are saying. This is serious, and we need to have help."

Getting Them to Emergency Care

Don't go behind their back with decisions but calmly insist on professional assistance.

If it is an emergency, and they are a threat to themselves at that moment in time, you must see it just like any other medical emergency.

If you aren't sure what to do, calling 988, the Suicide and Crisis Lifeline, in the U.S. will connect you with people to guide you and the person at risk in how to receive the care needed and steps to take. You don't have to do it alone.

This is a threat to their life. Tell them that you need to go to the hospital with them. That you care about them and this is serious. Go with them and be their support person walking in to get the care they need.

Drive them to the emergency room, and go in with them. Do not wait and "see if they get better" elsewhere. Getting to medical care right away is important in a mental health emergency.

Stay with them in the emergency department as they are seen and await treatment and care (if they are okay with you being there).

You may need to help share what occurred for them and be able to support them as they wait for evaluation and care. (sharing information such as they have increased thoughts of suicide, suicide intent, or a suicide plan to hurt themselves, etc.).

You can be an advocate for them and a voice in the emergency room, which is incredibly important.

If they are admitted, it is important to find out where they will be and how to contact the unit before you leave the emergency department. For a psychiatric hospitalization, the patient is not admitted with their personal belongings, to include their phone. Their personal belongings are stored until they are discharged. Read more on hospitalizations in Chapter 12.

When Your Loved One is Resistant To Emergent Care

It can be a difficult road if your loved one is resistant to going to the hospital.

Validate their emotions and feelings while at the same time discussing their symptoms and the need to seek professional support and care. You can tell them you are in a difficult position and want to respect and support them while also getting them the care they need.

Remind them again that the symptoms they shared are serious, and you both need more support and guidance in making sure they get the help they need. Tell them you understand if they are feeling worried, and you are there for them. You will be right with them as you go to the ER together. Tell them, *"We need to go to the hospital for you to get the help and treatment you need right now. I'll go with you and support you."* If you are needing additional assistance, call 988 for assistance to help guide both of you in them receiving the necessary care.

Your loved one does need to give permission for treatment and be willing to go. It is better to be voluntarily admitted rather than admitted against their will.

When a person is admitted against their will, they have a certain number of days hold and are even more carefully evaluated before being released. Some are taken to behavioral health units (psychiatric wards) by police car, if they are a threat to themselves and are unwilling to go. It is not the preferred or desired way to head into care. I discuss additional topics on hospitalization in Chapter 12.

Keeping Trust Present

It is important *to keep trust present* in the relationship in order *to continue to be a support person to your loved one* when they come out of the hospital.

Again, keep the long-term focus in mind, but also consider the duty you have to come alongside and protect their life if they have emergent needs. Hopefully, you won't find yourself in that difficult position. If they are involuntarily admitted after having increased suicide risk but not wanting care, they will likely feel betrayed by you if you were a part of getting them care. This will make supporting them in the future quite challenging.

If you find yourself in this situation, hopefully over time your loved one will be able to come to understand the concern and care you had for them and the emergent need they had at the time. Be gentle and kind but also firm in acknowledging that the symptoms present then were serious. Validate their emotions and viewpoint also.

Don't let your loved one talk you out of emergency care or being checked out and talking to someone professionally in the emergency room. If they do try this, access 988, the suicide and crisis lifeline, for assistance or begin with having your loved one accept reaching out to their mental health therapist. Their life is too important to not reach out for the help and assistance needed when you are not sure or suspect increased suicide risk. Their life is too important to not access the urgent or emergent care they need.

Professional Accountability and Support For Your Loved One

By your loved one accepting a care decision, they are more likely to be willing to accept additional care decisions or advice communicated by medical staff or their mental health therapist.

You should not be floating on your own trying to make the right decision for your loved one and your loved one needs the accountability and support from their mental health professional. This is why creating a suicide safety plan right when they start with their therapist is incredibly important in order to guide you both in the midst of symptoms but not fully knowing what step to take. You both have support and guidance on the next steps.

You can more confidently take action steps and make decisions when you are aware of warning signs of suicide risk and what to look for and then also know what to do if symptoms worsen. You will not have to guess at what to do because you will follow a plan and seek out professional guidance at any point if you are unsure. Going to the emergency room to be evaluated if you are unsure is okay to do. It is better to be safe, than to miss increased symptoms.

Don't Go It Alone Even If Your Loved One Tries to Talk You Into It

Professional guidance and accountability from the medical team and mental health therapist gives confidence and reassurance to you as the caregiver, and it brings a wise and authoritative voice into your charged and stressful moment. You both can have action steps to take. There is more than one important voice speaking truth and guidance to your loved one.

This will help assist your loved one in getting the care they need, even if at first they are resistant to the idea of going to the hospital or worried about it. It is normal to be uncertain.

Remember—

- Be aware.
- Consider all three data points.
- Seek out professional support and guidance if you are concerned about increased suicide risk.

Never hesitate to receive help from professional care by asking your loved one for their permission to contact their mental health therapist or having them call, contacting the 988 suicide and crisis number for support, or going to the emergency room if you believe your loved one is in crisis and at increased risk of suicide.

Again, having a suicide safety plan in place is *incredibly important* and helps both your loved one and you, the caregiver, in taking the steps agreed upon before, for an urgent or emergent situation.

Chapter 11

EMDR AND OTHER MENTAL HEALTH THERAPIES

Song: "God Problems" by: Maverick City Music
(feat. Chandler Moore)

In Bessel van der Kolk's groundbreaking book, *The Body Keeps the Score*, he solidified the knowledge that the physical body holds trauma, and trauma is not just locked away in our minds, accessed only by thinking and cognition.[1]

The body-mind connection must be considered when approaching treatment for trauma, emotional pain, or any emotionally charged memory.

Van der Kolk says, *"...if mind/brain/visceral communication is the royal road to emotion regulation, this demands a radical shift in our therapeutic assumptions."*[1]

For us, EMDR Therapy (which interacts with the mind/body connection) allowed for powerful healing to take place after trauma and PTSD took over with triggers, trauma responses, and dysregulation. EMDR Therapy allowed for 'stuck' memories to become 'unstuck' and integrated with other life-events, in the long-term, autobiographical memory. [2] [3] This, in turn, decreased the "vividness and emotion associated with the trauma memories" and decreased the intensity of the responses in the future. [4]

In essence, *we began to get our life back through the work done in therapy.*

I'm grateful, and I want that for you and your loved one too.

I will be up front with you, friend, and let you know I am a strong supporter of EMDR, specifically for PTSD and trauma treatment. EMDR can be used for other conditions as well. I am biased, in a good way.

I focus more on it than other therapies in this chapter for two reasons. My strong support for EMDR comes from reading about and studying the neuroscience of trauma and the way EMDR interacts with a traumatic memory to resolve it.

Also, I have experienced EMDR's life-changing power in my own life for my PTSD and trauma and have witnessed the change and healing which took place in my husband's life with his trauma and PTSD through EMDR.

That said, I fully respect the road to healing many have walked using other therapy modalities and value the research done on EMDR and many other types of psychotherapies. Using evidence-based treatment is important. There is benefit and usefulness for the various therapies I share in the section called types of psychotherapies.

If you have received benefit from a different therapy than the one I benefited from—I am so glad! The reason we seek out psychotherapy in the first place is to work through past 'stuff' that is still affecting us today. EMDR is one of many therapies available to assist in your and your loved one's healing.

As you read this chapter and hear our story and learn about the different therapies, you will understand why I am such a strong supporter of EMDR. It was life-changing for us. I want life-change for you and your loved one too—whether through EMDR or another therapy.

In this chapter, we will focus specifically on therapy for trauma and PTSD. Finding a trauma-informed therapist and using trauma-focused therapy (TFT) is important for PTSD and trauma treatment.

Your loved one and their therapist/counselor/psychologist collaboratively making treatment and therapy decisions fosters a sense of agency (having a say over one's life and choices) for your loved one.[5] Exercising agency and being given choice are incredibly important for someone with a trauma background, where they lost choice or felt helpless in the moment(s) of trauma.[5] Having a voice can empower them in continuing to pursue their own healing.

In treating trauma and PTSD, van der Kolk, identifies "EMDR as well as…internal family systems, yoga, neurofeedback, psychomotor therapy, and theater" as therapies which "focus not only on regulating the intense memories activated by trauma but also on restoring a sense of agency, engagement, and commitment through ownership of body and mind".[3]

Agency is harmed by trauma, and these therapies can help restore agency and ownership over oneself.[3][5]

To not feel helpless anymore. To have a voice. To have a say—is a powerful feeling.

Regaining "ownership of body and mind" is significant.[3]

The VA and APA (American Psychological Association) both recommend an individualized approach to therapy with each client, and we will cover their PTSD treatment guidelines later in this chapter.

Van der Kolk also uses an individualized approach to each client, based on their specific needs. He may reference input from a client (client's drawings or writings brought in of memories they can't talk about yet) in their first therapy session to guide whether he adds, for example, "somatic processing, neurofeedback, or EMDR" into the therapeutic work.[6]

An individualized approach is based on the unique needs of the person and integrating the best therapy modalities for that specific person.

Individualized therapy is needed because *therapy is not a one-size-fits-all process.* What is best for one person may not be best for another in seeking treatment and healing.

My Free Gift to You—An E-Book Guide "How To Find A Mental Health Therapist"

I've already mentioned it before in this book, but I don't want you to miss this incredible guide! As an additional support to you and your loved one, I wrote an E-book guide with crucial steps to guide you through "How to Find a Mental Health Therapist."

Head over to:

amberjparker.com/theforgottencaregiver/gifts to access this free guide.

To make it easier, here's the QR code to access it quickly:

As mentioned before, this Free guide has the tried-and-true steps I took to find a mental health therapist for my husband when we were in the middle of crisis, and I was desperate to find the right treatment for him. I have used these same steps to find my therapists and subsequent therapists for both of us.

In this Free guide, I share my go-to websites to find a therapist and what steps to take, starting with the first step, *"Do I need a therapist?"*.

Don't wait to access it and learn the steps of finding the right mental health therapist for your loved one or yourself.

Our Journey with Different Psychotherapies

Throughout our lengthy season of mental health caregiving, I navigated and supported Josh through a number of mental health therapies for his trauma, PTSD, depression, alcohol use disorder, and suicidality.

In order of when they were introduced, he underwent the therapies, from first to last: CBT, CPT, DBT, and finally, the one that truly made a difference for his trauma and PTSD—EMDR Therapy.

[CBT: Cognitive Behavioral Therapy, CPT: Cognitive Processing Therapy, DBT: Dialectical Behavioral Therapy, EMDR: Eye Movement Desensitization & Reprocessing]

He also later did intensive, outpatient EMDR therapy integrated with IFS (Internal Family Systems) and Neurofeedback for alcohol use disorder and suicidality.

Josh's condition worsened with CBT and significantly improved with EMDR. I'll share that story later in this chapter.

My hope is for your loved one to have access to EMDR Therapy first, rather than fourth, as my husband did.

For my PTSD and complex trauma, I searched for a therapist for myself who would support my spiritual faith and integrate it into the EMDR session. I already had researched EMDR and had seen its effectiveness for my husband. I knew EMDR therapy was the most effective treatment for me to pursue as well. I had done a cognitive therapy prior to that time which was supportive but didn't process my trauma.

I underwent trauma-focused EMDR therapy. It had cognitive elements incorporated at the beginning of the session and at the end of the session. Part of the EMDR preparation was to identify negative or positive cognitions or feelings and rate them.[7] I would rate my feeling on the SUD (Subjective Units of Disturbance) Scale and rate the VOC (Validity of Cognition, 0 to 7) of my thought—both were subjective ratings I gave my therapist after we identified a negative cognition or emotion for me.[7][8] We would also determine which trauma memory or emotion I would focus on during the EMDR session.

The SUDs scale subjectively assesses the level of distress a person feels about a memory or event (from 0 to 10), prior to EMDR and following EMDR.[8]

I also did intensive, outpatient EMDR Therapy sessions integrated with Neurofeedback for trauma and PTSD with the same cognitive preparation. During the Neurofeedback portion, specific questions would be asked prior and occasionally during the Neurofeedback also. Neurofeedback focuses on brain waves, using electrodes attached to the scalp.

Types of Psychotherapy (Mental Health Therapy)

There are many different types of psychotherapy (mental health therapy). In this chapter, our focus is on psychotherapies specifically for trauma and PTSD.

Trauma-focused therapy (TFT) is any therapy used to treat trauma.

Of the mind-body focused therapies, EMDR (Eye Movement Desensitization and Reprocessing) Therapy interacts with the limbic system and mind-body connection. EMDR Therapy uses bilateral stimulation (both sides of the body) while the person focuses briefly on the trauma memory itself which allows for re-processing and integration of the trauma imprints and emotional memories.[4] The intensity of the negative emotions and memories decrease as a result.

'Stuck' trauma memories become 'unstuck'.[2]

Several other therapies which interact with the mind-body connection are: Polyvagal Therapy, Sensorimotor Psychotherapy, and Somatic Experiencing.[9] Polyvagal Therapy has the person focus on what they are feeling in their body, rather than the details of trauma.[1] It uses awareness and focuses on a sense of safety being present.[10] Brain Spotting is a therapy with similarities to EMDR.

One of the cognitive therapies is CBT (Cognitive Behavioral Therapy). According to the APA (American Psychological Association), in PTSD treatment, CBT focuses on a client's negative thoughts, emotions, or behavior resulting from the trauma (the effects of the trauma memory) to desensitize the person to them, and shift to more "balanced and effective thinking patterns" and improved emotions and behavior.[11] It interacts with cognition and thinking (the rational brain).[2] CBT challenges or reframes the negative thoughts and beliefs for positive or healthier thoughts/cognitions, and it uses homework to help work through the problematic beliefs, thoughts, or behaviors.[2][12]

Variations of Cognitive Behavioral Therapy include: CPT (Cognitive Processing Therapy), PE (Prolonged Exposure), CT (Cognitive Therapy), and TF-CBT (Trauma-focused CBT).

Cognitive Processing Therapy (CPT) uses discussion of the trauma and specific techniques to address the client's negative beliefs.[13]

Prolonged Exposure (PE) Therapy gradually exposes an individual to trauma-related stimuli (situations, objects, etc.) being avoided in order to desensitize the client to the negative thought, emotion, or behavior through repeated exposure.[14][15] CBT is also considered a type of exposure therapy due to the homework and repetition used to reinforce concepts.

Other powerful therapies are IFS (Internal Family Systems), DBT (Dialectical Behavioral Therapy), and Neurofeedback. IFS uses 'parts work' based on the idea that our mind is like a family network with different parts (and split-off parts as a result of trauma), and change to one part can impact the other parts.[9] Neurofeedback uses specific brain waves with electrode wires attached to your head at specific locations (similar looking to an EEG test). DBT focuses on mindfulness and emotion regulation techniques.

This is not an exhaustive list of available therapies but a starting point for you and your loved one in seeking out therapy. Research further on your own starting with the resources in the Appendix at the back of this book.

My charge to you is to pursue the treatments and mental health therapies needed to achieve your and your loved one's therapeutic goals, alongside the guidance of your mental health therapist/counselor/psychologist.

Factors to Consider with Psychotherapy

There are many factors to be aware of in starting psychotherapy.

First, mental health therapy takes time and commitment. Consistent appointments with a trusted mental health clinician are vital for therapy work to make effective progress for the person (the client). The clinician may be called a licensed clinical social worker, a therapist, counselor, or even a psychologist. Weekly 1-hour appointments are a common spacing of appointments. Sometimes, twice-a-week appointments or therapy appointments lasting a few hours per session (for intensive sessions) may be needed.

Cost of therapy and insurance coverage are other factors to navigate. It can take time to find a mental health therapist/counselor/psychologist who's in-network with your insurance and specializes in the types of therapy and conditions you need. For us, much of Josh's mental health therapy was done through the VA system. All of my mental health therapy was paid for out of pocket, without insurance. Some of Josh's later therapy was also paid for out of pocket. Paying out of pocket can cause financial burden and be an additional struggle to navigate.

Therapy sessions can be physically, emotionally, and mentally tiring which is why I find it important to prioritize rest and time to just "be" after a therapy session (no matter what type of therapy is done). The clinician will likely offer different positive coping strategies and encourage self-care.

I always tried to decrease what was expected of me as much as possible the day of therapy (after the session) and the day following the therapy session. I would decrease my to-do list and incorporate rest, comfort, journaling, creating with art, or time in nature into those days.

A Quick Neuroscience Refresher

If you recall from Chapter 4, there are two different memory systems: the rational (cortex-based) memory system and emotional (limbic-based) memory system.[16] What we typically think of as thoughts are cognitive or rational thoughts in the dorsolateral prefrontal cortex.[16]

Emotional memories, including trauma, are stored in the limbic system, and these emotional memories must be accessed and retrieved there also.[16] The amygdala, hippocampus, and other parts of the limbic system are involved in trauma memory storage and retrieval.[17] The amygdala, as well as two brain regions not mentioned before, the ACC and PCC, are all involved with emotional processing and emotional memory (The anterior cingulate cortex (ACC) and posterior cingulate cortex (PCC) are other parts of the complex limbic system).[17] [18] Refer to this chapter's references for further information.

Because of the anatomy of the brain, the emotional information and memories in the limbic system can't be directly accessed by conscious thinking (rational part of the brain—the dorsolateral prefrontal cortex).[16] This is because there is not a direct connection from the dorsolateral prefrontal cortex to the emotional brain and amygdala.[16] In order to access where these emotional memories are stored, a limbic-focused therapy would be needed.[16]

The Effectiveness of EMDR Therapy

EMDR therapy is effective because it accesses where emotional memories are stored, where trauma is stored, and helps desensitize, re-process and integrate the memories, thereby decreasing negative emotions and physical symptoms being experienced by the individual.[2] [19]

In this section, we are going to get a bit more technical. If it's too much, jump to the end of this section and read the last few sentences before moving on. Otherwise, keep reading! It's amazing how EMDR works.

The APA (American Psychological Association) describes EMDR therapy as: *the person focuses briefly on the trauma memory itself while simultaneously using bilateral stimulation (like eye movements)* which allows for *"a reduction in the vividness and emotion associated with the trauma memories."*[4]

Francine Shapiro, the late originator and developer of EMDR, shared the way processing occurs in EMDR was through: the Adaptive Information Processing (AIP) model.[13] The AIP model helps explain how rapidly clinical results can be achieved with EMDR therapy and with consistency of response to it, via adaptive resolution.[13]

According to Shapiro, "rather than addressing the client's *reaction* to the disturbing event—as biofeedback, exposure therapies, or relaxation training do—EMDR therapy focuses on the memory itself."[13] The effect on the targeted memory and information associated with it seems to occur spontaneously, which then impacts the client's *reaction* also.[13]

EMDR's therapy model is guided by the belief that the negative cognitions and behaviors are only symptoms of the "physiologically stored memory".[13]

By focusing on the memory itself, the thoughts and behaviors will improve as a result of the memory being processed and resolved effectively.[13] Van der Kolk corroborates this stance, calling the cognitions "cognitive flashbacks" like visual flashbacks, seeming to be residue from the trauma, and better treated with EMDR than with CBT.[2]

And so—the impact of the memory and intensity of it can spontaneously adapt and change as the memory becomes effectively resolved through EMDR.

Unprocessed memories and stimuli are thought to cause the negative emotions and behaviors.[13] When EMDR therapy accesses the limbic system, a person's emotional memories are accessed, and these distressing thoughts, beliefs, emotions, and/or memories can finally be processed and integrated into the neural network.[2][16] Integration puts these memories and fragments back into the proper place they should have been placed at the time the event originally occurred.[2] Exactly how this occurs on a neurobiological basis is continuing to be studied and researched. Reading about brain scans showing activation of specific areas in the brain in connection to trauma memory and before and after trauma treatment is fascinating.[3][17] Refer to the references from this chapter for more information.

The trauma imprints and negative emotional memory can be integrated/resolved into the long-term, autobiographical memory— where past memories are supposed to be—to learn from and connect with other memories or emotions.[3][20] To be fluid with other memories.[2][19]

Another way to describe this is: **EMDR helps a 'stuck' memory become 'un-stuck.'**[3]

The memory is not immoveable anymore but instead can adapt and have flexibility, as it should, to be 'learned' from as other memories are learned from.[3] [20] The idea of neuroplasticity.[19] The negative memory (and connected thoughts and emotions) is re-processed and integrated/resolved, which decreases the negative impact it continues to have on the person.[20] PTSD symptoms and trauma responses can decrease.

Through EMDR, 'stuck' trauma memories become 'unstuck' so the trauma can be in the past, rather than constantly a part of the present.[2] [3]

The Bilateral Stimulation of EMDR Therapy

During EMDR, bilateral stimulation occurs on both sides of the body in an alternating fashion while the client focuses briefly on the traumatic memory, feeling, etc.

The bilateral stimulation for EMDR can be done a few different ways—with eye movements, vibratory paddles, or auditory tones. A therapist can guide the client's eye movements back and forth by having the client follow the therapist's finger to specific points on the left and right, while the client's head remains stationary.

The bilateral stimulation can also occur with vibratory paddles in each hand that buzz one and then the other. Auditory bilateral stimulation uses a sound playing in one ear and then the other with headphones. Bilateral tapping could also be done. Each person has different preferences of the modality that helps the most.

EMDR's bilateral stimulation facilitates the access of your emotional memory in your limbic system.[19] The re-processing and integration allows for the memories to not cause as intense of responses in the future as new neural connections are formed. The vividness and negative emotions associated with the trauma memory can decrease. [4]

My Experience With EMDR

For me, I needed to be able to close my eyes to focus during the EMDR session and found holding the vibratory paddles the most helpful for my sessions. Discussing with your therapist about which is most helpful and trying auditory, eye movements, or vibratory out can help delineate the most effective modality to use.

Prior to starting, the therapist would guide me on what to focus on during the EMDR portion. We would then begin the EMDR, with occasional inputs or simple questions from the therapist to guide my session. At the end of the session, I would be asked what came up for me during it, and my therapist would talk briefly with me, helping me process what came up. A coping technique or other education would be shared before we finished our therapy session.

By talking with my therapist briefly at the end of the EMDR session to process the session or by bringing in cognitive-focused elements into the session, this seems to have engaged the part of my brain connecting the emotional brain to the rational brain (medial prefrontal cortex, responsible for self-awareness).[16] [20]

I grew in my self-awareness and would try coping techniques out when triggered and noticing a trauma response or when a stressful moment would occur between sessions.

Two Powerful Positives of EMDR

For combat Veterans and civilians alike, who have experienced trauma and struggle with PTSD, it can be very difficult to talk about the events which occurred and talk about thoughts, emotions, and behaviors connected to their trauma or PTSD.

With EMDR Therapy, a person doesn't have to talk as much as in cognitive 'talk' therapies. During EMDR itself, the person is quiet and focusing inward. There is some talking before and after to set the session up well.

The bilateral stimulation with guidance from the therapist allows for the brain to rewire and integrate the traumatic imprints, for the brain to begin to heal itself. Having to talk about difficult events and emotions can be a big factor in someone being resistant to starting therapy or for stopping therapy, especially in the Veteran community.

While any trauma-focused therapy is difficult, EMDR Therapy decreases the burden of having to talk or write about the events or thoughts/emotions connected to it.

Another positive is EMDR does not require homework like CBT usually does. This means focused interaction with the trauma is confined to the therapist's office while coping strategies and self-care are used between sessions.

These positives should be considered when your loved one and their therapist are discussing what therapy to begin in determining their individual's needs and how to decrease their emotional distress during and between therapy sessions.

VA/DoD PTSD Guidelines

EMDR is one of three top therapies recommended by the VA/DoD for PTSD and Acute Stress Disorder.

This is great news. The fact that EMDR Therapy is one of the three top treatments by the VA/DoD is extremely promising for Veterans and the military community at large.

Here is the current 2023 VA/ DcD Clinical Practice Guidelines (for the management of posttraumatic stress disorder and acute stress disorder) which recommend with strong evidence:

Cognitive Processing Therapy (CPT), Eye Movement Desensitization and Reprocessing (EMDR), and Prolonged Exposure (PE).[21]

All three psychotherapies are recommended as first-line treatments.

For Veterans and military members to have access to EMDR Therapy as one of the first-line PTSD treatment options is significant!

When I was searching eight years ago for an EMDR therapist experienced with combat trauma and war PTSD, it took me over 6 months to find one. Such a long search was stressful and felt an eternity in the midst of mental health issues. In fighting to get my husband better, time was of the essence. There weren't EMDR therapists available at our VA nor could I find one in private practice with experience working with combat Veterans.

We finally discovered there was a psychologist at the VA who did EMDR, and Josh finally got in to see the psychologist and have access to EMDR work. The reduction in his PTSD symptoms was dramatic.

Individually Focused Therapy & APA Guidelines

An individualized treatment plan is crucial and finding the best therapy for your loved one to begin with is incredibly important—whether it is EMDR, CPT, or a different therapy. There is research for trauma and PTSD treatment which supports EMDR therapy as well as research supporting CBT, TF-CBT, PE, and CPT for trauma and PTSD treatment.

The current professional guidelines from the APA (American Psychological Association) for PTSD treatment recommend CPT, PE, and TF-CBT (all cognitive therapies) as first-line treatment and suggest EMDR Therapy, Narrative Exposure, or CT (Cognitive Therapy) as second-line treatments.[15] Professional guidelines are evidence-based practices based on many factors which guide clinician's treatment and therapy practices.

EMDR's focus on briefly accessing the trauma memory itself in order to effect change in the memory which then impacts the emotions and thoughts connected to the memory also, make it a powerful and different treatment option from cognitive-only based therapies.

My hope is for you and your loved one to have access to EMDR therapy as one of the initial PTSD treatment options available to you.

I believe EMDR Therapy should be available as one of the initial PTSD treatment options, not to replace cognitive therapies, but to allow individuals access to the power of limbic-focused therapy like EMDR right away.

The APA guideline encourages clinicians to use collaborative decision making, support patient preferences, and provide their patients with PTSD treatment options.[15] What this means for you, friend, is you (and your loved one) have a voice in your treatment—a collaborative voice, alongside your clinician. You are able to ask and advocate for a specific type of therapy. Your clinician would value your input as you collaboratively discuss the best course of psychotherapy—and they offer their professional insight. If they aren't trained in the type of therapy discussed, they can refer you to another clinician trained in it. Hopefully, the new clinician will take your insurance.

Finding a clinician who takes your insurance and offers a specific therapy can take time, so don't wait to start the search.

Finding the Best Therapist

Whatever therapy is done, it needs to help you or your loved one with achieving therapeutic goals and seeing improvement. You can read over the types of therapy I shared in a previous section to remind yourself.

Sometimes, the difficulty is finding the best fit in a *therapist*, rather than the *type of therapy* being done.

This doesn't mean a therapist isn't good at what they do, but maybe the therapist-client relationship doesn't connect well.

Trust and rapport between the therapist and client are important for effective therapy to take place.

I talk about this step of finding the right therapist in my free E-book guide: "How to Find A Mental Health Therapist."

You've likely already downloaded it. If so, I hope you are finding it useful in your search for the right therapist.

If you haven't yet, there's no reason to wait. It is a valuable adjunct to this book.

You will get on my email list to receive additional offerings from me as well.

Access your copy via the link:

amberjparker.com/theforgottencaregiver/gifts

Let me help you and your loved one as you search for the right therapist or counselor in your healing journey.

Staying Within the Window of Tolerance

For effective therapy to occur, the client must be able to stay in the window of tolerance for the client to not become overwhelmed and to receive benefit from the therapy.[2] Window of tolerance is a term used to describe a person's ability to tolerate the topics brought up in therapy in order to continue effective treatment, while not becoming too overwhelmed by them.[2] [9]

If someone is significantly dysregulated with worsening suicidality, trauma-focused therapy would need to be halted, while utilizing emotion regulation skills, mindfulness with DBT (or a similar therapy), and other techniques in order to stabilize the client and give them regulation tools needed prior to continuing with any trauma-focused therapy.[22]

At any point along the way—if a client has worsening suicidal symptoms, intention, or plan, it would be necessary to seek immediate emergency care and evaluation for hospitalization.

Before further trauma-focused therapy is conducted, the client would need to learn and grow in coping skills and additional regulation techniques through therapy. This would help offer the support needed to initiate trauma-focused therapy again, in order to keep the client within the window of tolerance and able to benefit from the therapy, without having worsening mental health symptoms or dysregulation.[19]

Our Personal Experience with CBT for Trauma

Using a therapy that is powerful but not the correct one for a person can exacerbate or worsen their condition.

We found this to be true with our own experience of CBT for trauma. The trauma-focused CBT used for my husband's trauma worsened his mental health symptoms significantly. Our experience with CBT homework was my husband doing his homework at home. He'd be re-living his trauma at night at home without an experienced therapist guiding him back to safety. I hated it because it was dangerous and felt very unsafe.

It wasn't safe, in fact... In order to face the CBT homework, he'd drink alcohol and be completely out of it, in a dark place mentally, and then want to start a fire in the backyard fire pit. Often, I couldn't talk him out of it and watchfully tried to guide him away from injury. It wasn't easy.

Fire, alcohol, and deep emotional pain don't mix well.

I was left as the caregiver and wife, to care for our kids upstairs and then rush back downstairs to keep him physically safe, while I felt helpless and trapped, unable to stop the CBT homework which caused such significant emotional distress in him. He had to finish it for his therapy session. He'd pass out, or I'd help an incoherent person up the stairs and to bed because he'd relive his trauma without an experienced therapist guiding him back to safety. And so, he used alcohol to try to cope.

Our experience with CBT was it forced my husband to relive his trauma over and over in homework and then talk about it during sessions, again continuing to increase his emotional distress and mental health symptoms. For my husband, his trauma and PTSD symptoms got worse and worse. His depression worsened too until the day he finally planned to end his life. That set off a whole host of additional problems.

There was a better treatment for him—one that did not require reliving his trauma through the therapy homework or continually talking about the experiences and memories surrounding the trauma. It was EMDR therapy.

We didn't get to have him do EMDR therapy until a year later, but it was life changing. After only three or four sessions, his symptoms were reduced significantly, and he felt so much better.

Caution with Trauma-focused Therapy for Suicidal Patients

Clinicians are cautious to utilize trauma-focused therapies for patients with suicidality due to the risk of worsening symptoms and risk of suicide (and rightly so).

There is research beginning to identify ways to use trauma-focused psychotherapy or TFT (trauma-focused therapy) for patients with suicidal ideation.[22] This obviously must be done cautiously, with heightened awareness for any emotional dysregulation or increased suicidal symptoms.

Trauma therapy would be contraindicated for someone actively suicidal (increased risk or worsening suicidal symptoms).

A suicide safety plan must be agreed upon by the client and the therapist, and the client's caregiver(s) should also be knowledgeable of the safety plan and what steps to take in case of worsening suicidal symptoms, intention, or plan.

Our Experience with DBT and Mindfulness

For us, Josh began DBT as a way to navigate mindfulness and work to stabilize his mental and emotional turmoil after his first two suicide psychiatric hospitalizations. After these psychiatric hospitalizations, he couldn't continue trauma-focused therapy.

He was ill enough that the only focus had to be stabilization of his suicidality. Mindfulness in DBT was important during this time.

DBT's focus is on mindfulness and emotional regulation techniques as well as distress tolerance.[3] It was an important therapy for the dysregulation and suicidal symptoms present.

As his symptoms stabilized more fully over many months using DBT alongside medications, he had additional hospital stays for increased suicidal thoughts and increased risk. This was improvement because these hospital stays were not for an emergency with a suicide plan and/ or suicide attempt. These stays were for increased suicide risk due to increased warning signs and symptoms. We followed his suicide safety plan and got him care and inpatient hospitalization before a plan or attempt occurred.

It was extremely necessary for him to have a hospital stay to help manage those increased thoughts and emotional distress, in order to stabilize him again and allow him the immediate mental health support he needed.

Hope Finally Breaking Through for Us

Finally, I found a psychologist who had experience with combat trauma and EMDR treatment. It took over six months from the time I began actively searching for a therapist or psychologist with this expertise in our area before I found one. Waiting that long was disheartening and difficult as I knew he needed the therapy and couldn't get it for him. Amazingly, my husband underwent three to four sessions of EMDR and made more progress in those sessions than he had through many CBT sessions and the other months of therapy.

Hope was palpable.

Maybe our dark tunnel would have some light at the end of it, after all. There was finally healing to grasp ahold of.

Research studies support the phenomenon we experienced of a few EMDR sessions improving PTSD symptoms significantly.

Your Dark Night & Tunnel

Friend—If you are in the dark night and the middle of the tunnel right now, eking it out one mental health therapy session at a time, know that I see you. Keep persevering.

Advocate for and pursue trauma-focused therapies for trauma and PTSD. I would love for your loved one to start with EMDR—whether it's for yourself or your loved one. It may be another therapy is better for them to begin with though. Making therapeutic decisions collaboratively with their clinician is important.

With my own EMDR therapy, I walked through excruciatingly painful re-living of my own dark moments, my trauma, my wounding, my scars in order to find some healing on the other side… soon enough we'll talk about my scars in this book (Chapter 16).

My healing is on a continuum, just like my husband's is.

Your healing and your loved one's healing are also on a continuum, friend.

We are moving towards healing and growth.

Yes. *Our healing is on a continuum.*

I will never say I'm fully "healed" because the scars I have from what I've walked through will be there. More healed. Still present.

I'm not the same person I was at the beginning of this, going into the battle.

It has changed me.

In therapy, I faced my trauma, memories, and emotional pain. It was hard, but I knew my therapist would support me, empathize with me, guide me, and champion me.

I didn't have to be my own advocate in her office.

I could just bring me—Wounds, scars, and all.

And just be.

That is a powerful gift.

REFERENCES

1   van der Kolk, B. A. (2014). *The Body Keeps the Score: Brain, Mind, and Body In the Healing of Trauma.* Penguin Books, 80, 88.

2   van der Kolk, 222-224, 230, 248.

3   van der Kolk, 238, 256-258, 272.

4   "EMDR Therapy." APA Clinical Practice Guideline for the Treatment of Posttraumatic Stress Disorder. https://www.apa.org/ptsd-guideline/ treatments/eye-movement-reprocessing. Accessed 5 June 2025.

5   van der Kolk, 97-98, 205.

6   van der Kolk, 241.

7   Shapiro, F. (2018). *Eye Movement Desensitization and Reprocessing Therapy: Basic Principles, Protocols, and Procedures.* 3rd ed. The Guilford Press, 31.

8   Brayer, R. (2023). *The Art and Science of EMDR: Helping Clinicians Bridge the Path from Protocol to Practice.* PESI Publishing, Inc., 67-71.

9   van der Kolk, 26, 218-220, 282-283.

10 Porges, S. W. and Porges, S. (2023). *Our Polyvagal World: How Safety and Trauma Change Us.* W. W. Norton and Company, Inc. 118-119.

[11] "Cognitive Behavioral Therapy." APA Clinical Practice Guideline for the Treatment of Posttraumatic Stress Disorder. https://www.apa.org/ptsd-guideline/treatments/eye-movement-reprocessing. Accessed 5 June 2025.

[12] "PTSD Treatments." APA Clinical Practice Guideline for the Treatment of Posttraumatic Stress Disorder. https://www.apa.org/ptsd-guideline/treatments. Accessed 5 June 2025.

[13] Shapiro, F. (2018). *Eye Movement Desensitization and Reprocessing Therapy: Basic Principles, Protocols, and Procedures. 3rd ed.* The Guilford Press. 15-23.

[14] "Prolonged Exposure for PTSD". National Center for PTSD. https://www.ptsd.va.gov/professional/treat/txessentials/prolonged_exposure_pro.asp . Accessed 5 June 2025.

[15] "APA Clinical Practice Guideline for the Treatment of Posttraumatic Stress Disorder in Adults." https://www.apa.org/ptsd-guideline/ptsd.pdf. Accessed 6 June 2025.

[16] van der Kolk, 178, 207-210.

[17] Gvozdanovic, G., Stampfli, P., Seifritz, E., and Rasch, B. (2017). Neural Correlates of Experimental Trauma Memory Retrieval. *Human Brain Mapping,* **38:** 3592-3602.

[18] Bari, A., Niu, T., Langevin, J., and Fried, I. (2013). Limbic Neuromodulation: Implications for Addiction, Posttraumatic Stress Disorder, and Memory. *Neurosurg Clin N Am.* 2013 Oct 10; 25(1):137-145. https://doi.org/10.1016/j.nec.2013.08.004.

[19] Brayer, 2-13.

[20] Shapiro, F. (2012). *Getting Past Your Past: Take Control of Your Life with Self-Help Techniques from EMDR Therapy.* Rodale, 74.

[21] "VA/DOD Clinical Practice Guidelines: Management of Post-Traumatic Stress Disorder and Acute Stress Disorder Quick Reference Guide". https://healthquality.va.gov/HEALTHQUALITY/guidelines/MH/ptsd/VA-DOD-CPG-PTSD-Quick-Reference-Guide.pdf . Accessed 22 February 2025.

[22] Burback, L., Dhaliwal, R., Reeson, M., Erick, T., Hartle, K., Chow, E., Vouronikos, G., Antumes, N., Marshall, T., Kennedy, M., Dennett, L., Greenshaw, A., Smith-MacDonald, L., and Winkler, O. (2023) Trauma focused psychotherapy in patients with suicidal ideation: A scoping review. *Current Research in Behavioral Sciences 4*, 100102. 1-13.

Chapter 12

PSYCHIATRIC MEDICATIONS & NAVIGATING PSYCHIATRIC HOSPITALIZATIONS

Song: "Surrounded (Fight My Battles)" by: Michael W. Smith

We've had our fair share of experience with behavioral health medications, also known as psychotropic or psychiatric medications. My husband has been on many different medications, and at one point, his cocktail of psychotropic medications was a lot—specifically following hospital stays for suicide attempt or plan and when his suicidality symptoms, severe depression (Major Depression Disorder), and PTSD were full blown and needed to be brought under control for therapy to have a chance to work. He didn't stay on the number of medications he was on long-term. They shifted and changed as his symptoms and conditions required.

It's not a one-size-fits-all when it comes to treating mental health symptoms and diagnoses. Different therapies and medications are used for different symptoms and conditions, and the same one won't always work for everyone. Decisions need to be made together, collaboratively with the patient/client and provider/therapist working together. When the patient/client feels empowered and supported, they will be more invested in reaching the treatment goals they decide on together.

A trauma-informed approach is powerful in the medical provider office and the mental health therapist's office.

A Holistic Approach to Treatment

I find a holistic approach important for trauma and PTSD treatment. The three-pronged holistic approach of medication, psychotherapy, and faith in God is a powerful combination for healing. I have experienced the power of integrating my faith in God with psychotherapy for my own healing. It is powerful.

In this three-pronged approach, faith and belief in God bring hope, purpose, and a significant reason to live and allow for healing the spiritual aspect of oneself. We'll look at faith in the next chapter. Therapy brings guided healing and the facing of trauma, other emotional pain, or difficult memories in order to allow the brain to begin to heal. Medication allows for symptoms to be managed and decreased while the therapy work is done.

In caring for a person dealing with suicidality, medication allows for the person's symptoms to be cared for and lessened so the person can stay alive, alive long enough for the psychotherapy to begin to do the healing work needed to stabilize, build distress tolerance, offer coping strategies, and then address underlying issues present, such as trauma.

If worsening suicidal symptoms and dysregulation occur, then trauma-focused therapy must be halted to stabilize the client and help them to keep growing in coping techniques such as emotion-regulation techniques and mindfulness with DBT or a similar therapy.

Hospitalizations may be needed to stabilize your loved one at different points. A hospitalization would be needed in the case of emergency and increased suicidal risk. Refer to previous chapters regarding those topics.

If trauma-focused therapy could continue at some point, the number of medications the person was on would likely change or lessen as the therapy treatment worked. My husband was prescribed many different psychotropic medications, throughout our mental health crisis battle.

Managing Psychotropic/ Behavioral Health Medications

There are many classes of psychotropic or behavioral health medications. I won't be covering the names or classes of medications here. You can research and read about them and discuss them with your loved one's medical provider or psychiatrist.

The medications prescribed will be discussed with the psychiatrist or other behavioral health medical provider to appropriately manage the symptoms your loved one has.

The issues we navigated for my husband were trauma, PTSD, self-medicating, depression, and suicidality. The specific issues you navigate may be different.

For us, there was a cocktail of medications he was on as time progressed, especially after the suicidal hospital stays had occurred. There were different classes of medications used for different purposes and reasons. It took time for the providers to dial in the right grouping and doses of medications to treat the symptoms my husband was having and decrease side effects or avoid adverse effects of each medication. Navigating which medication to use and identifying whether a side effect was able to be tolerated or was adverse took time and energy.

There is not a one-size-fits-all approach with behavioral health medications and can't be when there are complex symptoms and co-morbidities present concurrently. While certain medications are first-line treatment for a condition, if they aren't well-tolerated by a patient, then a different medication will be used.

Switching psychotropic medications usually requires tapering down (decreasing the dosage of a medication rather than abruptly stopping it) due to adverse effects from stopping it immediately. Tapering up is also common.

Having appointments with a psychiatrist to manage the medications and address any side effects is necessary when a person takes psychotropic medications for mental health conditions. Psychiatrists are specialists in managing psychiatric conditions and know how to titrate up or down the different medications and which medications to change a patient to if there is a need to change the medications.

The Purpose of Psychotropic Medications

The purpose of psychotropic medications, *in my viewpoint,* is to treat the symptoms the patient is having in order to stabilize them enough for other underlying issues to be treated with psychotherapy.

The medicine won't fix any underlying trauma or other issue, but it will help manage the person's symptoms for them to begin healing the underlying issues through therapy.

For many months for us during increased suicidal ideation, attempt, plan, and hospitalizations the focus of therapy was only stabilization for my husband, not treatment of his underlying trauma. Trauma work had to pause until he was more stabilized and in his window of tolerance (able to tolerate the topics brought up in therapy but not become too overwhelmed by them).[1]

If his therapy treatment was focused on trauma work during that time, it would have increased his emotional distress, increased risk of worsening suicidal symptoms, and it wouldn't have been safe or effective for him. He needed to learn coping strategies through the mindfulness work in DBT at that time.

Psychotropic Medication Duration- Long Term versus Short Term

An important and sticky discussion point is how long does a person need to be on a medication for a mental health condition or symptoms. This question has the wrong focus.

When it comes to psychotropic medications, one person may need medication always (long-term) and another person may only need medication for a short time or a specific season of life. This determination of the patient's medication needs is decided as a team, with the patient and the psychiatrist (or behavioral health NP or PA or possibly with their primary care provider) involved.

Asking how long they need to be on a medication is like trying to predict whether a person on thyroid medication will need to be on the medication long-term, or not.

The answer: Time will tell. Symptoms will tell. The patient's condition and management of symptoms will inform that determination.

I, personally, have a thyroid condition and am on thyroid medication indefinitely, likely long-term. To apply the same approach to a mental health diagnosis is appropriate: time will tell. Symptoms and how the diagnosis progresses or improves will tell. There are many people who need to be on depression medications long-term. That's okay. All of our bodies are different.

Let's stop viewing psychotropic medications through a different lens from other classes of medications.

Psychiatric Hospitalizations

It's important to demystify the mystery surrounding an inpatient stay at a psychiatric ward (behavioral health unit). Most people don't have any understanding of what to expect if their loved one needs care for an emergent mental crisis and is admitted to a behavioral health unit. The unknown can feel scary and stressful. I understand.

This section is for the express purpose of you knowing better what to expect when your loved one is admitted for a psychiatric hospitalization.

Do not use this information in choosing whether your loved one will or will not go to a psychiatric ward (behavioral health unit) or seek medical care for worsening mental health symptoms or mental crisis.

Any hospitalization for a loved one is stressful and difficult to navigate, whether for a mental health or physical condition. If your loved one was in the ICU for a serious physical condition, it would be overwhelming and stressful. A psychiatric hospitalization is also stressful and overwhelming. In both instances, your loved one needs professional inpatient care in order to stay alive and get better.

Do not hesitate to take your loved one to get immediate emergency care for a mental health issue if they have increased risk of suicide or increased mental health symptoms.

Seek out professional care. Call 988 for assistance. Go to the nearest emergency room.

You want your loved one to live and stay alive. Get them to the help they need to stay alive and get better when there are increased mental health symptoms. Do not wait.

Being in a behavioral health unit helps keep your loved one alive and away from items they may use to harm themselves.

The purpose is to protect them and help stabilize them with medication to manage their present symptoms, have interaction with the professional care team, and set up their outpatient support for when they are ready for discharge to include: a therapist for psychotherapy, a psychiatrist to oversee their care and medication management, and any additional mental health support needed.

In this section, I don't share every detail about our experiences. The information I do share is to help you be better prepared when you do take your loved one for emergent care due to worsening mental health symptoms and crisis.

If your loved one has increased suicidal risk and is a threat to themselves, taking them to the ER is the typical location to go to. Once at the ER, if your loved one is deemed a risk for suicide or having increased mental health symptoms, there may be additional security in place to watch them. Sometimes, they will be put in a room to be supervised more closely from the nurse's station.

A psychologist or other mental health professional from the behavioral health unit is contacted to come to the emergency department and conduct a psychiatric evaluation. This can take a while with waiting for each step of the process.

If your loved one is deemed to have increased risk for suicide or other mental health conditions requiring hospitalization, finding a psychiatric open bed becomes the next step. They may be admitted to the current hospital or be transferred to a different behavioral health unit at a separate facility.

All your loved one's personal belongings are gathered in a bag and securely stored away from them, to include their cell phone. This is different from your loved one being admitted to a medical unit (where they'd still have access to and be able to contact you with their cell phone).

If you or another support person are not present with your loved one the whole time they are in the ER and up through the time of their admission to the behavioral health unit or their transfer to another facility, you will have no idea where your loved one is sent (and with HIPAA, medical personnel from the ER won't be able to tell you where your loved one is if you call later that day or the next morning). I have experienced this firsthand as the advocating caregiver.

This can be quite upsetting. Your loved one will also not be able to contact you and tell you since they do not have their phone with them and do not have access to making a phone call until they are settled on their behavioral health unit.

Advocate for Your Loved One in the ER

The ER is usually the first step for your loved one getting to where they need to be in a mental health emergency—admitted to the behavioral health unit.

For my husband's first two hospitalizations, I was present with him in the emergency department up until he was taken to the unit he was admitted to. Another time, a close friend of ours was the support person at the ER with him. A fourth time I was not present in the emergency room with him, but he still was admitted to the unit he'd been on before.

The last time, though, I didn't have childcare and so drove him to the ER at the hospital where he'd been admitted into the behavioral health unit in the past. We walked him inside, and he was taken back to be seen. I felt confident, knowing he'd go to the behavioral health unit and receive the care he needed.

This time though the psychiatric beds were full, and he had to be transferred elsewhere. He requested to be transferred to a large psychiatric hospital in the area, but his voice was not listened to as to which hospital he was transferred to. Without a loved one or support person with him to advocate for him, he was sent to whichever psychiatric hospital the medical staff decided to send him.

He didn't have a voice for his own care, presumably because he had presented with suicidal intention. This should not be.

Now, why do I share this story with you?

This experience highlights the difficult topic of mental health self-advocacy in an emergency. Keeping the person alive and safe are primary goals in a psychiatric emergency.

That said, I believe collaborative decision making is still possible in mental crisis, even if the only input a patient has is what facility to be transferred to when a psychiatric bed isn't available at the current hospital. A person being able to exercise a small amount of agency and choice in the middle of a personal crisis can help their sense of overall wellbeing during an overwhelming situation.

There are also additional reasons why you or a trusted support person being with your loved one in the emergency department can be very important. It is not only to advocate for their care.

Being present with your loved one is a way to mentally and emotionally support them during a very difficult time. It's possible they may be too emotionally distraught to communicate their medical or psychiatric history well to the staff. They may forget to communicate daily medications they are on. You can help communicate their needs. Advocating can be as simple as asking for water if they need water while waiting in the ER.

You can be their voice and advocate—to communicate their history with staff, any request or question they have, and to know where they will be transferred or admitted to and how to contact the unit. **I encourage you to plan to be with your loved one or have a support person with them in the emergency department** *if at all possible.*

Leaving the ER with the behavioral health unit's contact information is also important. Every time I took my husband to the ER, I checked and double-checked with the staff for the correct phone numbers of the unit he'd be on and additional information, such as visiting hours, calling hours, etc. One hospitalization, I found that some of the information I received from a staff member was old information about the unit's phone number and visitation hours. Thankfully, I double-checked and received the right information before leaving the emergency department.

Don't leave your loved one or the ER without the name of the unit or facility they will be on and the phone numbers to contact the unit or facility as well. Verifying the specific unit they are admitted to is important.

Hospitalization—The Behavioral Health Unit/ Psychiatric Ward

During your loved one's hospitalization, ask questions of the social worker, medical assistant, or other staff for how the facility is organized schedule-wise and program-wise so you are knowledgeable of their schedule and rules in order to support your loved one from the outside and come alongside them during their hospital stay.

Knowing visitation hours and visiting your loved one is incredibly important also. There are specific schedules and times for activities during the day.

The length of stay on a behavioral health unit depends on the severity of symptoms, how the patient is doing while on the unit, their response to medication, and whether their symptoms improve, worsen, or stay the same. The psychiatrist or behavioral health NP or PA will make treatment decisions, including determining when the patient is able to be discharged.

Your loved one would be on the psychiatric unit in order to have a psychiatrist start them on medication for the different symptoms they have, titrate different medications up to a therapeutic dose, and help your loved one detox from alcohol or another substance, while watching for adverse effects such as seizures. Your loved one's medications may not be appropriately managing their symptoms, and therefore being in the behavioral health unit will allow changes and modifications to their medications. Many people in a behavioral health unit are on multiple psychotropic medications.

After your loved one is released and discharged from the hospital, they would follow-up with a psychiatrist for monitoring symptoms and managing the psychotropic (behavioral health) medications. The doses may be titrated up or down or a medication may be changed to another medication depending on your loved one's symptoms and the psychiatrist's management of their condition(s).

Social workers, mental health therapists, psychologists, behavioral health nurses, Psychiatrists, and Nurse Practitioners (NPs) and Physician Assistants (PAs) are all medical professionals who may work on these units.

Often social workers or therapists will conduct group meetings on different days of the week as well as manage discussions with family members for the patient's outpatient care once they are discharged. A nurse may also be a part of these discussions. A psychologist may see a patient one time or more than one time in a stay. The Psychiatrist, NP, or PA will round each day and make decisions on patient care, to include medications, management of symptoms, and determine when a patient may be able to be discharged. The psychiatrist will usually talk to the loved one or family member of the patient concerning their condition prior to discharge. This is obviously with permission from the patient.

Once Your Loved One is Hospitalized

Once your loved one is admitted to a behavioral health unit, they are not able to leave the unit because it is a locked unit. They do not have their personal belongings with them when admitted and don't have access to their own phone or a room phone in their hospital room. There will usually be one or two central phones in a main area for all patients to use during specific phone hours. They will wait in line before they can call you. If you know the phone hours, I recommend calling right when that time begins and asking for your loved one by name. When they are admitted, you may be given a special code or number to say when you call to indicate you are a person your loved one is okay talking to. This is for the privacy of your loved one. Without the special code, the staff will not confirm whether a person is a patient at their facility or unit, for confidential and HIPAA reasons, in order to protect the privacy of the patients. Be aware of this and be patient and gracious to the staff person on the other end of the phone, though I know you are worried about your loved one.

Finding out the unit's specific rules on personal belongings allowed for your loved one and items they may desire (such as a Bible or paperback book to read, slip-on shower shoes, and new underwear or socks) can assist your loved one's transition to the unit and make their stay more comfortable for them. The staff will check any belongings coming onto the unit for safety before passing them onto your loved one.

In my experience, no shoelaces, drawstring clothing items, or belts were allowed, nor were pens or pencils allowed, due to safety risks. Only crayons were used for writing. I brought him socks, underwear, t-shirts, and pants without drawstrings. I also brought him paperback books and his Bible to read.

Ensuring the safety of all patients is important. Different facilities may have different rules.

Visiting Hours

While not everything is the same from one behavioral health unit (psychiatric ward) to another, it is helpful to have some understanding of what visitation hours may look like. Each facility conducts visitation a little differently.

I have been buzzed into a room with lockers where I placed my purse and personal belongings, to include my cell phone, in a locker, and then after that, I was buzzed onto the unit. In the unit, I would meet with my husband and visit for the time allowed.

Visitation hours vary but may be 2-3 hours in length at the same time each day. Some facilities don't have visitation hours on the weekend or may only have one weekend day offering visitation hours (due to the social workers not working on the weekend days).

There are a limited number of visitors allowed per patient at a time. One unit only allowed two visitors for a patient at the same time. Visitors had to be age 18 or older. We would visit in the main area and have conversation just the two of us or might have disruptions from other patients and be distracted by interactions going on in the main space with many people present in it. Sometimes we had time in a visitation room where we were able to talk, without disruptions.

Patient Organization on Unit

Facilities are organized differently. Some facilities have all the different behavioral health conditions on the same unit. This can be troubling as a unit can become loud and noisy depending on patient outbursts or strong negative behavioral symptoms (yelling, throwing of items, etc. by a patient). Negative behavioral symptoms of one patient can be agitating or upsetting to other patients. Witnessing other patients' outbursts or negative behavioral symptoms can be stressful for your loved one.

Being aware of this potential for your loved one can help you as you talk with them while they are inpatient, ask them how they are doing, and support them in such a new and very different environment.

Some facilities have dementia patients separated unit-wise from other mental health conditions. While I am only discussing adult hospitalizations in this chapter, for patients under 18 needing psychiatric hospitalizations, different hospital systems implement different age cut-offs for a pediatric patient being on an adult unit versus a pediatric unit. It is not always the age of 18 for separation; sometimes it is much younger. If your loved one is under 18, find out the cutoff age for adult units versus pediatric units to help guide your advocacy and decision-making for the psychiatric unit or facility your pediatric loved one will be admitted to. There may not be choice sometimes due to bed availability or the number of psychiatric units available in your area.

Do Not Wait in an Emergency—Seek out Care

After all that I just shared, I must stress to you this important point—

Do not wait to get your loved one to emergency care if they are having increased mental health symptoms, including increased suicidal risk.

In a mental health emergency or if you aren't sure, it is always best to seek out professional medical care.

Your focus is to keep your loved one alive and for them to have the chance to get better.

Call 988 for help (the Suicide and Crisis Lifeline). Go to the nearest emergency room.

- **Be prepared**—Know the warning signs of increased risk of suicide and 988.
- **Take action**—Keep your loved one alive. Be pro-active and supportive.
- **Be brave**—Get the help needed for your loved one. Take them to the emergency room.

A psychiatric hospitalization is stressful and overwhelming.

If your loved one needed to be in the ICU for a life-threatening physical condition, it would be stressful and overwhelming also. Realize this as you consider your loved one's psychiatric (behavioral health) hospitalization.

Remember, the purpose of a psychiatric hospitalization is to keep your loved one safe and alive while managing their mental health symptoms with medication and connecting them to outpatient support so they can move toward discharge and being cared for in an outpatient setting.

Hopefully, what I shared dispelled some of the mystery surrounding a psychiatric hospitalization and some of what may occur if your loved one is admitted. This is not an exhaustive discussion on hospitalizations but will better prepare you.

Remember—My purpose in sharing with you is to better prepare you in supporting your loved one through a hospitalization. Do not use what I shared for choosing whether your loved one will or will not go to a psychiatric ward (behavioral health unit) or seek medical care for worsening mental health symptoms or mental crisis.

You want your loved one to live and stay alive. Get them to the help they need to stay alive and get better when there are increased mental health symptoms. Do not wait.

Get your loved one to emergency care and keep your loved one alive.

And now, we will shift focus to you, the caregiver.

The next 4 chapters of this book are on caring for yourself, the caregiver. Make sure to reference Chapter 3: Caregiver Burden and Protecting Against Burnout as well, as it lays the groundwork in caring for yourself. We'll begin by talking about faith in Chapter 13.

I pray you are blessed, strengthened, and empowered in your caregiving journey, my friend.

REFERENCES

1 van der Kolk, B. A. (2014). *The Body Keeps the Score: Brain, Mind, and Body In the Healing of Trauma.* Penguin Books, 220-222.

PART 3: CARING FOR YOURSELF, THE CAREGIVER

Ch. 13—16

Refer to Ch. 3 also

Chapter 13

MY FAITH, SPIRITUAL BATTLES, & PRAYER

Song: "Take It All Back" by: Tauren Wells, We The Kingdom, Davies

I didn't start my faith journey and relationship with God during my husband's mental health battle. I'd been walking with God for a long time before.

God had been with me through significant battles already that built my emotional, spiritual, and mental resilience and my faith and trust in God.

Let me share a bit of my faith background with you.

I was born into a Christian family, and my parents valued their Christian faith and valued raising and guiding us by Biblical truth. They sacrificed financially to put me and my siblings through a Christian education.

I accepted Jesus into my heart at age 4 in kid's church service. It was real.

I wanted to follow God. I know the blessing my parents gave me and my siblings laid the groundwork for my continued pursuit of God.

I remember in high school praying earnestly with another friend over a mutual friend for the Lord to work in their life.

Being at a private Christian school meant I memorized Bible verses and talked about the Bible at school. I went to a Christian university also and received a Bible minor in addition to my Biology and Chemistry degrees and Psychology minor.

After college, I remember the Lord showing Himself faithful when I didn't have the money for an Anatomy graduate program, and I told the Lord if He was leading me in it, He would have to confirm that decision by providing a scholarship. I cried tears of disbelief, amazement, and thanksgiving when in opening the envelope, I found a full scholarship for the program. The Lord confirmed above and beyond my prayer request.

God showed Himself sovereign in leading the way and providing for me. I walked through a long-distance relationship with Josh, and then a 6-month deployment while I was in my Physician Assistant Master's Program and planning my wedding, not knowing if my to-be husband would make it home alive. He was in harm's way.

A time supposed to be full of joy and connection was filled with hardship, stress, and a deep dependence on God for me. We married and then moved a lot with the military after I graduated from PA school. We started over every 6 months to a year in a new place, me trying to find yet another PA job in the beginning of my career, not to mention state licensure changes with each move.

I faced two more deployments for him, one with children. I prayed prayers of protection over him as he'd scramble due to a call on deployment real-time.

None of these seasons were easy.

Why do I share this with you?

I share because of the idea of:

Resilience. *Rising to challenges. Facing struggles.*

How we respond to the challenges we face determines our growth.

I had the example of how my mom and dad rose to their challenges, medical and otherwise. They adapted to the new challenges. They prayed. They sacrificed. They leaned in and caregave and advocated and stood in the gap and prayed through their own battles. They were committed to their faith and their God. They shifted with change and were resilient.

Having examples in our life of others who have been resilient in the face of challenges in their own life and seeing how they have held onto their faith is incredibly important as we walk through our own battles.

I just shared a few of my hardships and trust in God stories from my life with you for you to see a window into my faith background and what came before this battle against suicidality. There were many other answers to prayer and God stories.

The Lord was apparently already growing my faith and resilience through previous battles I thought were the hardest (the first deployment while in PA school and preparing for a wedding) until this one came and became one of the most challenging and personally depleting battles I have ever faced.

How we approach the struggles in our life matters.

How we approach our struggles and choose to interact will have significant influence on whether we grow as a person through them or stagnate and stalemate.

I Am Human

I dealt with fear, uncertainty, struggle, emotional pain, overwhelm, and many other emotions through the different battles I'd already faced in my life. Every battle and struggle I'd already faced mattered. How I chose to respond to and approach them mattered.

I chose to lean into God for strength. I chose to trust Him, to pray and ask big things of Him—to cry out to Him and find community and solace in the Psalms in the Bible. It was a choice.

I knew the outcome might not be what I prayed for, but that didn't mean God wasn't still faithful or that He didn't care about me.

God was for me. God was with me as He always had been before.

This new battle seemed insurmountable, overwhelming. But God was in it with me too.

Relying On God

God is in your battle with you too, friend. If you haven't been relying on Him in past struggles for help or strength, it's not too late to pivot and choose to talk to Him and tell Him about your struggles.

He is there and desires to come alongside you, no matter your past or how many times you've rejected or ignored Him before. He will hear you, and He cares deeply about everything you are walking through.

He cares about your loved one who is struggling with suicidality as well.

What Does a Faith Journey Look Like

The first step in a faith journey with Jesus is having a personal relationship with Jesus.

We are all sinners, meaning we make decisions that dishonor and go against God. Sin requires a consequence, death. The consequence has to be paid. It can't be ignored. Jesus is fully God and fully man, and He died on a cross for the penalty for our sin. He was without sin but paid the consequence, death, for the sins we had committed. He rose again on the 3rd day conquering sin and death and making a way for us to have eternal life and a right relationship with God again. When we accept Jesus' free gift of salvation, when we submit our own will for His, believing in Him, we can have relationship with Him.

> *"If you declare with your mouth, "Jesus is Lord," and believe in your heart that God raised Him from the dead, you will be saved. For it is with your heart that you believe and are justified, and it is with your mouth that you profess your faith and are saved"* (Romans 10:9-10).

Asking Jesus into your heart is the way it's talked about with children, and that idea and principle is still valid no matter your age.

You can pray: "God, I need you. I'm sorry for living life without you. Forgive me of my sins. I believe you died for my sins and rose again from death to save me. Come into my heart and change me, Lord. I want to live for you now. I submit my will to yours."

If you are saved, you now have the Holy Spirit's power within you to help you and guide you. When a person becomes saved and has a relationship with Jesus now, the Holy Spirit is who dwells inside of them. The Holy Spirit is the comforter, the One who guides, the One who quietly speaks to us to follow in obedience to His voice. Those who don't know God relationally can't understand it because it is spiritually understood.

Being saved gives you access to the same power that raised Jesus from the dead. You have access to that same power because you have the Holy Spirit within you.

The Holy Spirit's power within me has been my ultimate source of strength through every significantly overwhelming moment. He has renewed my strength, friends.

I wouldn't have made it through without my faith in God and His strength and presence.

I want that for you too. You need strength beyond yourself, a faith to hold you strong.

After starting a relationship with Jesus and having the Holy Spirit within you, a faith journey encompasses continuing to grow in knowing Jesus and finding others who also know Jesus to interact with and grow in relationship with Him together (fellowship with other believers).

A faith journey means not trying to figure out the answer to your issues by yourself but choosing to ask God for guidance. It means spending time with God and reading the Bible to hear directly from Him in His word since the Bible is God's inspired words to us. The Bible is active and powerful today.

A faith journey means talking to God about your life through prayer and daily choosing to place your trust in the One who is faithful and will never leave you, the One who comes alongside you and fights your battles for you.

Spiritual Battles

When I originally found out about Josh's PTSD, self-medicating, depression, and later suicidal ideation, I wanted to call out the cavalry, spiritually speaking.

I knew what we were fighting against was bigger than he or I could handle on our own, physically or spiritually.

I knew we had to fight this battle in the spiritual realm as well as the physical, and I also knew our adversary, the devil, was stronger than we were.

The devil wasn't, however, stronger than my God.

> *"Finally, be strong in the Lord and in His mighty power. Put on the full armor of God, so that you can take your stand against the devil's schemes. For our struggle is not against flesh and blood, but against the rulers, against the authorities, against the powers of this dark world and against the spiritual forces of evil in the heavenly realms. Therefore, put on the full armor of God, so that when the day of evil comes, you may be able to stand your ground, and after you have done everything, to stand"* (Ephesians 6:10-13).

It is clear to me that one of the devil's schemes against any of us is suicide. To tempt and coax someone into death.

Another passage says:

"The thief comes only to steal and kill and destroy. I came that they may have life and have it abundantly" (John 10:10, ESV). This passage is Jesus speaking and the thief referred to is the same adversary as above, the devil.

We need the full armor of God to be able to stand against the devil's schemes and plans.

We can't fight against the leviathan of suicidality on our own and in our own power, or even just in the physical realm of medical and therapeutic interventions.

I strongly believe that fighting against this battle simultaneously using the power of God and the amazing therapeutic interventions available today, that we can make a difference in people's lives being ravaged by trauma responses, PTSD, and suicidal thoughts, intention, plans, and attempts.

Faith plus therapy.

We won't be facing it alone in our own power, anymore.

The Devil's Goal

There is a spiritual battle going on for your soul and for your very life. The devil's goal is to steal, kill, and destroy your life in every possible way.

I have seen his many attacks and attempts to do just that to my family, to my husband. When our eyes are opened to life not just being about what we see and touch (the physical realm), we begin to have spiritually minded 'eyes'. We begin to realize a battle is waging against us and our families which is bigger than us.

God is stronger than the adversary, though. We must, as the Ephesians passage says, be strong in the Lord's power. We can tap into God's power to fight against the devil's schemes against us, including fighting back against suicidality, in any way we can.

If that doesn't convince you of the enemy's goal (death and destruction) and of the need to fight on all fronts and from a spiritual stance, as well as from a medical and psychotherapy stance, read this:

> *"Be self-controlled and alert. Your enemy the devil prowls around like a roaring lion looking for someone to devour. Resist him, standing firm in the faith, because you know that your brothers*

throughout the world are undergoing the same kind of sufferings" (1 Peter 5:8-9).

The devil, who is the enemy, is seeking someone to take down. He is on the hunt, as it were. When we acknowledge that reality, we can choose to combat it by tapping into the One who is all powerful—God.

We don't have to be fearful of that knowledge, but aware. This scripture passage says to be alert. To be focused. To be on the lookout for attack.

It is wise to anticipate an attack in some way from the enemy, the devil, so that you can be ready to fight against it when it comes, not in your own strength and knowledge, but in God's.

If the devil can't take your life or the life of your loved one, then he's going to try to steal or destroy something else in your life. He may try to destroy your health, steal your joy, throw attacks of anxiety or depression at you, break down your closest relationships, steal your financial security, job security, relational security, or maybe even your spiritual security.

Maybe the enemy can shake or destroy your belief and reliance on God because the circumstances in your current reality look bad.

Let's take a look at the armor of God which helps us stand in the day of evil and stand against the attacks of the devil against us. The passage describes the armor as the armor a Roman soldier of the time would have worn and adds faith elements to each piece of armor.

A belt of truth, breastplate of righteousness, feet ready to take the gospel of peace, shield of faith, helmet of salvation, and sword of the Spirit, along with prayer (from Ephesians 6:14-18). The end of this passage mentions *flaming arrows of the evil one,* indicating attacks should be expected and will come. The sword of the Spirit is the word of God, the Bible.

"And pray in the Spirit on all occasions with all kinds of prayers and requests...be alert and always keep on praying for all the saints" (Ephesians 6:18).

While I would love to go deeper into discussion on the different types of armor shared here, I will instead encourage you to study it more fully on your own. You can read a commentary which will help explain more fully what the passage means looking at the original language of the passage and historical information of the time also.

The point I want for us to take away from this section is there is a spiritual battle occurring for every human being on earth. The spiritual battle is not one we can see. The devil wants to take you down in any way he can. God is the One who has power to overcome the evil one, and we can fight in God's strength and in His power.

We are not promised what the future holds or the hardships or battles we will face on earth. We will face trouble in this world, but *we can take heart and comfort in the knowledge that Jesus has overcome the world* (adapted from John 16:33).

If you are a believer in Jesus and have accepted His gift of eternal life, you can tap into *the same power that raised Jesus from the dead* because it's the same power in the believer (from Ephesians 1:19-20). We fight in God's power.

I, for one, am glad I am not fighting my battles in my own strength, with my own knowledge, or by myself. I am so grateful to lean into God's power because my own power and strength dries up pretty quickly alone.

Growing In Prayer

I want to focus more fully on prayer and how prayer allows us to tap into God's power in our battle and crisis.

The Bible passage from the last section ended with:

> *"And pray in the Spirit on all occasions with all kinds of prayers and requests…be alert and always keep on praying for all the saints"* (Ephesians 6:18).

As mental crisis continued and suicide threatened my husband's life with ideation and worsening mental health, prayer became a constant companion for me. I had prayed before constantly through a deployment over my husband's life, and God heard those prayers of protection.

In this new and different battle, I grew in my prayer abilities in major ways over the almost two years of ongoing mental crisis caregiving.

As time continued with suicidal ideation and then plan and attempt and continued ideation, Satan would bring new ideas to my husband in the night for ways to end his life. Spiritual warfare prayers were necessary. Every night, before we would go to sleep, I would pray over my husband. I prayed protection over our home and over each of our children. I prayed against any attack of the evil one. I prayed scripture, God's very own words. I prayed over my husband's life. I prayed over his mind and for the Lord to protect his mind as he slept, for no nightmares to come in the night. I prayed against any scheme of the devil against his life.

I knew the battle was bigger than us though, and I needed other prayer warriors to come alongside us in battle over the night. Every night for quite a while when that battle was intense, I texted a few specific prayer warriors to also pray over him every single one of those nights. Their prayers alongside my prayers surrounded my husband, surrounded our family, and lifted our arms up.

In the mornings, I would check in with my husband and ask about the night, nervous, hoping there hadn't been any attacks or new ideas thrown his way. I was always amazed and so grateful when my husband would share many mornings that he had no nightmares. I knew it was the Lord who had answered our prayers and brought miracle after miracle of him not being plagued in the night.

There were also nights where his report would be a discouraging report, and he would share he had nightmares about death and new ways to end his life. Those were moments of discouragement and coming alongside him in support and leaning even more heavily into listening to praise music and praying over him. God was still faithful and was still at work. I continued to trust Him.

I sought the only One who could turn the tide against what the enemy's plans (death) were for my husband.

I knew God was sovereign and in control and therefore, leaned into His power, trusting Him with the battle we faced. As I said before, we also pursued medicine and psychotherapy at the same time—all three were very needed.

Fighting from all fronts is incredibly important in facing the battle against suicide.

We were fighting for life and for healing.

"Do not be anxious about anything, but in everything, by prayer and petition, with thanksgiving, present your requests to God. And the peace of God, which transcends all understanding, will guard your hearts and your minds in Christ Jesus" (Philippians 4:6-7).

There is this phenomenon in prayer and true reliance on God, in the walking with God through the deep valleys and darkness of our life, that His peace can come over us and comfort us in situations and moments where there is no peace present, physically speaking.

God can protect us, our heart and mind, and help us in the midst of the uncertainty and struggle we face.

Yes, even in the midst of our loved one fighting against suicide.

Chapter 14

SAFE, TRUSTED, AUTHENTIC COMMUNITY

Song: "For My Good" by: Maverick City Music,
Naomi Raine, & Chandler Moore
(feat. Todd Galberth)

As humans, we are built for community and to offer support and receive it from others. Throughout my husband's mental crisis battle, I had a small, trusted support system. I had a few specific trusted people in my life, ones I knew I could trust implicitly.

My parents supported us countless times. My dad and a few key friends came to our aid in desperate moments. Other family members and close friends also supported in tangible ways and through prayer support which was desperately needed also.

Those who knew the mental health battle we were walking through at the time were not many, and it couldn't be many in order to keep Josh feeling emotionally safe, physically alive, and continuing toward healing—the goals at hand.

Community Is Not Just For Times Of Crisis

I was already in community and in a trusted faith-based group before crisis hit. I also had to build community in the midst of our crisis period after a move to a new place.

We are not meant to do life in isolation. When calamity hits, we need to have close people to turn to for help and vice versa. The antiquated and prideful view that "I can't ask for help" is wrong. It's a lie from the enemy, designed to keep you trapped and isolated, so he can do more damage in your heart and life.

We need community in crisis. Some community is slowly built up over time; other community is built in the midst of crisis.

True community is predicated upon the tenants of being safe, trustworthy, and authentic.

If we don't have it presently, we have to begin to look for the types of people who will offer this type of community.

As we open up authentically, we will find the other people reciprocating with their own life and story. In so doing, connection and true support is found.

In my story, I had a few safe, trusted people in my life, and yet, I still needed more support, emotionally and tangibly. I still felt incredibly alone and was alone caregiving for my loved one and caring for my family most of the time. It was overwhelming and exhausting and didn't let up.

Counteracting Isolation

Isolation is the enemy of peace.

The days and weeks I was more isolated from other people, Satan could infiltrate my thoughts more easily and drift me off course.

When I was plugged into community with strong believers in God, it bolstered my faith and increased my strength. I was grateful for the strength-infusing and weary-lifting aspect of true community. It was wonderful and an honor to share in praying for each other's struggles and battles. We would bear each other's burdens (from Galatians 6:2) and pray on each other's behalf.

Society says to do it alone and show you are strong; however, *we are not called to carry our own struggles alone.*

God is, in fact, a relational God. God has built community into the construct of a faith community and into the societal construct at large because God made us for connection and community. We have to choose to enter into community. It takes action on our part.

When it isn't possible to spend quality time with trusted people, stepping out of isolation and into society is still helpful. Going to the grocery store, another store, the library, or another public space and having small interactions with other people can be helpful and uplifting. A kind interaction with the clerk or fast-food person can be the small encouragement needed to know you are not alone.

Don't disqualify small interactions or being in proximity with others.

Small interactions can have big impact against isolation's negative power in our lives. You need connection and to be in community.

Don't give into the temptation to pull back from others… I would recognize myself pulling back from others to conserve my energy, recharge, or because I was exhausted. It was important for me to recognize my pulling back stance and actively force myself at times to text a person back or reach out to someone else to connect.

There were times to focus on and create rest for myself, but *I had to proactively identify when exhaustion caused me to retreat and isolate from others.* This was not always healthy, and I had to fight against that tendency and fight towards connection. It had to be a balance.

What Does Authentic, Trusted, Safe Community Look Like?

Finding supportive community can be difficult. It takes time to find a group that is authentic, trustworthy, and emotionally safe to share thoughts, feelings, and emotions in.

It takes time for trust to develop and for others to prove their trustworthiness and vice versa.

Don't rush into friendships and relationships sharing and opening up all of your fears and secrets. You will likely get *emotionally "burned"* or be betrayed, gossiped about, or judged unfairly if you enter relationships and friendships without taking time to discern trustworthiness before opening up.

Trust takes time to build and needs a proven track record of consistent decisions and actions to stand on.

Take time to open up. Be discerning. Be wise about who you share your painful burdens and wounds with to not be wounded even further.

It takes time for trust to develop and for trustworthiness and confidentiality to be proven in a relationship.

It is a reciprocal commitment of each person entering into that commitment to hold what others share in that space as sacred and honored information. The information shared is to be held close, protected, and those having been trusted with the knowledge will help support and care for the story they've been entrusted with.

Confidentiality and Information Shared Is Not Yours to Share Elsewhere

What is shared in a trusted, safe community is not to be shared outside the group except in very specific crisis circumstances such as immediate need for action to be taken with an abusive situation or if child abuse is occurring or an immediate threat of harm to another person or the person themselves (increased suicidal risk or warning signs of suicide or homicide). Those types of scenarios would be wise to discuss as a group when forming the group and how those types of situations may be handled (bringing it up openly, coming alongside in support of the person who shared about it, offering assistance, determining an appropriate way forward for assistance and professional help of the specific issue, and being accountable to each other).

By and large though, crisis moments will hopefully be a rarity but still important to plan for and discuss.

Entering into a trustworthy, safe community is focused on reciprocal sharing and supporting of each other's real-life struggles and circumstances and trusting others to protect that information shared and hold it in strict confidence. The information shared with you is not your own to share with other people outside that group, and the same goes for the information you share in this type of group. It is supported, cared about, and valued.

May you find this type of group even if it's only one or two other people. It doesn't need to have many people in it. Four to seven people is a good number for this type of group—big enough for a community feel, but not so big that it is difficult to know what is actually going on in each other's lives.

A group or other relationship can disintegrate quickly after years of careful building up if issues are not addressed as they occur.

If ruptures are not repaired and cared for, they can be additive in nature and the disintegration of the connection can occur quickly.

True humility, gentleness in tone, and mutual respect with truth are necessary elements for repair after rupture. Sincere apologies and forgiveness are also necessary for repair.

Every relationship or group of friends will traverse some aspect of disagreement, offense, or issue (even Paul and Barnabas did in the Bible), but we must learn how to navigate them with humility, gentleness, respect, and truth.

Trustworthy Friendships

I would love it if we had easy ways to verify another person wouldn't betray our trust or share our secret shared confidentially… with a mutual friend or possibly as a prayer request with other people in the group or a different group without permission.

These situations do happen and cause breakdown of trust and openness in friendships and relationships. We should never need to fear that the private details of our life shared in confidence and in trusted friendships would be slipped or openly conveyed to others in accidental gossip, "just so's you know", "you may want to talk to so-and-so as they are going through something similar", as prayer requests with unconnected people or mutual friends, or any other version of not confidently protecting the privacy of a dear friend, confidante, prayer group person, family member, or other individual in our life we have opened our hearts and pain up to. This can apply to and occur in extended family units also.

Not everything is everyone's business.

Being aware of the issue of sharing confidential information without consent *is important in order to limit our own personal culpability and decrease the likelihood that we would do it ourselves.* May we be trustworthy friends and prayer warriors in other people's lives.

A verse in the New Testament says, *"Carry each other's burdens, and in this way you will fulfill the law of Christ"* (Galatians 6:2).

Authentic Community

To be authentic is to show up vulnerable and honest, without a filter or curated carefully selected presentation of self.

We come together as we are. We don't put on a "face" or a "mask" to put up artificial protected walls around us or in front of us.

No. We choose to say 'This is me' and face the risk of being rejected, judged, criticized, or deemed too much or not enough.

There is risk in being authentic and vulnerable.

There is also great reward. The flip side is when we open up, truly, about our real self, fears, wounds, pain, and past, and choose to be real and another person also chooses to do the same, we then have the beautiful privilege of being seen. Being really seen by another. Not pretending anymore, not being alone, not being an island, but being known, fully known.

To be seen, truly seen, and known by another person is incredibly scary and also *delightful, rewarding, and uplifting all at once.*

When the other person fully enters into the same with warts, scars, and wounding not fully healed yet either, in realness, rawness, and speaking truth

- 254 -

into each other's hearts, without judgment, condemnation, or rejection... **We receive the gift of acceptance**. Of true love.

This brings to mind the widely known William Shakespeare's quote from Sonnet 116 on love:

"Love is not love which alters when it alteration finds."[1]

Yes, this is true love. Authentic, vulnerable community which gives full acceptance and does not turn away from blemish or wart, which speaks life into each other, willing one another towards more. Towards growth. Towards truth. Towards wellbeing.

It is a gift not to be tossed away, but to be regarded, held close, and accepted.

It is not easily found, in truth. And yet, because of its rarity, it is most treasured when actually found.

It may be for a season, rather than a lifetime, to be a part of a group like this.

Curt Thompson, who I've mentioned before, leads 'confessional communities' which are fully authentic and real groups with powerful life-changing impact. It sounds amazing when you have experienced this type of safe, authentic, trusted group without judgment, condemnation, or rejection.

I have experienced this type of group in my own life, and it has been life-altering in the best way and life-giving.

What This Looks Like In Christian Circles

In Christian circles, this type of community requires an honest sharing and connecting on sins in our life, strongholds, addictions, struggles, habits, worries, fears, and any temptation we continually fight against. Spiritual warfare can be alive and well, but when we surround ourselves with like-minded believers who are fighting for God's kingdom and His will in their life and others, we can find strength and sustainment in our battles.

If you only ever brush over prayer requests lightly and do not enter into true vulnerability and openness about your real life and real struggles with each other, then there is no way to have the rich friendship and fellowship I am describing. It takes humility and self-awareness for us to see ourselves, the good and the bad, at the same time and be fully honest about our real lives and the challenges we face. And choose to reciprocally see others in the same way.

I'm sure I've given some of you a lot to consider as you thought you were just reading about finding community so you could have support during mental crisis.

It is far beyond that.

We need deep, authentic community support in every aspect of our lives—in our thoughts, emotions, attitudes, moods, spiritual practices, and in our healing from wounds and pain.

When we gather in this type of authentic, connected, fully known and seen community—*God meets with us.*

Shame disappears because there aren't hidden things in the shadows someone is afraid of having uncovered or someone finding out about.

Condemnation disappears because we can seek God's forgiveness and have other believers speak truth to us and over us about how God interacts with whatever we have done in the past that we have sought forgiveness for. We can begin to see ourselves and others through God's lens and perspective.

Secrets disappear because, well, there are none.

We also receive the gift of accepting ourselves in this environment also.

Others are able to speak truth into our circumstances from their own experiences and faith journeys with God but also speak truth into our life and heart from scripture. God can speak through other believers to encourage, exhort, and keep us accountable and point out any areas we may be struggling in, gently and lovingly. We can do the same for them. We lift each other up. We pray for the areas we each are falling short in and give each other equal time to share. We do not show favoritism in lifting one's struggle, situation, or life as more important or prioritized or in always giving one person more time to share than the rest. When there is a crisis, we surround that person with love, care, and tangible love. We weep with those who weep and rejoice with those who rejoice.

This type of group and connection takes time to cultivate. You can start out with sharing a little bit and supporting and praying with others and then as time continues and trust develops and confidentiality continues, opening up more. It is okay to go slow as you grow a trusted, safe, authentic community.

Safe Community

A safe community stands on trustworthiness, confidentiality, and being able to share without being judged, condemned, rejected, or diminished.

You should feel emotionally safe to share, and others should also feel emotionally safe to share with you. It is a two-way commitment. In a safe friendship, relationship of any kind, or group, you will know what you share doesn't go beyond that person or group of people. It is a protected, safe space to be open and vulnerable with one another. This creates a sense of security and safety which is important for continued relational growth.

A Community For a Season Or Seasons—Only God Knows

This community with a certain group of people may not continue long-term. It may be needed only for a specific season of your and their life.

Don't try to keep grabbing ahold of a group that was life-giving if it begins to naturally disband. It doesn't always disband for negative reasons. Sometimes, God is trying to lead each of you toward what He has next for you.

During one particular season, I found I kept trying to bring a group back together after it disbanded because it had been so rich, but life had moved on. Continuing together was not what God had planned. What I couldn't see was God was trying to lead me to the next group I needed for a specific season that was incredibly difficult in my life. If I had begun to look for a new group earlier than I did, I would have likely found the new group more quickly and would have saved myself some extremely lonely and isolating months for myself.

God knew what He was doing.

I was looking backward, but God was trying to lead me forward because He knew what was coming up ahead *that I didn't know anything about yet.* God was preparing the way before me.

I learned a lesson through that time. Keep looking for where the Lord is leading and don't settle for the good He already brought you to as it may only be meant for a season for you and the ones you are with. That isn't bad. It often can be how God grows us.

We like to get comfortable and stick to what is familiar. God doesn't call us to the familiar, though.

Our faith and trust can grow exponentially in the unfamiliar and uncomfortable places, if we choose to be open to what God is doing in our life.

God is transforming and growing us to be more like Him as He leads us.

He wants to use us to further His kingdom, not for us to get comfortable in groups that are comfy and familiar. If those groups keep sharpening us and pushing us forth into where God is calling us to, then, yes, those groups may be ones for multiple seasons and years.

We don't have the ability to predict what God will use or how long He will call us to one spot. As we sharpen and grow, God may be calling us to different people in order to use us in their life in a way that couldn't have happened if we'd stayed put where we were.

Let us trust that God has good plans for our life, above and beyond what we can see presently before us.

Let us get comfortable with being ready for the next direction, being willing to be called and to go, as Abraham was called by God in the Bible. At the time, he was called Abram, and he was a man who

God called to go to a place He would show Abram. Abram didn't know where he was going, but he trusted the One who had called him. Abram's faith was counted to him for righteousness. What a beautiful picture and testimony of God's faithfulness.

I guess, friend, what I am urging you to do right now is to not be complacent. To not stay in a group or a spot because you like it and it was or is familiar.

Be open to where the Lord leads for you to be challenged in your faith, be able to see your weaknesses and strengths, and be in authentic, safe, trusted community of faith-building people like you.

We only get this one life. *Let us not squander it.*

- Let us allow the Lord to lead us how He will.
- Let us choose to seek out others for community and support.
- Let us choose to be authentic and share more openly as we discern the trustworthiness of the other person or people and vice versa.
- Let us create a space where true connection, trust, and support flourish.

REFERENCES

[1] Shakespeare, W. "Sonnet 116." The Sonnets, 1609.

Chapter 15

NAVIGATING SUPPORT AND BOUNDARIES IN CRISIS

Song: "Fear Is Not My Future" by: Maverick City Music, Kirk Franklin, Chandler Moore (feat. Brandon Lake)

How do we implement community? How do we step out of isolation and protective modes in crisis and begin to let people in, truly? It can be easy to say safe, authentic, and trustworthy community is something to aspire to or 'good for you for having it'.

The stepping out and risking rejection, judgment, condescension, advice-laden, minimizing, or overbearing responses from others can cause even the most desperate of us to pause, before reaching out—to stop, recoil, and continue trying to eke it out on our own.

We can't control others' responses, and in that, there is risk in reaching out. But—there is also the potential of great reward too.

I encourage you to try it, small at first, the reaching out for support. Even better, try accepting help from others (gasp), especially if you have been conditioned to only ever be the one "helping" others but never wanting to bother anyone else with your own struggles or needs. You will be amazed by the difference letting others into your struggle makes.

Reaching Out When In Need

I am personally grateful for others' help and support in the midst of crisis. If you tend to "go it alone", I encourage you to shift your mindset away from the idea of how can I get through this without "burdening" another person.

Instead, choose to reach out to a trusted person and share your need—whether a prayer need, physical or logistical need, or emotional need. It is a healthy and good practice. If they are able to come alongside and help you or know how to meet a specific physical or logistical need you have, they will. You don't have to be alone in determining a solution for a problem or need.

A trusted friend can share the emotional weight of a burden, even if they aren't able to support tangibly.

They will be blessed by coming alongside another's need, as I am blessed when I come alongside and help someone also.

There are many times in my small group Bible study, where prayer requests and life burdens are shared with each other for prayer support and emotional support. It makes a difference to not feel alone in struggles.

When close, trusted friends offered assistance to me in our crisis, I accepted their help if I was able to. These were people already sharing in community with me and my family when crisis hit. This is one reason why having community and people you trust in your life on a regular basis is important. You support one another in times of need. This should be a reciprocal sharing of each other's burdens, to accept their assistance when you are in need and to offer help and assistance likewise to them when they are in need.

If you don't have someone to reach out to like that, brainstorm and consider where to find people like this in your current life and place you live. Then, take the next step and try a group out and begin to get to know other people in it.

Types Of Support Needed

When mental crisis occurs or is ongoing, whether hospitalization has occurred, or life is very tumultuous with caregiving for your loved one, you need support from others.

You need both tangible and emotional support, as well as spiritual and prayer support.

Tangible support comes in the form of hands-on help, whether meal assistance, watching kids, helping with cleaning, schedule issues or conflicts, supporting your loved one going to an appointment or the hospital, or just giving a hug.

I can't stress the need for community enough, friend, in order to have some of the support you need.

God's Support

Having faith in God is incredibly important and was what got me through such desperate and difficult moments that had no end in sight. God strengthened and upheld me. He carried me and gave me guidance and wisdom.

I hope you have belief and faith in God in order to derive the strength you need to get through this. If you don't yet, it's never too late to start a relationship with Him. I shared how in Chapter 13.

I encourage you to just start talking to Him. He'll listen. He hears you. Start seeking Him and find a church to be a part of. The church is where I find the safe and trusted community that has been so incredibly impactful through crisis. Find a church and join a small group or Bible study to start being a part of. If one church doesn't fit well, keep searching until you find one with welcoming, authentic community and strong Biblical teaching. Finding community is so crucial. You can't do this alone friend, at least not very well. As you do begin to find community and navigate asking for help and having others offer help and vice versa, here are some important considerations.

Boundaries In Crisis

While you do need support and help in crisis, it is not necessary or wise to accept all offers of help, friend. It is important to use discernment and have boundaries in the midst of crisis and difficult circumstances. In fact, it is necessary to have boundaries in your life at all times. Boundaries are not bad. They are healthy.

A boundary is just a delineation between persons—their feelings, emotions, thoughts, physical distance, responsibility, choices, and desires. It creates order and allows for mutual respect in relationships.

A boundary is where one person stops and another begins. To know your own needs and speak up for them is healthy and good.

For the caregiver, boundaries are also crucial in their relationship with their ill loved one. Having limits and boundaries for how much you can give helps protect your own wellbeing. It can help protect against enabling a loved one in negative choices as well.

Realizing when a choice or responsibility is not yours to make and therefore not 'owned' by you, brings freedom.

"Who owns this? Do they, or do I?"

I've learned a lot from Henry Cloud from his book *Boundaries* and his social media posts and videos.

You don't have to give someone unlimited access to your life or your loved one's life but instead can place healthy, relational boundaries to protect you and your family's wellbeing.

Accepting help and assistance from people who provide not just tangible support, but safe emotional support for you and your family, is incredibly important.

Reserving Your Energy- Assessing Emotional Energy Too

Tangible and emotional support are important, along with spiritual and prayer support for you as the primary caregiver of mental crisis.

Identify the people in your life who are safe and validating of you. Are they both emotionally and tangibly supportive of you and your ill loved one? If so, they will be a trusted support person, a trusted secondary or tertiary caregiver in your lives.

You, as the primary caregiver, must reserve your energy and resources and can't drain your energy by interacting with people who do not give emotional support to you, regardless of how close a relationship they have with your loved one who is ill. If you still need their help, then find a way to limit the help or interaction so that your energy to fight for your loved one's life and wellbeing is not drained by additional battles and emotional fights or conflicts.

If someone, often a close friend or family member of the person who is ill, comes with their own needs and agenda in crisis, they will deplete you and drain you of your emotional and physical energy, even if they were 'trying to help.'

You do have a voice that matters as the caregiver and a right to stand up for your own wellbeing in the middle of crisis.

The focus cannot be solely on the ill loved one, and you don't have to be forced into help situations that are not safe or supportive of you also.

You are allowed to say 'No' to help offered.

You are allowed to fight for your own peace. You are not obligated to accept help just because of a person's familial or close friend relationship to your ill loved one.

You have my permission, friend, to decline and say: *"No." "Thank you for the offer. We appreciate the thoughtfulness. We'll let you know if we need the help you offered."*

I learned this lesson the hard way over the years and the number of crisis moments we had and have spoken with others regarding this same struggle in their own life as well. I'm sure some of you are also struggling with this added and difficult dynamic of crisis.

Pro-actively recognize and protect your and your family's emotional and physical health needs in crisis.

You can respectfully decline help and hold your boundary when needed.

Safe people will accept your answer with graciousness and understanding.

The people coming alongside in support must be people that you also feel safe around, friend. You have a voice too and your needs are also important as the primary caregiver of your loved one.

Those who are emotionally safe will likely respond to you declining an offer of help with graciousness and easy acceptance, knowing you'll let them know if you need help.

Other people will get angry about you not accepting their offer or they will be offended and may even attack you verbally when you decline their help, and that is okay. You aren't responsible for their response. You can tell them you have to focus on what is best for you and the ill loved one and won't be able to interact with them presently with regards to their upset.

Remember, you don't have extra emotional energy to offer to these types of conflict. You don't have to respond to them even. You do not have to accept help out of obligation or 'to be nice.'

This is a form of people-pleasing and often denies your own needs in the process. If someone is upset, you could say: *"I'm sorry you are upset. I hope you can support from a distance. I have to focus on our health presently."*

If they won't leave you alone, you can block, delete, stop communicating, or whatever you need to in order to protect your peace and not be distracted from your most important job and role presently— to care for your loved one struggling with mental health illness.

Remember—you are in crisis right now, in a battle for life. Your focus must be to keep your loved one alive. That is your priority.

Your own wellbeing and mental and emotional health are also a high focus and extremely important so you can keep caregiving without entering burnout. You don't have extra time and energy to manage other conflicts that may come up with people who have other opinions and ways of doing things that are not helpful or supportive of the primary goals—the wellbeing of your loved one and you (and your children if you have children).

If your ill loved one doesn't understand your decisions, explain to them what your priority is and why you are choosing to decline an offer for help or stepping back from a person presently. Hopefully, your ill loved one can respect and accept that you need to also feel supported and have the energy to caregive for and support them, while navigating your other responsibilities as well.

To reiterate—the focus must be on the wellbeing of the ill loved one and you, the primary caregiver, and your children if you have them. That is it. Those are the people with priority and focus in crisis and in ongoing mental health caregiving—what is best for both of them and their health and wellbeing.

The caregiver often gets pushed to the back and forgotten by everyone, *including themselves.*

Fight for yourself and your wellbeing, friend. Research in fact backs up this fact. If there are increased stressors, it will add to your caregiver burden and affect your ability to continue in your role effectively. If you enter burnout and have nothing left to give, you won't be able to offer effective care and support to your loved one.

Just in case you need to hear it in a different way—

It is okay for you to thank someone for their help and decline it. You are not being mean. You are making wise, discerning decisions.

You must protect your emotional strength and fortitude as the caregiver when in a mental crisis battle. No one will likely protect it for you.

You Don't Need To 'Host' In Crisis.

Another important point to realize is:

You don't need to 'host' in crisis.

You don't need to place societal expectations on yourself or your children to have added stressors and to-do's above and beyond the bare minimum of what is absolutely needed for doing life during crisis.

Protect your rest, your children's rest (if you have children), and your ill loved one's rest.

In order to have strength, you must rest to re-energize what is depleted. People may want to come over and be 'with' you continuously if your loved one is in the hospital during crisis. Be very protective over your time and energy. You are allowed to kindly and respectively tell others you need rest or need downtime. You are not required to 'host' people, nor should you feel obligated to, if they come over. If someone is interacting in that way, cut the time short in a kind and gracious way in order to give yourself necessary rest.

If someone brings a meal or food or groceries over, catch up and talk for a short time in a gracious way, and offer gratitude, thanking them again for bringing the items they did, and then share you are needing to rest. Be willing to share your need with them. You have to verbalize your need so they are aware of it. Thank them again for their thoughtfulness and support.

Be gracious and kind, while also communicating your emotional and physical needs.

This honors yourself and preserves a boundary for your emotional and physical reserve.

Set Pride Aside In Accepting Help

If you are someone who struggles with accepting anyone's help, please set that idea or belief aside. It often stems from a sense of self-sufficiency which can be rooted in pride to be unwilling to accept others' help.

To never accept help also robs others of the blessing of coming alongside. Again, try to only accept the help from those who will be emotionally supportive rather than emotionally draining for you. *You do not have to accept everyone's offer for help.* You are allowed to have a voice and an opinion. Those whom you do accept help from, be grateful and show thankfulness to them.

If you accept help when you typically haven't in the past from anyone, know this is a moment of growth for you and an opportunity for the Lord to be working on humility in your heart in allowing others to support you. It can feel vulnerable if you aren't used to accepting help, but it is a wonderful growth opportunity and moment of connection in that relationship.

For those whom you decline offers of help from, make sure to thank them kindly for their thoughtfulness. You can let them know if you think of something you could use help with, and if they are people who pray, ask for their prayers. Prayer should never be underestimated.

Prayer is incredibly important and necessary work in the midst of mental health crisis battles.

As you can see, support comes in many forms and all are needed by the caregiver of mental crisis.

Using discernment in who to give access to yourself and your family, even in the name of "helping", is incredibly important for preserving your energy and your emotional and physical wellbeing.

Be willing to ask for help and support from others. Be willing to accept offers for help as well. You are able to live life, even in crisis, by working to identify needed boundaries and honor those boundaries.

To have ownership of only what you should, and to release all other responsibilities you were never supposed to handle, is wonderful and freeing.

Chapter 16

MY INDELIBLE SCARS & MENTAL HEALTH STRUGGLES

Song: "The Truth" by Megan Woods

When we are vulnerable about the deepest most painful parts of ourselves, we welcome others into a sacred space.

In that space, for a moment, they too will find a piece of themselves and take a step toward healing in their journey also.

Here is my poetic offering to honor our journeys.

Communing Together with Our Wounds & Scars

May we honor this space, friends, the space of sharing openly about our wounded selves and our journey on the path toward healing.

Not a destination yet reached, but one continuing to go along—humbly, truthfully, with a few more friends along the way.

Friends who have their own scars too and bravery in healing.

Friends who get me in ways that only those who've walked the jagged path of suicide caregiving also understand—

A knowing nod, a sigh after silence, a brief hand on the shoulder.

Yes, brokenness came, and in the breaking came a different kind of beauty—one only truly known by those who have suffered a similar breaking.

Add in a faith element and the beauty transcends as Jesus Himself descends along the path—the One who knew the deepest kind of suffering, trauma, and pain.

May we be like Him as we commune together, resilient, on the path toward freedom.

The path toward healing. The path, the way.

The Light illuminating ahead and leading the way.

Amen.

Vulnerability and The Path To Healing

When one person chooses to share vulnerably, they welcome others into vulnerability and healing as well. Shared connection, sacred ground. The communing of stories of pain brought out into the open in safe and reciprocal places. May we extend deep compassion and a safe space to honor the journey each has traversed. Pity never has a place here.

To extend pity is to distance yourself from another's pain and story. Compassion, empathy, and the gift of presence are instead needed.

Entering into another's story with compassion, a desire to understand, and an openness to personal growth and self-learning is to *step into hushed holy ground,* a place for healing and wholeness, a place for God to *show up in redemptive pieces of Himself.*

May you see me first and then may it begin to reflect yourself as you find bits and pieces of your own fragmented, broken self along the way to glue back together again also.

To heal, slightly differently from before, a little more scarred, a little more resilient, maybe even a little more wise.

A Profound Impact

Being a caregiver for mental crisis had profound impact upon me. I had walked through many battles prior, but this one was its own kind of debilitating, overwhelming, exhausting battle without an end in sight. A battle that consumed my life because it was a battle that had consumed my husband and was trying to take his life. I gave it my all, sacrificing every bit of my energy and reserve, and the sacrifice was great. The impact upon myself was great too.

My vulnerability and openness sharing with you here is not something that came naturally to me, by the way, but it was a learned way of sharing as I have practiced opening up vulnerably about my pain and story.

When we are vulnerable about the deepest most painful parts of ourselves, we welcome others into a sacred space.

In that space, for a moment, they too will find a piece of themselves and take a step toward healing in their journey also.

I Had To Be Perfect. A Survival Belief

A significant negative belief that came out of my almost two years of crisis caregiving was—

the belief that I had to be perfect and couldn't make mistakes.

I had to be perfect in my interactions with my husband. I couldn't be human. I couldn't make mistakes. I couldn't mess up. I couldn't disagree. I couldn't enter into conflict. If I made a mistake, he would die.

A byproduct of that was we couldn't have an actual relationship with each other anymore because any conflict, disagreement, or negative interaction between us would be the catalyst for him heading down a suicide pathway in his thinking.

This belief was based in reality and formed from experiences and interactions we had where that did occur. It also significantly affected my view of myself as well. I was a 'trigger' for him.

The weight of that knowledge was heavy for me.

As time has lengthened between then and now, and since I have done my own EMDR therapy work on my experiences and on this belief and its significant effect upon me, I have a more balanced viewpoint of what was occurring during that heavy crisis time period.

I would alter my prior statement of: "I was a trigger for him." now. Let me explain.

A Person, Themself, Is Not a Suicide Trigger

Conflict between us or a negative interaction for him could be actual suicide triggers for him.

I, myself, as a person, was not a 'trigger.'

My existence and personhood are not, in and of themselves, reasons for someone to head down a detrimental path to suicide. A person is not a reason someone ends their life. Instead, their response to a conflict or interaction with another person and ultimately their reaction to being upset and emotionally distraught can lead someone down an increased suicidal pathway, toward suicidal intent.

Toward an emergency.

Neither I, nor you, friend, are responsible for our loved one's suicidal thoughts, suicidal intent, plan, or attempts.

Coming to terms with that truth is incredibly important.

Becoming free from the first negative belief (I was responsible) and trading it for the actual truth (I wasn't responsible for his suicidality) was pivotal for my healing.

I had begun to own the lie that I was responsible for his suicide plans and attempts. That I had to be perfect or he would die.

It took me processing and dismantling those lies in EMDR therapy for me to separate myself and my personhood from my loved one's illness.

I finally knew I wasn't responsible for my husband's suicidal thoughts. I knew I didn't cause his symptoms. They were a byproduct of and connected to his trauma, PTSD, depression, and the lies and beliefs he was struggling with as a result of his own experiences. And yet, I still had felt responsibility over his increased suicidality.

The truth was though, I didn't have control over his choices or actions. I didn't have control over his feelings.

I Don't Have Control Over Another Person, Only Myself. And the Same Applies To You.

I don't have control over another person—their choices, actions, or inner world of emotions or thoughts—and neither do you.

The only person I had control over was myself, but I first had to recognize and accept that I was human. I had to give myself grace. My negative belief of having to be perfect or he'd end his life was based in real experiences that we walked through, but that belief was based in the idea that I had a way of controlling the outcome of him staying alive (by my being perfect) which was not the case. Again—

- I only have control over my choices, reactions, and decisions.
- I don't have control over another person's feelings, perceptions, actions, decisions, or reactions to events.

The same is true for you. Read over these powerful "I" statements again, and say them out-loud, as you apply them to yourself.

The truth is you don't have control over your loved one's feelings, perceptions, actions, decisions, or reactions either, no more than I do.

This is a crucial truth to grab ahold of—one that took me therapy to internalize.

I didn't have the ability to see into my loved one's brain and his mind and know, for sure, that he wasn't heading down a suicide pathway one day from another, or one moment to another.

Not having control, or even the ability to access our loved one's brain and true thoughts, feels scary when we know our loved one is struggling with suicidal thoughts often and there is the potential for increased suicide risk.

The truth in my situation was: I was my husband's support person, his caregiver, walking through one of the most difficult and life-threatening unpredictable battles alongside him, and I was doing everything I could to care for him well. I was asking the Lord for wisdom and seeking to do my utmost to care for him well and not miss any signs.

You also are doing all that you can to support your loved one. Accept that truth and when you aren't sure of what to do, always reach out for professional assistance, professional guidance on the next best course of action. Look at the additional resources I offer in the Appendix in the back of this book.

988 is the U.S. Suicide and Crisis Lifeline. It is an important number to contact for help and assistance. They can guide you in what to do to support your loved one.

Relational Difficulty, Stress, and Emotional Capacity

There will be difficulties that occur in life and there will be disagreements or opposing viewpoints in any relationship. That is a part of life.

As the caregiver, it is important to decrease and limit the number of conflicts or difficult discussions you have with your loved one, knowing their mental and emotional capacity to handle stress is lessened and relational discord or conflict can cause emotional distress and increased negative mental health symptoms. To discern and let alone or not address a number of disagreements that may be important is not easy. It is hard to be quiet when you would normally talk through an issue together and come to a decision or compromise. To not have that ability any longer because your loved one may head into suicidal intention is difficult.

Finding a safe space and friendship to vent those changes and struggles to is helpful. I pray it is not forever, because we want our loved one to begin to heal through therapy and begin to get better. Healing takes time, and we have to persevere in it. We have to hang in for the long haul and the hope of our loved one slowly getting better. I pray it is not always so difficult.

Know that walking the path of mental crisis caregiver is one of the hardest roles you will have and also is one of the most vital roles you will hold for another person.

In a mind already struggling significantly with suicidal ideation even a small rupture or small disagreement, in a close relationship, could be the upset to cause increased suicidal thoughts and increased risk of suicide.

What I realized through therapy and healing was the idea of me being a trigger did not have to do with me specifically but the fact that I was my loved one's closest relationship. A differing opinion or conflict of any kind could increase symptoms, and not necessarily within our relationship, but even in another relationship that mattered to him.

Difficult In the Long-term

As I mentioned, I carried such a significant weight and burden of perfection throughout that time to try to not "give away" a differing opinion, negative feeling, or dissenting thought with him unless it was a moment that was too important to not be addressed.

This approach is not sustainable long-term, nor was it healthy for me. It was incredibly unhealthy for me to ignore and set aside my own voice and thoughts continuously. I know the Lord used my survival approach at that time to protect Josh's life, but I later had to deconstruct those beliefs that came from life in survival.

Deconstructing survival beliefs takes time and focused psychotherapy.

The belief I had to be perfect and needed to hide away my differing thoughts was deeply ingrained in order to protect life. It wasn't overcome easily. EMDR therapy with cognitive elements guided me slowly on the path to healing this inner wound and dismantling a belief that served me for a time to protect my loved one but wasn't healthy for my own personhood.

I denied my own self, and it had ramifications for me.

There was hope though because through the EMDR therapy, I began to accept my own humanness again. I began to stop *expecting perfection* of myself. I began to allow myself the grace of making mistakes, asking for forgiveness when needed, and not being wound so tight to keep myself in check and not "mess up".

There was freedom in setting down that survival belief and again picking up a healthier, inner balanced approach.

I could accept who I was, my strengths and my weaknesses, and show up more fully and authentically as myself in my own life.

Walking On Eggshells

I walked on eggshells around him, figuratively speaking. It was stressful. It was tiring. I yearned to have my best friend back, the one I was close to and had married and started a family with.

Our relationship suffered. How could it not? Our roles became caregiver and loved one struggling, with attempts at being a family and a married couple. Attempts to be 'normal' at times. It was challenging. It was exhausting. It was tense.

My heart aches when I look at pictures from that lengthy crisis season. *The smiles on faces and seemingly beautiful moments of a young family bely the torment and chaos that swirled around each moment.*

The cries out to God for help, the uncertain questions in the dark of what to do and whether medical care was needed urgently right then or not was weighty.

The angst. The worry. The love.

The strong living out of my vows to "love in sickness and in health". I had no idea the "in sickness" part for me would be loving through serious mental health illness. It was a battle we were in for his life, and I supported in every way possible.

The chaos and turmoil of constant hypervigilance, checking in, and never being "off" as the primary caregiver affected me.

Navigating broken trust, lies, hiding, and self-medicating of himself affected me.

Saving his life during a suicide attempt affected me. Trauma. Trauma responses. Avoidance of my trauma triggers. All were some of my symptoms.

Stressful night, after stressful night, nursing a baby and running down to make sure he wasn't going to do something dangerous. The alcohol and trauma CBT homework concoction was a terrible mix. Him having to relive his trauma at home without the guidance of a therapist present was terrible for me, and as I've recently realized—those nights were traumatic for me. The additional caregiver burden they added also was significant.

"I Have PTSD"

It took time for me to identify and accept the label and diagnosis of PTSD for myself. I saw the signs of it but pushed it aside because my husband had trauma and PTSD.

Did I also?

I had been through very stressful and difficult circumstances prior to that time already.

I didn't have trauma from them, however.

Deployments, miscarriages, many moves and transitions with the military and my job.

I didn't have my own advocate, so it was difficult to determine if yes, I truly did have PTSD or not as I observed and recognized the symptoms within myself.

I didn't have my own sounding board. I didn't have my own caregiver to come alongside and support me, to graciously and kindly share observations they had and suggest a potential struggle I might be facing.

I was forced to be my own friend and support person and speak truth to myself. There was no one else to do it.

I had to ask myself those questions and identify a potential struggle I was now facing as well. The PA in me began to know deep down I was in fact showing signs of a trauma response and as time went on, of PTSD.

As I observed myself, assessed my own self, I began to determine that, *Yes, I think I did have PTSD.* I had secondary trauma as well as primary trauma.

Primary trauma are the specific events I experienced that were traumatic for me. PTSD developed from them for me.

Secondary trauma is the secondary impact on a person in caring for and managing their loved one's trauma, PTSD, or other mental health conditions.

It took me a while to come to a place of determining I wasn't overreacting to say I had PTSD.

The first time I actually said it out loud I said it a few times out loud.

"I have PTSD".

"I—have PTSD."

In some ways, it was a relief to accept this diagnosis that supported the symptoms I had been dealing with and experiencing. As a provider, I knew how to diagnose it, and I knew I had it.

It was hard but necessary to name it. To name out-loud that I had secondary PTSD from caregiving for my husband—that I had dealt with my own mini-trauma events, continuously, day in and day out, night after night.

To say out-loud I had primary PTSD from two primary trauma events was a monumental moment for me. A scary but important moment. A moment of revelation and relief.

There was relief to know I wasn't broken and irreparable.

There was a reason for my symptoms. There was relief in naming the symptoms I was having and being able to identify my own pain and focus on my own healing, my own therapy, my own help too.

If I could name what I was fighting, then there was a path forward to heal it.

You Are Your Own Advocate & Caregiver

I had to be my own advocate and caregiver.

The caregiver of others and the caregiver of myself, too.

The same is true for you also. It's not fair, but it's reality.

And, friend, it's hard to fight for yourself too when you are already fighting for the best care for someone else. It's sometimes much easier to just focus on fighting for your loved one getting better and the help they need.

I often didn't have any more energy or emotional, physical, or mental capacity to focus on getting care for myself also. I often didn't have additional support to care for my kids so I could go to my own therapy. After setting up childcare so I could support and be present for some of my husband's appointments, it was difficult to find additional time for me to go for myself. We dealt with medical issues for a child and had to be specific with who cared for our children as a result. My husband was already missing time from work to go to his own appointments, and he had to make that time up. He didn't have the ability to support me going to my own therapy appointments also.

I share this logistical issue with you because you may have other unique challenges you face different than ours that make pursuing your own care difficult as well. It's easy to say go get therapy. Sometimes the logistics are more challenging to navigate. Keep pursuing it and making time for it and carving money out for it in whatever way you can in order to find healing for yourself too.

The Strong One Reaching Out

It can feel vulnerable and even awkward as the strong one to reach out for mental health help. You may feel embarrassed or wonder what you will tell people if someone finds out you went to therapy or counseling.

Pause that thought.

Consider this instead—

Someone who is strong for others needs support, self-care, and recharging too.

Being able to face difficult, hard things doesn't mean the hard things don't have a lasting imprint upon you.

To ignore or dismiss this reality will actually diminish your long-term strength and may lead to burnout or more substantial mental health conditions for you over time.

Processing with a mental health therapist and facing your own feelings and emotions for the circumstances you are walking through is incredibly important for continued resilience, strength, and perseverance.

As a mental health crisis caregiver, you need to have someone in your corner focused only on your health and your needs so that you can continue forward in all the strong and amazing ways you are showing up for your person. For your family. For your community.

Friend, going to therapy, means you will keep on being a mighty caregiver warrior in the mental health battle for your loved one's life. The painful moments, struggles, emotions, and thoughts will keep piling up, rather than diminishing. It's much easier to work through them when you haven't waited for a long time before.

For me, I discovered when I did EMDR therapy, my capacity improved and increased for my present struggles and caregiving. When I began to process through old pain and stuck emotions and memories, it freed up my current capacity.

If you feel that burden on your shoulders from current burdens or from old wounds and old events, memories, and emotions, know those old "things" are present with you and affect your present ability to show up well for your own life.

You know, by now, I am a huge proponent of EMDR therapy. It helps stuck emotional memories become unstuck and be integrated into the neural network, thereby decreasing the impact of the memory.[1]

It helped to decrease the intensity of my trauma responses. Even when I did have a trauma response, I could use the positive coping techniques I learned in EMDR therapy to help limit how long I was affected by the response.

I want EMDR therapy for you also, friend. I want the experiences you've walked through to not affect you as significantly as they do right now.

Resurgence Of Symptoms & Marled Scars

Obviously, I'm not going to lie and say I don't have resurgences of symptoms because that isn't true. It is important to be truthful about reality. Once we have been through something deeply painful that changed us forever, we aren't the same person we were before.

But—**God can heal those deep gaping, festering wounds from our painful experiences.** *Those deep gaping wounds can be transformed to marled scars.*

There will always be telltale signs of the battle we have faced, but if we have walked through our own healing therapy journey, we can view those experiences differently because we are now different too.

We have come through the refining fire and have chosen bravery to walk through and face the pain again in therapy, not because we want to be in pain, but because we desire to process and integrate those painful parts, in order to become free of their hold on us.

I did this process myself through intensive EMDR sessions with cognitive elements and my faith integrated with it. I also walked through faith-based healing work focused on becoming free from the pain and hurts of my past. With an integrated faith and EMDR focus for my healing, God did a work within me mentally, emotionally, and spiritually as I pursued my own healing work with Him and with the help of my therapist.

It was important and necessary work—all of it. I am grateful and thankful I pursued both.

Reservations & Resistance To Seeking Therapy For Yourself

I know you may want to ignore it friend. I get that. It's very difficult to pick up the phone and make that first phone call. I've been there.

I also know that **if we don't deal with the painful things of our past, they will** *continue to affect our present life and our future,* **whether we realize it or not.**

They will affect our beliefs and how we show up in our relationships, how we parent, and how we offer and receive love.

Our past wounds affect our present and future life.

Unless we choose to be brave and face them.

Another question or reservation that held me back was I was so consumed with caregiving *"When could I go, and when would my care fit into the schedule?"*

You may also tell yourself that it's selfish for you to have care because "you are doing okay". We already addressed this earlier.

If you don't care for yourself, no one else will, and you will begin to head toward burnout, where you can't offer care to anyone anymore.

Burnout is when you have no more capacity and nothing left to give.

Money and financial strain can also be a barrier to seeking therapy. Sometimes a group doesn't take your insurance or it takes time to find a group, therapist, or psychologist who takes your insurance and offers the therapy and treatment you are seeking, such as EMDR therapy. I will tell you we paid out of pocket for most if not all of my treatment and some of Josh's also.

Seeking healing affected our finances. I'll be honest with you—we went into debt for it. We desperately needed it though, and time couldn't wait. I wouldn't have done it differently. I know of more resources now than I did then certainly. I'm not advising you to go into debt, but rather to consider seeking out therapy in the same context as if your loved one needed a medical surgery right now, and it couldn't wait—you would fight and find a way to make it happen. Your mental health and your loved one's mental health is incredibly important to both of your wellbeing.

I encourage you to ask and search for groups that can offer sliding scale, a lesser fee, or if it's a therapy or psychology group connected to a church, sometimes even free psychotherapy, to include EMDR therapy. EMDR therapy is more widely offered now than it was when I originally searched for it years ago. It is possible. It often takes searching and asking and calling many places to find the place you need to go. Don't give up.

I have found there are many groups who may not take your insurance or bill insurance but will create a bill or superbill for you to submit to insurance yourself for possible reimbursement. You would pay the group and then receive the superbill showing the amount and payment which you would then submit to your insurance. Ask a group or practice about sliding scales, lesser fees, and the ability to submit a superbill afterwards to your insurance. There is no guarantee your insurance will reimburse you for the costs you incurred, but you can try. With one group, we received a portion of reimbursement from our insurance after submitting one of the superbills. I wish it were easier to access necessary care that is needed for mental health therapy. Keep fighting for the care you and your loved one need. Do not give up. Be resourceful and find a mental health therapist, friend.

In the slight chance you haven't received my free guide for you yet, here's the link for your E-book guide "How To Find A Mental Health Therapist".

You deserve healing and the opportunity to work through and process the difficult circumstances you have walked through.

Go to my website to receive your Free digital E-book and Spotify Playlist:

amberjparker.com/theforgottencaregiver/gifts

This E-book guide is for your personal use. If you live outside the United States, you can still apply the guidance and one of the websites I offer in the resource to find a mental health therapist to help you in your healing journey.

Don't delay. Grab your guide.

Survival Living

When you are in the middle of crisis, you are living from one day to the next focused on immediate needs. The immediate needs for your kids, yourself, your loved one. This can sometimes be a trauma response.

Making long term plans or even a few months in advance plans are difficult because your day-to-day survival is all you have the ability to focus on. You don't know what next month will look like or even two weeks from now. You are focused on your loved one's changing and up and down symptoms and how they affect your life. This is survival living, survival mode.

Survival living doesn't mean you are doing great. It does mean you are getting from one day to the next and giving your loved one all that you have, usually without anything left over. Survival mode puts a lot of stress on your body and your energy. Often, your sympathetic system (the one with fight or flight mode and adrenaline) is continually on because you are constantly on alert, "on duty", as we talked about before. Giving all that you have to care for your loved one seems commendable, but it is not healthy or sustainable and will lead to burnout.

You must attune to yourself and the emotional, physical, mental, and spiritual needs you have to stay healthy.

Seeking Your Own Healing Is a Gift.

It isn't selfish to get your own help and seek your own healing. I hope I've stressed that point enough so it begins to sink in for you.

Seeking your own mental and emotional healing is actually a gift to those whom you love. It's a gift to yourself to choose vulnerability and the path of healing for yourself. It's a gift to put your actions where your words have been and do the incredibly hard task of picking up the phone and making the phone call for yourself. Making that call to talk about why you yourself need therapy. Why you yourself need healing. To talk about the pain and memories you've shoved down because there wasn't time to deal with it. The emotions and struggles you had but couldn't process before because you had to set them aside in order to fight for your loved one's life.

There is never a 'too late' moment for your own healing. A moment to be honest with yourself and lay down the mask of *'doing it all'* and *'being the strong one'*.

You are strong to seek out your own therapy. You are brave.

It's okay to enter into a safe place of healing and vulnerability, in your own psychotherapy, friend, in order to come out on the other side more resilient and a force to reckoned with.

Go To Mental Health Therapy Focusing on the Why Behind Your Going

Don't be afraid to go to therapy yourself. Don't ignore your emotions, your feelings, your pain, your experience. Do the EMDR therapy work.

Don't shove your emotions down deep and carry on with a plastered smile on your face. Don't do it. Pause and ask yourself what you are struggling with. Where the pain is.

You will have to walk through the painful experiences and moments again in therapy... And friend, I know it's brutal.

Remind yourself the reason you are facing the pain this time is for a different reason—not just to hurt and feel pain, but to reach the other side. To obtain healing. To not have to ignore or numb the pain or wound whenever it tries to overwhelm you. To not fight against it but learn ways to cope that are life-giving. To live with more freedom. With more joy. With more life. It's the only way to freedom. Freedom. Resiliency. Hope on the other side.

I am cheering you on friend and know you can make that first mental health therapy call for yourself because you have already done such incredibly hard things prior to now. You are a strong person who has fought hard for their loved one and deserves to be fought hard for as well.

You, yourself, are the one fighting hard for your own self. I know that's not fair, but that's the reality and may need to be accepted in order for you to get the healing that you also need.

So—accept the reality and step forward toward healing.

Take a deep breath, hold it for 3 seconds, and exhale slowly over 3 seconds—Then, go, be your own best friend, your own advocate, and speak the truth to yourself about your need for therapy and don't delay. As you learned in Chapter 3 and Chapter 9, you just used my favorite positive coping strategy: boxed breathing. For a more detailed description of how to use it and why it decreases stress in the moment, go to Chapters 3 or 9 to read further.

What It Means To Have a Mental Health Therapist

To have your own mental health therapist—Think of it as having someone in your corner, that is there just for you. It's true.

I have been so deeply blessed to know my therapist is just for me and has my best interests and mental health in mind. It gave me a safe space to put down my necessary mask and carefully curated interactions.

It gave me room to *breathe* and to begin *healing*. It gave me an ally.

I am transformed as I bravely move forward, facing pain and memories I never had the luxury to process yet.

It is a gift, friend.

What Healing Begins To Look Like

The other side is so much more wonderful—the side where the wounds are finally closing and forming scarred tissue, hardened—less naïve or beautiful—but oh so much more resilient and truly glorious.

There may still be some pangs present of what was from before, like bumping a physical scar on a hard table could cause shoots of pain to spread.

Likewise— *'Bumping' your trauma on a trigger could activate your fight or flight response, making your body head into 'danger' mode.*

Or a trigger or detail could make the wave of grief and loss of what was changed forever overwhelm you for a moment. And you have to catch your breath, take a pause, and sit with it for a moment, or moments. Not try to push it off or distract yourself with something else. Instead, give the trigger and feeling of grief or loss the space to be present or offer grace and presence to the physiological fight or flight activation in order to calm it.

Maybe you need to write it out in a journal to process and make sense of it or to catalog it, so you have it written down to discuss it with your therapist. Be gracious to yourself in the moment. Acknowledge that what you are experiencing makes sense. It is a normal response and should be expected occasionally, even after walking through extensive therapy and healing. It's possible you would benefit from a maintenance EMDR session or sessions to explore that trigger and symptoms to lessen the intensity of it in the future.

Hopefully, you see the correlation between a physical wound that has become a scar and a mental/emotional wound that has gone through considerable healing through therapy.

How to Find A Mental Health Therapist

Now, if you aren't sure what to do or how to go about finding the right therapist for yourself, as I mentioned before—I've already done the work for you. If you haven't grabbed your E-book guide yet, **you need to get it.**

It's free and will assist you and your loved one in your healing journey.

Here's the link and QR code to your Free E-book guide:

"How To Find A Mental Health Therapist"

amberjparker.com/theforgottencaregiver/gifts

The link and QR code are also in the Appendix at the back of the book.

Remember, you can do hard things friend. I'm cheering you on. Run after your own healing and health too! You deserve it.

REFERENCES

[1] van der Kolk, B. A. (2014). *The Body Keeps the Score: Brain, Mind, and Body In the Healing of Trauma.* Penguin Books, 222, 230.

PART 4: CONCLUSION: A MORE BALANCED APPROACH

Ch. 17

Chapter 17

LIFE AFTER CRISIS: RELAPSES, RESILIENCE, & REDEMPTION

Song: "Look At What the Lord has Done" by:
The Belonging Co, Shantrice Laura

Song: "I Thank God" by: Maverick City Music, UPPERROOM, (feat. Dante Bowe, Maryanne J. George, Chuck Butler, & Aaron Moses)

As you continue on the path towards healing for your loved one and yourself, there may come a moment where you begin to breathe a little easier, feel a little more 'normal', and wonder how on earth you made it through all of 'that.'

For me, I felt grateful. These lulls were such a needed respite.

Even in a healthier place, there can be challenges. There can be uncertainty of your loved one getting worse again as well as trying to figure out your relationship again with them.

What does it look like when you stop being 'caregiver' and 'ill loved one' and go back to 'wife' and 'husband'? [insert parent, child, or other pertaining relationship]

You are both changed from what you walked through. It will take time to learn a new way of doing life together again with a more balanced, healthier approach.

We are still living out this chapter, and as such, I hope you can glean what you need as you continue to find a new way forward, together, a little more healed, continuing toward growth, truth, and authenticity. As you continue to use positive coping strategies to handle stress and emotional pain... as you support one another.

When You Think Crisis Is Over—Relapses & Resurges

I would caution you to *not assume* your loved one is fully in remission from suicidality, even if your loved one appears to be doing well or says they are doing well.

A relapse is possible. Another dip into mental crisis is possible.

Be aware of and identify warning signs of increased suicide risk if they occur.

This is not to live in fear, but to live in reality. Being in remission from suicidality is cause for celebration. It means either symptoms may never come back or symptoms could come back at some point in the future. I share this so you don't live life unaware.

I knew it could happen because it already had in someone's life a few removed from us. A Veteran who was a mental health leader helping so many find healing ended up dying by suicide during the same time as our lengthy battle with suicide. It was devastating and shook me to my core. It affected Josh significantly as well. It was devastating.

It made me realize to always be aware. To never assume.

It gave me a different outlook—to be thankful if my husband was getting better but always aware of the potential for relapse.

I share this important point also because suicidality relapse happened in our life too. Relapse happened for Josh years after the initial lengthy and intense time of suicidality caregiving.

My husband had another suicide plan which was halted. And I came to his aid to help him receive the emergency and in-patient mental health care he needed. We could have lost him. Again.

I had always stayed aware of the potential of a suicidality relapse. It was still overwhelming and surreal when it occurred, and we were back down the painfully familiar and difficult path of emergency care and hospitalization. Of being simultaneously thankful for life and overwhelmed by crisis returning and the necessary care ensuing, the in-patient and out-patient care.

Research On Mental Health Relapses

The research supports this phenomenon of a mental health relapse for those hospitalized for treatment of mental illness.

~30-50% of those who are hospitalized for mental illness *will have a relapse of symptoms in the first 6 months after hospitalization.*[1]

50-70% of those hospitalized for mental illness treatment *will have a mental health relapse in the first 5 years after discharge.*[1]

These statistics are for all mental health hospitalizations and not suicidality-specific.

The takeaway is that **a high percentage of people requiring hospitalization for mental illness have a relapse within the first 5 years following discharge.**

Being aware of this potentially happening for your loved one is important. Encouraging your loved one to be aware and identify and communicate with you if they begin to have symptoms return can help with crisis prevention—by treating early. As the caregiver, you will also need to keep awareness of symptoms in order to recognize increasing mental health symptoms for your loved one—to get them the care they need when they need it.

Significant predictors of a mental health relapse include: *"comorbidity with other mental illness, non-adherence to medication, shorter duration on treatment and experiencing stressful life events as well as a high disability score, and a single admission history."*[1]

It is necessary to be aware of risk factors for a mental health relapse and aware of mental health symptoms to identify and respond proactively if they are present.

Live Prepared and Aware.

I can't stress it enough, friend—Even if your loved one is doing significantly better or appears 'healed', stay aware and alert of suicidal warning signs and checking in with them.

This is not to live in fear, but to live prepared, with tools and knowledge to quickly recognize if suicidal symptoms return in the future. You can now come alongside other people struggling similarly with their loved ones, to help educate and support others in your community—with the knowledge you now have.

Don't live in fear. Live prepared and aware.

We covered symptoms of increased suicide risk in chapter 6, but I will share some of those symptoms again here because they are incredibly important to recognize.

Suicide warning signs as described by NAMI's website can include *"increased alcohol and drug use, aggressive behavior, withdrawal from friends, family, and community, dramatic mood swings, and impulsive or reckless behavior"*.[2]

Call or text 988 to reach the Suicide and Crisis Lifeline in the United States for assistance.

NAMI outlines **other suicidal behaviors** indicating an increased risk of suicide and psychiatric emergency. These are *"collecting and saving pills or buying a weapon, giving away possessions, tying up loose ends, like organizing personal papers or paying off debts, and saying goodbye to friends and family"*.[2] If these steps are being taken, seek immediate care from a healthcare provider or call 988 for assistance from the Suicide and Crisis Lifeline.

This is not a comprehensive list of suicide risk factors and symptoms.

Go to the NAMI website at www.nami.org (full link in the Appendix) and read further to educate yourself further on the risk factors and symptoms to be aware of for suicide and increased suicide risk.

AFSP shares risk factors for increased risk of suicide to include health, environmental, and historical factors which are extremely insightful and important to be aware of. Turn back to Chapter 6 to review those. You can also go to http://afsp.org/ to learn more.

Remember—**Live prepared and aware.**

When a situation with your loved one begins to feel deja-vu like, it may be because it is triggering memories for you and there are similarities to past moments when your loved one had increased suicide risk. Treat it as you would at another time there were increased mental health symptoms.

Identify increased suicidal risk, ask your loved one pertinent questions, and be a support to them. Use the three data points from Chapter 10 in considering and assessing, and always reach out to medical and mental health professionals for assistance, whether you are unsure about symptoms or you know your loved one needs immediate care.

Use 988, the Suicide and Crisis Lifeline, for guidance. Reaching out to professionals for assistance and recognizing increased warning signs for suicide have the power to save your loved one's life again and get them the help they need in crisis.

Be aware but not living in fear.

Be prepared and willing to check in with your loved one.

Maintenance Mental Health Therapy

Your loved one may be discharged from therapy after they've accomplished the goals determined at the start of psychotherapy. It may be helpful to ask the therapist about how to stay an 'active client' or if maintenance (less frequent) sessions are offered. This way if stressors or life events begin to affect your loved one's health, they can easily access therapy support sooner—before symptoms worsen or turn into crisis.

That said, many therapists and counselors have their clients graduate from their care and if therapy is needed at a later time, then re-establish care. One reason is to free up their sessions and schedule for clients who are presently in significant need or have been on the waitlist trying to get in. With a growing mental health burden societally, there is a shortage of clinicians working to meet the demand for psychotherapy. Your loved one can discuss this with their clinician and make a collaborative decision once they've reached their initial psychotherapy goals.

If your loved one takes a psychiatric medication, their 'maintenance' or check-in could be with their psychiatrist if they aren't seeing a therapist currently.

My encouragement for you is to continue to be *aware* of mental health symptoms and seek out care *pro-actively* rather than *waiting* until symptoms worsen.

If It Was Cancer

If you had cancer or another chronic illness and it was in remission, you'd get check-ups, possibly annually, to make sure you were still doing well. You'd do this because you wouldn't want your illness to resurface unaware and not be able to seek treatment. You would make decisions for follow-up with the knowledge and understanding that it could resurface. You would live your present life thankful.

In the same way, mental health crisis and suicidality can also resurface. Depression can worsen. PTSD can worsen.

To be aware and prepared is to be wise.

I would rather live life aware that suicidality could resurface and concurrently thankful we are doing well presently.

I can prayerfully ask and seek the Lord for full and total healing and for this type of battle to not come near our home again. In that, I can fully hold onto the truth that God is mighty and powerful and able to do far beyond what we can hope or imagine (from Ephesians 3:20). That is true. I am not in control of the future, but I can pray in faith.

I can live with the humility of how low we have been brought and thankful at the same time for where we are walking presently, *knowing that today is a gift.*

How we approach our today will impact whether we continue to stay on the path of health, healing, and wholeness, in all areas, but especially in the realm of mental health. We must not get complacent but instead be proactive with identifying when we are facing challenges and increased stressors.

It is important to be honest with those trusted people around us when we are not doing well. To stay plugged into support and connection with other people. To have accountability. To not be an island alone unto ourselves.

Do not be an island alone unto yourself.

Help Your Loved One Grow In Self-Advocacy

Be aware, be optimistic, be proactive. Being proactive means encouraging and supporting your loved one to continue in their mental health therapy and their self-care activities. Being intentional in pursuits to support both of your mental health needs and overall health is a powerful way to feel connected as you support each other and do life together.

Helping guide your loved one to be proactive in their own health is an important growth step in their journey. As they learn ways to care for themselves and self-advocate for their needs, they are empowered to keep momentum up and not allow setbacks to deter their goal toward getting better.

As they get better, it is not healthy for either of you if your loved one is fully reliant on you continuously to make sure they receive the care and treatment they need to (if they are competent and capable of taking on self-responsibility for some of their tasks).

This means they begin to become their own advocate and speak up for their needs, an important task to grow in.

We may, as the caregiver, advocate automatically in a situation for our loved one (as if on autopilot) if we've been supporting them in this way for quite a while.

As your loved one continues with therapy and healing, it's important to recognize this tendency in yourself and look for ways to encourage their self-advocacy. As they begin to gain skills in therapy and grow in their healing, they will begin to learn self-care tools like grounding, breathwork, and positive coping skills. They will learn ways to speak up for their needs and advocate for themselves.

Your loved one's growth in self-advocacy of their mental health and being proactive about their self-care will come slowly and naturally as they pursue treatment and healing. Encourage them in fostering those skills and applying them in their life while you continue to be a support. Doing so will empower them on their trajectory of improved health.

Recognizing this need and encouraging your loved one to speak up for their own needs and apply positive coping strategies when they are struggling helps them grow in self-awareness, self-attunement, and self-care. They become more resilient as they grow in their capacity to interact with their own struggles and counteract negative thoughts, feelings, emotions, and behaviors.

They still need your support. Don't worry, you aren't going anywhere. You are still coming alongside your loved one and being aware of their symptoms and helping them in any way they need. You are also encouraging them in growing in their abilities also. They still need you to support them and a professional team to care for them.

They will gain confidence and grow in trusting themselves as they learn positive coping strategies and when to reach out for professional help.

Your caregiver burden becomes *lighter* because the weight of care becomes *more evenly distributed.*

Don't force this if your loved one isn't yet at a place of healing to implement self-advocacy and apply self-guided positive coping strategies. This is a gradual process and one to encourage your loved one in with small steps towards self-advocacy and self-guided care. Celebrate the small steps. It's a process of learning together.

If your loved one's attempt at advocating and speaking up for their needs doesn't work in a situation, you are still there to support and speak on their behalf and for their best interests. Take it slow. Be encouraging and uplifting to your loved one as they grow in these skills. I pray your burden becomes a little lighter as your loved one begins to get a little better and you both grow together in navigating their mental health needs as well as your own needs.

You can now begin to live your life more balanced.

Having a healthier balance is important. It can be difficult to determine what that looks like when you've lived in survival mode for so long. Take it one step at a time.

Spotlight vs. Lantern Approach

A balanced approach considers both the loved one who is ill and the caregiver when identifying needs. It looks at boundaries of self.

Where do I end and the other person begin? What am I responsible for and they responsible for? Allowing your loved one to have increased ownership of their care is important as they get better.

My therapist shared with me about living more balanced with utilizing **a lantern effect** versus **a spotlight effect** on my loved one's needs.

This helped me significantly during my husband's most recent mental health struggle. I was able to consider in a more balanced way how to support him while not fully ignoring my needs and my children's needs. Instead of focusing fully and only on him, I focused with a lantern effect. A lantern effect casts more diffuse light which in this setting indicates balancing and considering everyone's needs, rather than only one person's struggle or needs.

A spotlight approach highlights and prioritizes one person's needs, at the detriment and dismissal of everyone else's needs.

In survival mode, I used the spotlight approach to caregive for my husband, but it had a significant toll on me. As I healed and then more recently used the lantern effect, I did what I was able to in supporting my husband with his PTSD symptoms, and then I focused on my children's needs and my own also. It brought a sense of peace as I prayed to God over what I had no control over. It was a healthier, more balanced approach, one more easily sustained, though, still very difficult.

[One important note: I don't share the spotlight and lantern approaches to be applied to interactions or symptoms regarding suicide. The lantern approach should not counteract any information on how to identify and respond to suicide warning signs or symptoms. I used the lantern approach in caring for PTSD symptoms. Always get the help needed for someone in crisis or with increased suicide risk. Always reach out to and contact mental health professionals or call or text 988 in the United States for the suicide and crisis lifeline. Respond to emergencies immediately and appropriately.]

Even in the midst of crisis, God was at work. There were glimpses of His fingerprints and His hand upon our lives.

Hitting Rock Bottom

God is working all things together for His good.

In our story of ongoing crisis, EMDR therapy was the ultimate turning point for us. It did, in a few sessions, what we could not accomplish in months with CBT therapy. It decreased Josh's symptoms in such a monumental way and brought my husband "back to me" for a time.

After he felt so much better following the EMDR sessions, he didn't continue doing therapy or having maintenance sessions. He didn't pursue mental health support. A few years down the road, he wasn't doing well again, and this time instead of taking his life and choosing to go down the suicide route, his PTSD and choices led him to leave me. We were separated for a time and worked to rebuild our relationship through marriage therapy. You can imagine the significant impact this season had on our relationship and marriage, even still today, after marriage therapy.

Trust in a relationship takes time, plus consistent action, to rebuild.

We are rebuilding bit by bit as we choose each other daily.

Fast forward another year and a couple months, and he planned a suicide attempt again. He'd been heavy into using alcohol but was hiding it from me. Self-medicating in large quantities. I knew he could relapse suicide-wise again. And he did…

What was different this time though was God needed him to hit rock bottom.

Josh needed to hit rock bottom in order for the Lord to do a miracle in his life of saving him in the psychiatric ward. The Lord needed to also free him from the grip of alcoholism taking over his life at that present time and *wreaking havoc* in our home. Alcohol addiction (i.e. alcoholism) had control over him.

I would rather Josh tell you this next part himself, but he has given me permission to share what God did for him. I am witness to the miracle in his life, and God allowed me to be an active participant in his redemption story.

Saul To Paul Redemption

Josh grew up thinking he was a Christian. I thought I married a Christian. But, in his words, when he was stripping off the things he didn't need in his life—God and religion were things thrown down.

We walked through a period of a few years where he didn't believe in God and didn't know if there was a God. He was agnostic.

It was incredibly difficult for us to do life as a married couple when we didn't even share the same foundation in decision making, how to parent our children, or who led our life. It was a silent battle because no one on the outside barely knew what was actually occurring within our home.

God was pursuing my husband and had not forgotten me or my desperate prayers.

When Josh hit rock bottom in the midst of addiction to alcohol, he went forward with a suicide plan to end his life. Thankfully, a picture of me and our kids flashed into his mind and stopped him before continuing. I supported him in suicidal emergency again and got him to the care he needed. There is much more to the story and a significant advocacy and spiritual battle that occurred while he was in the psychiatric ward.

I want to get to the crux of it, though.

In the psychiatric ward, Josh had an encounter with the Holy Spirit and laid down his will, asking Jesus into his heart and life truly for the first time.

We were not fighting against *flesh and blood* but were in spiritual warfare—a war over *his very own spirit and eternal life.*

Josh came to know the Lord in the psychiatric ward. That was over two years ago.

It was hard to wrap my mind around him never being a believer truly before, but I have now reconciled that.

I have seen evidence of a changed heart over two years' time in ways I never saw before in our relationship or in my time of knowing him. He has laid down his way of doing things to pursue God. There is a humbleness and patience there that was not there before. A different way of approaching situations now.

It was a religion before and something he did, a culture he was a part of.

Now, it is a relationship and something that changed the depth of him on the inside, from the inside out—a heart change, a submission of will—with his behavior coming out of a transformed heart by the power of the Holy Spirit.

I can see the fruit of the Spirit growing within him now, in ways he couldn't do on his own. Seeing this begins to bring a peace and calm over my heart. A rest.

I am grateful he is growing towards health: mentally, emotionally, and spiritually.

I am encouraged and can pause in gratefulness knowing he is sober and continuing to add another month and another month of sobriety. He is over two years sober presently.

I don't have to continuously be on alert, ready for whatever chaotic or uncertain interactions or events may take place.

It feels...safer. Calmer. Less tumultuous. The waves of crisis are abating.

I still make sure to ask him how he's doing if there's a risk factor for suicidal ideation or alcohol use.

Now—I do want to share a key point for those wondering why I'd slide these last important stories in at the very end of the book.

Well, the majority of this book is focused on our almost two-year lengthy suicidal crisis period. While there was a relapse with another suicide plan years later and struggles with alcohol abuse, the alcoholism and addiction to alcohol are not the overarching focus of the book. Alcohol use disorder and addiction are where our story led in recent years. An unhealthy relationship with alcohol had been present before then though.

Life can be messy.

There can be multiple struggles co-occurring. Finding help, resources, and treatment for each one is incredibly important.

We are all on a continuing path of healing and growth—mentally, physically, spiritually.

On this side of heaven, we can humbly recognize we will never arrive at a place being fully healed and whole We are on a continuum of healing and growth in this life, as we persevere and pursue healing, health, and wholeness.

"Let us run with perseverance the race marked out for us" (Hebrews 12:1b).

We can choose to continue to grow and be changed, transformed, knowing it is a lifelong pursuit.

As my husband and I talked about this book, we knew that offering tools and insight on suicidality and trauma *rang hollow* without the life-giving truth of Jesus and sharing the testimony of *God's miraculous calling of my husband in the psychiatric ward.*

A Saul to Paul moment as I call it.

As Josh put it: *"I had peace in a place where there was no peace"* all of a sudden.

God was at work for good as Romans 8:28 testifies. The transforming power of the Holy Spirit was at work.

The reason I share this testimony is this:

We overcome by the blood of the Lamb and the word of our testimony (adapted from Revelation 12:11).

Declare What God Has Done

We are to declare what God has done in our life.

I knew our story wasn't just for us while it was taking place. I just didn't know when or how it would be used to impact others. And now, I know.

Even though my husband came to have a relationship with the Lord in a miraculous way and I can see God's hand in our life, it doesn't mean our life is now magically easy and devoid of any impact from the experiences we had.

We still have ripple effects and mental health challenges at times, not emergencies though.

In pursuing healing, we both underwent intensive EMDR treatment alongside Neurofeedback, and my husband did IFS with his EMDR and Neurofeedback.

We also entered into authentic and rich faith community focused on growing with God and identifying our past to be dealt with and brought before the Lord to be healed from. With Josh's heart change, he actually wanted to be at church and involved in studying the Bible which was the opposite from before.

God was at work spiritually in both our hearts and lives, and God was at work healing our minds/brains through EMDR therapy. Neither of us will be fully healed on this side of heaven.

Neither will you, unless the Lord does something fully miraculous. He is certainly able to. He has done his share of miracles in the Bible and even in our life.

Peace and relief enter my heart as I accept the truth that our life is not tumultuous from mental health battles and crises at this present moment in time. We can continue to heal, grow, connect, and find grounding. We can work on our relationship and the ways it was impacted for the negative—a slow building up and choosing of each other daily, of changing old patterns of interacting for new, healthier ones. Of building trust and connection, once again. Of choosing each other, daily.

On our marriage healing path, a powerful tool we used and are still using is the Enneagram. The Enneagram is a personality tool which shows positive and negative traits for each personality. This tool allowed us to see our failings and our strengths in order to accept ourselves and accept each other, and it fostered understanding of each other and ourselves in ways we couldn't have done otherwise. By knowing ourselves and others more fully we can have compassion for ourselves and others. We can enter into a more authentic way of living with each other when we are open about our positive and negative qualities. Each personality type has them. In knowing our negative potentials, we can offer those to the Lord to ask Him to help us overcome them daily and continue to mold us into a reflection of Him in our actions, thoughts, heart, and spirit.

And now, I am so incredibly grateful. I don't know what battles on the mental health realm we will still face, but I'm sitting in the beauty and grace the Lord has given for right now. For this moment in time.

This slight calm in the storms we have has allowed me the space to focus on writing this book, this book of hope and a friend's hand reaching down into the darkness of the battle you are currently traversing alone.

And friend—can I say—you aren't walking alone anymore. I'm here. To help come alongside you, to offer guidance, to pray for you, and to help you know you are not alone. And you never have been alone. More important than me, God is present. He is there within your battle.

Call out to Him. Speak to Him. Tell Him your troubles. He hears you. Even if you have never talked to Him before, you can right now.

We can ask Him for guidance, for help, for wisdom, for strength. And He gives all of that to us. Your burden is too heavy for you to carry it on your own. Let Him share the weight and carry you and your loved one with mental illness.

> *God is the One who heals the brokenhearted and binds up their wounds* (from Psalm 147:3), and *He is the One who can heal all our diseases* (from Psalm 103:3b).

> *God is the One who redeems my life from the pit and crowns me with love and compassion, who satisfies my desires with good things* (adapted from Psalm 103:4-5a).

Abundant Life and The Good Shepherd

One last verse for you is this:

> *"The thief comes only to steal and kill and destroy. I came that they may have life and have it abundantly"* (John 10:10, ESV).

Satan has come at my family in almost every possible way to steal, kill, and destroy. There are many more ways he has attacked our family than what are in the pages of this book. If Satan couldn't take life, he tried to destroy something else.

Jesus, on the other hand, came for us to have life. Not just life, but *abundant life.*

Overflowing life, life led by and protected by the good Shepherd as John 10:11 talks on.

Psalm 23 also speaks of the Lord as our Shepherd who cares for us in just the ways we need—refreshing our soul, watching over us, protecting us—to the point where surely goodness and mercy, or goodness and forever love, will follow and pursue us all the days of our life. (adapted from Psalm 23)

> *"Surely your goodness and unfailing love will pursue me all the days of my life, and I will live in the house of the Lord forever"* (Psalm 23:6, NLT).

Let it be so. Amen.

My Parting Words For You

Truths to Internalize for Life Balance: My Parting Words to You, My Friend.

1. You are brave. You are a warrior. What you are doing for your loved one in supporting them through this often-silent battle is remarkable. Accept that truth. It will carry you on the hard days.

2. Educate yourself. Don't wing it. Look up the organizations I shared and read their education, pamphlets, and other information on suicide, warning signs, and so many other vital topics. Many offer support for you also, the caregiver, the family member. Take advantage of their offerings. By educating yourself with correct knowledge, you will be empowered in the moments of uncertainty or overwhelm. You will know where to turn to for help and guidance on when to seek professional care or emergency care in crisis.

3. Next—You are not in control. You can't control your loved one's thoughts, decisions, or actions.

4. You are human. You are not perfect and can give yourself grace when you mess up or make a mistake, as you seek to repair, ask forgiveness, or reconcile an issue.

5. You are a support to your person, but you also have to find support for yourself.

6. No one will likely advocate for your care, so you have to my friend.

7. Connect with and find groups with people who are walking through similar battles. There are support groups for family

members beginning to pop up and form in different areas because the need is becoming recognized.

8. Don't isolate yourself. You will be tempted to. You must have community around you—not so they know all of your details, but so you are not alone and have positive human interaction.

9. Get your own therapist. Don't justify or deny the significance of what you are walking through. Don't minimize your own journey and experience. It is hard.

10. Caregiving for mental crisis changes you. You will not be the same person who began the journey. I pray that what you have walked through will foster resilience and a voice of advocacy for your loved one and others struggling as well as those who are in your shoes too. I pray it builds compassion within you.

11. Give yourself grace. Don't be so hard on yourself.

But truly.

Do all that you can to caregive and support your loved one well, and then, don't beat yourself up for being human yourself.

You are also growing, trying, fighting, learning, and you're in a battle you never knew you'd be up against. Keep persevering. Day by day. Moment by moment. You aren't alone in your battle anymore, friend. You chose to pick this book up, and I'm so glad you did. I pray you and your loved one are blessed.

Remember, you are not alone in your battle.

-Amber

REFERENCES

1. Phillips, R., Durkin, M., Engward, H., Cable, G., and Iancu, M. (2023) The impact of caring for family members with mental illnesses on the caregiver: a scoping review. *Health Promotion International,* **38** (3), June 2023, 1-23. https://doi.org/10.1093/heapro/daac049.

2. Risk of Suicide. NAMI, National Alliance on Mental Illness. https://www.nami.org/about-mental-illness/common-with-mental-illness/risk-of-suicide/ Accessed 14 February 2025.

APPENDIX—ACCESS TO FREE E-BOOK, PLAYLIST, & RESOURCES

1. **My Author Website**
   amberjparker.com

   Check out all the pages!

   Sign up for my email newsletter.

   Reach out to me regarding speaking engagements or collaborations.

   View the speaking or about link to connect.

2. **Join My Email Newsletter**

   Sign up for my email newsletter!

   Joining my email newsletter is the best way to stay in touch with my offerings and continue to be encouraged through an integrated faith and neuroscience perspective. You can sign up at **amberjparker.com or choosejoyinthemidst.com**

3. **Blog: Choose Joy In the Midst**
   choosejoyinthemidst.com

   Yes! I have a blog and write on faith and resiliency in hardship as well as mental health topics integrating faith, neuroscience, and psychology. I hope you are blessed by my words.

4. **Connect on Social Media**

   Instagram: **@amberjparker_**

   @choosejoyinthemidst

   Facebook: **@amberjparker**

   @choosejoyinthemidst

   YouTube: **@amberjparker**

5. **Shop: Beautiful Truth Design**

   My shop, Beautiful Truth Design:

   Beautifultruthdesign.com has mugs, journals, and t-shirts with powerful faith and mental health messages to empower you in your battle.

   Purchase my signature "You are not alone in your battle" statement on a variety of items!

   Treat yourself and buy gifts for others to encourage and empower!

   Having truth to focus my mind on in the midst of crisis was incredibly important which was why I started this store and began designing items—to give you that same opportunity!

6. **Your Free Gifts- Spotify Playlist and E-book Guide**

   Here are your Free Gifts to accompany this book.

   They are companions to this book and will support you and your loved one in your pursuit of healing and wholeness.

   They are my thank you for purchasing this book.

- **"You Are Not Alone In Your Battle"** Spotify Playlist
- **"How To Find A Mental Health Therapist"**–your Free E-book guide

Access them at my website:

amberjparker.com/theforgottencaregiver/gifts

To make it easier on you, here's the QR code to access them:

Once you input your information, you will receive an email with the playlist link and E-book guide.

Check your spam folder if it has not come through.

- The "You Are Not Alone In Your Battle" Spotify playlist will empower and encourage you as you listen to it.
- Your Free E-book Guide "How To Find A Mental Health Therapist" will be an invaluable help as you navigate the steps in finding a mental health therapist, counselor, or psychologist for your loved one and/or yourself.

Included in this guide are the steps I took when we were in crisis, and I desperately needed to find Josh the right therapist. I researched and searched and figured it out on my own. I have used these same steps when I was searching for my own therapist.

It's free because I don't want a financial barrier to keep you from receiving your E-book guide.

Again, receive your Free digital copy of "How to Find a Mental Health Therapist" and a link to your Spotify playlist at this link:

amberjparker.com/theforgottencaregiver/gifts

You will receive an email with access to these invaluable gifts.

Check your spam folder if it has not come through.

This guide is for your personal use. You are welcome to share the link to sign up for it with others who have this book and want the free guide.

Note: If you live outside the United States, you can still apply the guidance and one of the websites I offer in the resource to find a mental health therapist to help you in your healing journey.

Don't delay. Grab your gifts.

Additional Resources

You will need additional resources and support beyond my book. I needed support myself from many different avenues.

1. Additional Books

I am sharing a list of some of my favorite authors and one of their book titles I have appreciated underneath their name. Take a look. Buy a few and try them out. Each author has positively impacted me, and I deeply respect each one on this list.

They write on a variety of subjects.

A. Henry Cloud, Ph.D. and John Townsend, Ph.D.

   "Boundaries: When to Say Yes, How to Say No, to Take Control of Your Life"

B. Alison Cook, Ph.D.

   "I Shouldn't Feel This Way: Name What's Hard, Tame Your Guilt, and Transform Self-Sabotage into Brave Action"

C. Bessel Van der Kolk, MD

   "The Body Keeps the Score: Brain, Mind, and Body in the Healing of Trauma"

D. Curt Thompson, MD

   "The Soul of Shame: Retelling the Stories We Believe About Ourselves"

E. John M. Gottman, Ph.D. and Joan DeClaire

"The Relationship Cure: A 5 Step Guide to Strengthening Your Marriage, Family, and Friendships"

F. Ian Morgan Cron & Susanne Stabile

"The Road Back to You: An Enneagram Journey to Self-Discovery"

G. Jennie Allen

"Get Out of Your Head: Stopping the Spiral of Toxic Thoughts"

H. Lysa TerKeurst

"Uninvited: Living Loved When You Feel Less than, Left Out, and Lonely"

I. Ann Voskamp

"Gifts & Gratitudes: A Year of One Thousand Gifts"

J. Christine Caine

"Resilient Hope: 100 Devotions for Building Endurance in an Unpredictable World"

2. Additional Mental Health Books

Here are additional book recommendations specifically on mental health, trauma, PTSD, mental crisis, negative thoughts, etc. Some are difficult reads due to the subject matter but have great mental health information. I have learned a great deal and grown in my knowledge as well as my pursuit of healing and health through these authors.

Let me know which books you purchase below that also impact you for the good.

A couple of these will be repeated from the above list.

"The Body Keeps the Score" by Bessel van der Kolk, M.D.

"Once A Warrior, Always A Warrior" by Charles W. Hoge, M.D., Colonel (Ret.), US Army

"Rewire Your Anxious Brain" by Catherine M. Pittman, Ph.D. & Elizabeth M. Karle, MLIS

"The Soul of Shame" by Curt Thompson, M.D.

"I Thought It Was Just Me (But It Isn't)" by Brene Brown, Ph.D., MSW

"Conquer Your Negative Thoughts" by Daniel G. Amen, M.D.

"Getting Past Your Past" by Francine Shapiro, Ph.D. (The discoverer of EMDR therapy)

"What Happened to You?" by Bruce D. Perry, M.D., Ph.D. and Oprah Winfrey

3. **Websites**

Here are some important websites to reference regarding mental health, PTSD, alcohol use disorder, suicidality, and veteran care.

A. https://www.mirecc.va.gov/visn19/lethalmeanssafety/

B. https://www.mirecc.va.gov/visn19/lethalmeanssafety/evidence/

C. https://www.mentalhealth.va.gov/docs/data-sheets/2024/2024-Annual-Report-Part-1-of-2_508.pdf

D. https://www.mentalhealth.va.gov/docs/data-sheets/2024/2024-Annual-Report-Part-2-of-2_508.pdf

E. https://www.nami.org/about-mental-illness/common-with-mental-illness/risk-of-suicide/

F. https://www.nimh.nih.gov/health/statistics/suicide

G. https://www.psychiatry.org/patients-families/ptsd

H. http://afsp.org/

I. https://www.ptsd.va.gov/

J. https://dictionary.apa.org/

K. https://www.aa.org/

L. https://al-anon.org/

M. https://nida.nih.gov/nidamed-medical-health-professionals/screening-tools-resources/chart-screening-tools

N. https://www.veteranscrisisline.net/

O. https://healthquality.va.gov/HEALTHQUALITY/guidelines/MH/srb/index.asp

P. https://healthquality.va.gov/HEALTHQUALITY/guidelines/MH/ptsd/PTSD-Assessment_508.pdf

Q. https://www.ptsd.va.gov/professional/assessment/adult-sr/ptsd-checklist.asp

R. https://www.garysinisefoundation.org/

4. Podcast Recommendation

One podcast I've learned a lot from and believe you will too is:

The Best of You hosted by Dr. Alison Cook.

She artfully discusses difficult topics, weaving psychology and faith into the fabric of the show.

5. Professional, Government, or Nonprofit Organizations

When you are reading and researching online, please make sure the information you find is from a reputable medical, educational, nonprofit, or government website to ensure the information you are reading is accurate. Use reputable evidence-based information to inform appropriate treatment decisions.

These organizations include:

U.S. Department of Veterans Affairs

National Center for PTSD

SAMHSA- Substance Abuse and Mental Health Services Administration

NAMI- National Alliance on Mental Illness

AFSP- American Foundation for Suicide Prevention

NIH- National Institute of Health

NIMH- National Institute of Mental Health

American Psychiatric Association

American Psychological Association

AACC- American Association of Christian Counselors

AA- Alcoholics Anonymous

National Council for Behavioral Health

National Council for Mental Wellbeing

PTSD Alliance

DBSA- Depression and Bipolar Support Alliance

Community of Hope

Rethink Mental Illness

The Brain and Behavior Research Foundation

The Jed Foundation

Reboot Recovery

These organizations are wonderful ways to connect with other people with similar struggles. It is powerful to meet people walking through a similar battle as yours or your loved one's as a result of connecting to an organization.

In Closing:

This is not an exhaustive list of organizations, websites, or books but a starting place for you as you continue your research and learning.

When you are reading and researching online, please make sure the information you find is from a reputable medical, educational, professional, or government website to ensure the information you are reading is accurate. Use reputable evidence-based information to inform appropriate treatment decisions.

Your role in your loved one's life is important, and your growth in understanding how to navigate suicidal ty and PTSD is vital for both of your wellbeing.

Be Blessed, friend.

ACKNOWLEDGEMENTS

I first must acknowledge God, not tritely at all. God is the ultimate One to give honor to in this book becoming a reality.

Here's why:

This book was a prayer offered up to the Lord in the midst of deep waters and overwhelming suicidality caregiving. It was a whisper even: *"Please redeem our story."*

God knew the timing and the waiting and the additional painful seasons of my life which would occur between then and now. God also knew the healing and trauma therapy work that had to take place and the work that had to occur in my husband's heart and life before we could ever get to a place where this story and these words could be shared. The breaking and reshaping of me also.

That prayer whispered up so many years ago didn't seem like a possibility with the torrent of additional battles and struggles which rushed in.

And yet, *God is a God of the impossible.*

I knew the moments I was witness to of God's miraculous power and prayers answered and Holy Spirit leading were not moments meant for private reflection. They were not meant to be just our stories but stories of a God who sustains, who brings life and a way forward in the midst of darkness and pain—Our stories were meant for you.

God had to work in order for this book to take place.

Josh and I both had to be in a more healed place, personally and relationally, for this book to become a reality.

A redemption story is one where the painful moments and broken shards of angst can turn into purposeful and renewed bits. *The pain turns to purpose.*

And so—this book became—the redemption and sharing of our story to help you in your time of need.

Thank you to Josh and my kids for all the time we sacrificed for this book to become a reality. The weekend days that were my workdays, the evenings, mornings, and squeezed in moments.

Thank you to my mom and dad who supported and cared for our children, asked how the book was coming along, believed in this message, prayed for, and cheered me on in this new venture.

Thank you to my family and Bible study friends for praying over me and my family against spiritual attack throughout the writing and editing of the book.

Thank you to those who follow my blog *Choosejoyinthemidst.com* and the ones who first encouraged and thanked me for writing on trauma, triggers, and the amygdala as well as mental health. You helped me know my words mattered and were making a difference.

Thank you to my writer and author friends. I had no idea I needed friends like each of you. The way we celebrate and pray for each other, support each other's writing and messages, speak into each other's lives, and discuss deep and difficult topics, I am so grateful. You know who you are, dear friends.

Thank you to hope*books Publishing and Brian Dixon for your message and vision. Thank you for the coaching and shaping of each of us, not just as authors, but as individuals embarking upon a new path to share our hope-filled message with the very people who need it most. Thank you to Hope Dover for overseeing our manuscripts as they come to life. Thank you to my developmental editor, copy editor, and each person on the team working to make this book become a published reality.

Thank you to my beta readers. Josh, you were my first beta reader and the one who's feedback was most crucial as this was your story too. Thank you for being brave.

Thank you to each person who offered insight and perspective, encouragement and feedback. It was invaluable.

Josh, thank you for being my second eyes on the manuscript at the very end, offering important insight, edits, formatting it before it was sent on for official formatting, and ultimately believing in this message and cheering me over the finish line. I'm grateful to be doing this work with you.

Thank you to each of my endorsers. Thank you for supporting my book publicly and offering your name and words in support of this message. I'm grateful for your insight and wisdom. Your words are powerful.

Thank you to my book launch team and book launch manager. I couldn't get this book to those who desperately need it without all of you sharing its message with others. Thank you for believing in this message and supporting it. I am deeply appreciative.

Thank you to my readers. Many of you will find me for the first time through this book, but others have been faithfully following along on social media or my email list.

Thank you to my new and seasoned readers for listening to my perspective and being willing to lean into a message to see and support those hidden in the shadows, silently fighting a battle against suicidality and trauma. Thank you for being willing to learn alongside me and be open to integrating neuroscience and faith for healing.

If you are the one in the battle right now fighting for your loved one or yourself, know you aren't alone.

Not anymore. I'm grateful you are here.

Blessings,

Amber